WeightWatchers®
PointsPlus®2012

Canadian
Dining Out
Companion

D1108807

PointsPlus®

2
PointsPlus®
value ™

Per 2 slices

Indeed

They're powered with wholesome goodness.

They're delicious with all your favourite sandwich fi

And, yes indeed, they're as tasty as they loo

Weight Watchers
Multigrain

Weight Watchers
00 % Whole Wheat
de blé entier

Weight Watchers
White • Blanc

WeightWatcher

CONTENTS

Introduction

Weight Watchers® Dining Out Companion

Let 2012 be your best year ever!

Dining out is part of life – a wonderful part! And whether you're losing or maintaining your weight, it can be a part of yours! The trick is to be prepared. And that's what this book is all about.

With a wealth of dining out foods listed from A to Z, and over 40 restaurants to choose from, there's just about something for everyone here.

Know where you're going? Find it in our **Restaurant Menus** section. Our extensive list of national chain restaurants will help you make wise choices even before you get there!

Your restaurant not listed? Our **Dining Out A-Z Food List** of items commonly found in restaurants is the best place to start.

Haven't decided yet where to go? Use the listings to find a chain or cuisine that allows you options. Or use them just to get some great ideas. That way, deciding once you get to the restaurant will be easier.

In this book you will find:

Dining Out Essentials, FAQs, and Do's and Don'ts
- Easy ways to plan, figure out the *PointsPlus*® value, and gauge portion sizes when you're out and about
- Answers to those ever-popular questions that come to mind
- Guidelines to help make choosing what to order easier

Dining Out A-Z Food List
An alphabetical *PointsPlus* value guide to hundreds and hundreds of restaurant foods (Weight Watchers® Power Foods are identified by a green pyramid [▲])

Ethnic & Regional Favourites
A comprehensive listing of popular ethnic and regional dishes, organized by cuisine for quick and easy reference

Restaurant Menus
The *PointsPlus* value for thousands of menu items from over 40 restaurant chains

INTRODUCTION

A note about restaurant offerings:
Since most of the restaurants listed in this book have locations in different parts of the country, keep in mind that a restaurant chain's offerings may vary by location. And all items featured in each restaurant's menu listings and photos may not be available at every location.

Trademarks of restaurants and photographs of menu items are used with permission of the owners of such trademarks and photographs. Inclusion of the restaurants and photos in this book does not imply endorsement or sponsorship of such restaurants or menu items by Weight Watchers International, Inc.

A note about the *PointsPlus*® value for each listing:
The ***PointsPlus*** value for each food in this book was calculated by Weight Watchers International, Inc. using the most current nutrition information provided by the participating restaurants at the time of the book's publication. However, since restaurants may revise their menus, recipes, or serving sizes from time to time, feel free to ask for nutrition information or to check the restaurant's website for updated information. Then, find the ***PointsPlus*** value by using your ***PointsPlus*** Calculator or, if you're a subscriber to eTools, the calculator on WeightWatchers.ca.

One more thing to keep in mind:
Certain foods, especially sugar-free ones, may contain sugar alcohols, which can impact the total ***PointsPlus*** value of the food. These ingredients – and also regular alcohol – are not typically included on food labels or in the nutrition information supplied by participating restaurants. As a result, you might notice discrepancies with the values you see in your lists in this book and the values you calculate with your ***PointsPlus*** Calculator or online. For the most accurate ***PointsPlus*** value for sugar-free foods and foods containin alcohol, you can feel confident using this book, your Program materials or, if you're a subscriber to eTools, the database on WeightWatchers.ca.

DINING OUT ESSENTIALS

Dining out is a part of life that every person should enjoy. And a key to eating out successfully while losing weight is…planning.

Planning ahead
...when it's a special occasion

Many dining-out occasions are special: birthdays, dates, celebrations. And the fact that they're special means they're scheduled. This means there's lots of time to prepare. That preparation, you'll find, is a huge help when it comes to staying on track with your weight-loss efforts.

Here's how to do it

Research the restaurant. If you know where you're going, decide ahead of time which items will work best for you. If the restaurant is a chain featured in this book, you're in a great position to make wise choices. If not, look online, or call and ask the restaurant to fax/email a copy of their menu (maybe even their nutrition information!), so you can study up.

Prepare yourself by picking items in advance with the best *PointsPlus®* value for you. With earlier access to the menu, you can determine the *PointsPlus* value before the waiter is standing over you waiting for your order. This way there's less pressure, and you'll be more likely to pick something smart, rather than just *something*.

Track in reverse. Imagine taking note of what you'll order, and tallying how much you'll use of your weekly *PointsPlus* Allowance, before you even pick up the salad fork. Remaining mindful of how your choices will fit into your plan will help you make smarter choices.

Save room for splurges. You can choose anything, as long as you make room for it. When you know you have an occasion coming up, you may want to:

- Save some of your weekly *PointsPlus* Allowance

- Earn activity *PointsPlus* values to swap for food

- Try to use fewer *PointsPlus* values on your other meals and snacks that day

Planning ahead
...when it's everyday dining out

Not every restaurant meal is a special occasion. Eating out can be a great last-minute back-up plan, and sometimes – for work, or for whatever reason – it's the only option. If you find yourself eating out often, you're not alone.

The good news – planning for everyday dining out is the same as special occasion dining out. Plus, you can:

Look for restaurants that work. After some experience with eating out on plan, you'll notice that some restaurants simply make it easier for you. Their menus offer more options that work with your efforts.

Make it a game. Some people enjoy searching menus for items that will work for them – they look at it like it's a game they want to win. That kind of positive attitude helps: Instead of focusing on the foods you feel you can't have, look for foods you enjoy and feel good about eating.

Keep this book close by. If a time comes when you know you're going to eat out, and you haven't planned ahead, you're going to want to make some quick decisions. With easy access to so many restaurant menu items, planning becomes a piece of cake.

Figuring out
the *PointsPlus*® value

PointsPlus values are going to be an important part of
the equation when you dine out. That's why it's important
that you have on hand as many ways as possible to figure
them out.

This book should be your primary resource.

Before you check anywhere else, see if the restaurant you
intend to visit is listed in this book. If it is, meeting your daily
PointsPlus Target or using your weekly *PointsPlus* Allowance
will be as easy as paying attention to your portion sizes, and
tracking each *PointsPlus* value.

If you don't have access to *PointsPlus* value information
for the restaurant's menu items, see if the restaurant's
website features nutrition information for menu items,
or if the manager has the information. With the protein,
carbohydrate, fat, and fibre information per serving, you
can calculate the *PointsPlus* value yourself.

Can't get the information you need? Try to determine the *PointsPlus* value per serving of each ingredient. For example, if you dine at a local restaurant and order roasted chicken with fresh lemon and sage, you can determine the *PointsPlus* value for each ingredient, and then add those values together for a total *PointsPlus* value of the dish. The trick here is to ask the waiter exactly how the food has been prepared – what oils or sauces have been used, if any.

Determining
portion sizes

The *PointsPlus®* value for each item listed in this book, and in other Weight Watchers® materials, are for a specified portion size. It may or may not be the size of the portion you are served in a restaurant. In order to determine the correct *PointsPlus* value, you will need to be able to recognize portion sizes.

Portion control is important everywhere, but it's a special challenge at restaurants, where bigger is often considered better. Some places pile two, or even three, portions on a plate, for added value. Others offer unlimited refills. In other words, a "portion" at one place can be very different than a portion at another, which is also different than the portion you'd dish up at home. And it's unlikely that you want to carry a tape measure, measuring cups, or a food scale into a restaurant with you.

Your ability to accurately eyeball portion sizes can make a huge difference. So learn to "spot" portion sizes instead using these visual cues.

Fist = 1 cup

Thumb (tip to base) = 30 grams (1 ounce) meat or cheese

Thumb tip (tip to 1st joint) = 1 Tbsp

Fingertip (tip to 1st joint) = 1 tsp

Index finger (1st to 2nd joint) = 1 inch

Cupped hand = 30-60 grams (1-2 ounces) of nuts or pretzels

Palm (minus fingers) = 90 grams (3 ounces) of meat, fish, or poultry

Getting around
"bigger is better"

Large portions are a marketing strategy.

Restaurants often offer bigger portions to add value to their offerings. And it makes perfect sense. Restaurants spend lots of time and money researching what it will take for customers to feel they're getting good value for their money – so that they have pleasant experiences, and return for more meals.

That doesn't mean restaurants are out to get you – they're just doing their job. But it does mean that it's important that you be savvy about their strategies, and smart about making some strategies of your own.

Try these tricks:

Order appetizers as entrées. Sometimes, items appear twice on a menu: Once as an appetizer and once as an entrée. The difference? Portion size. Additionally, the entrée-size portion of a meal will often come with extra side dishes. If you order the appetizer-size portion you'll get a reasonable portion size, and you can pick the sides yourself.

Divide and conquer. Deal with large portions right away by getting rid of the extra food as soon as the meal arrives at your table. Ask the waiter to bring you a to-go box. Put at least half your entrée in the box before you start eating.

Share with a friend. Restaurants are accustomed to people splitting entrées. When you say you want to share, they'll often bring the plated entrée and two side plates. This is perfect, since side plates are usually better anyway for showing off a reasonable portion of food.

Be picky about plates. Restaurants buy big plates on purpose to show off their big portions. If the correct portion of your entrée looks silly on the giant plate, try not to let it bother you. Better yet, ask for a smaller plate. After all, you're paying! You should get what you want.

DINING OUT FAQs

Do you remember that teacher in school that said "no question is a silly question, except for the one that's not asked"? Well here are some "not so silly" questions for which we have some very practical answers.

Q: How can I make it through a restaurant buffet and stick to the plan?

Stop and look. In other words, don't take a morsel until you've looked over all of your options and determined which foods really appeal to you. Take your own walking tour of the buffet and eyeball the food options before digging in. This way, you're less likely to fill up your plate halfway through the buffet line, only to realize that a few of your favourite foods are at the other end.

Once you've eyed all of the goods, try the following tactics:

- Fill up your plate with a larger proportion of healthy foods: fruits and vegetables with a 0 *PointsPlus*® value, lightly dressed salads, shrimp cocktail, freshly carved skinless turkey breast.

- Round out your plate with small portions of a few special items or foods you don't make for yourself, but that you know you will enjoy.

Listen to your stomach. Sit for a while before you go back for round two. It takes about 20 minutes for your body to recognize that it's full.

Scratch the "I-must-eat-my-money's-worth" attitude. Yes, it's an all-you-can-eat buffet, but if you go overboard, the cost of going off your plan can outweigh the value of any uneaten food.

Consider ordering à la carte. Although your meal may end up costing as much as — or even more than — the buffet, you're getting built-in portion control.

If sweets are your weakness, plan for them in advance. Pick out your favourite dessert but cut it in half at the buffet table, or ask the server to slice it smaller for you.

Q: How do I handle sharing a bottle of wine with friends when I eat out?

A:

Plan for it. Meals out are often special occasions, and special occasions are often celebrated with a few drinks. If you enjoy a cocktail, a beer, or a glass of wine, by all means, partake. Just plan for it, and look for ways to partake for a lower **PointsPlus®** value.

- **If you choose to imbibe,** start your meal with the alcoholic drink, then switch to non-alcoholic, non-caloric beverages – seltzers, diet sodas, unsweetened iced teas. Or, drink water with the appetizers, so you have plenty of **PointsPlus** values available for a glass of wine with your entrée.

- **Instead of ordering wine by the bottle,** or sangria by the pitcher, order drinks by the glass. If your dining companions are in the mood to party, and the pitchers were ordered before you even got there, don't worry, you can still have fun. Just ask the waiter for a pitcher of water, too, and alternate alcoholic drinks with non-alcoholic drinks.

- **Know your limits.** The downfall is that drinking alcohol can impair your judgement. So the first secret to success is to try to avoid overdoing it.

- **Watch out for portion sizes.** If you're not sure how many millilitres of beer or wine are in your glass, or how many shots are in your martini, ask the waiter.

- **Many people have "their drink,"** a favourite beverage that they order every time they go out. If your drink has a higher *PointsPlus* value than you'd like, try to find a substitution that you like as much, or at least almost as much. For instance, a 100 millilitre (3 1/2-fluid-ounce) cosmopolitan has a *PointsPlus* value of 6. But a shot or jigger of berry-flavoured vodka mixed with seltzer and a twist of lime is also refreshing, and it has a *PointsPlus* value of only 4.

- **Plan for the *PointsPlus* value you want.** Your weekly *PointsPlus* Allowance or earned activity *PointsPlus* values come in handy at times like this.

Q: What do I do when I'm going to someone else's party and will have no choice of what is being served?

You may not have a choice of what is being served, but you always have a choice of what to eat. No, we don't mean that you should go hungry. You just might need to be a bit creative.

- **If you go to a wedding,** or some other special occasion, usually there are at least a few different options. Caterers can make substitutions and omissions just as well as restaurant kitchens can. If the hosts have arranged for chicken in a sauce, ask for the sauce on the side. The fish comes fried? Ask the waiter if your portion can be baked instead.

- **If you're eating at someone's home,** think about bringing a dish that you feel comfortable eating: Maybe a platter of crudités with a dip, or an interesting side dish for which you've already calculated the **PointsPlus®** value. Others are often excited to try something new, so don't forget to bring the recipe, because someone is sure to ask for it!

- **If there's no wiggle room at all on preparation,** simply use some of your weekly *PointsPlus* Allowance or eat a satisfying snack or meal before you head out so you can be satisfied with a small portion of the meal.

Whatever you do, Don't starve yourself! Weight loss isn't about deprivation. It's about making smarter choices. Just look for ways to eat wisely, and if you don't see any, try to focus on portion control. Then get up and dance and earn some activity *PointsPlus* values. It is a party, after all!

Q: When I'm eating out with a group I don't want everyone to know I'm trying to lose weight. How can I keep my "secret"?

A:

It may be easier than you think. Try these tips:

Suggest a type of restaurant where you know you can easily get a meal that works with your efforts. Tell the waiter what you're looking for up front so you don't end up picking apart every item on the menu.

Try: I've been looking forward to a nice piece of broiled fish with lemon. Do you have anything like that?

Be indirect to get the information you're looking for. That is, compliment food items that intrigue you and then ask a question about them so you can find out about their ingredients without being so direct.

Try: The mushroom appetizer sounds delicious. I love garlic sauce. What's yours like?

Have a rebuttal line ready if someone makes a comment about your special food requests. Say it like you mean it and be upbeat and positive, not defensive.

For example: I feel so much healthier eating this way. My clothes feel looser and my energy is through the roof.

Know the language. Some food names include clear giveaways of how they are prepared. Knowing how to classify these different preparation types can help streamline your selection process discreetly.

Usually Higher in Fat and Calories		Healthier Options
		Au jus (in its own juice)
Au gratin	Crispy	Baked
Battered	Fried	Boiled
Blackened	Hollandaise	Broiled
Breaded	Parmigiana	Grilled
Buttered	Scalloped	Poached
Creamed	Scampi	Roasted
		Steamed

Remember, a lot depends on your attitude. Be proud of yourself and focus on the positive health benefits you'll reap from losing weight and making wise food choices. If you're confident in your actions, others may be more likely to support your efforts as well.

Also, keep in mind that people make special food requests because of food allergies, health and weight issues, and simple matters of taste. And requests for food modifications are increasingly common as people become more and more health conscious. If you ask politely, you may be surprised how easily restaurants will cater to your requests.

Q: How do I keep from "giving in" when I see and smell things I think I just can't resist?

Whether you think you *can* resist or think you *can't* resist, you are right! So change your way of thinking, and you just might be surprised at the results.

Rehearse in advance. Rehearsing will help you improve your level of confidence before you even leave the house. And increased confidence will help you make wiser decisions.

Ask your Weight Watchers® leader about Mental Rehearsing, a tool from Weight Watchers Tools For Living, which will help you do just that. With Mental Rehearsing, you let expected challenges play out in your head and, also in your head, you practise responding.

Here's how mental rehearsing works:

- **Imagine yourself at a restaurant.** Picture it in your head, as though you're watching yourself in a movie.

- **Be specific.** What day is it? Where are you sitting? Who are you with? What are you saying? What exactly are you doing, and how are you doing it?

- **In your mind,** step into the movie and practise responding in the way the new, healthier you wants to respond. What do you see? What can you hear? How do you feel? What do you do?

- **Do this every day** before you eat out.

Try it! When you practise succeeding, even if only in your mind, you'll be more likely to succeed in real life.

Q: Can I really eat out and have the things I love while losing weight?

Absolutely! Instead of focusing on the things you can't have, focus on the things you can have. Just plan for them, making sure you know the *PointsPlus*® value of what you choose.

- If you know you can't pass up a particular food served in your favourite restaurant, then don't. If possible, find the *PointsPlus* value of one portion ahead of time, make sure you can "afford" it, and enjoy it guilt-free.

- Look at the **Dining Out A-Z Food List** section or **Ethnic & Regional Favourites** section of this book to help find the *PointsPlus* value of the food you want.

- Balance out the rest of the meal with items with a low *PointsPlus* value, and enjoy.

You'll be surprised to see how much you can enjoy eating out while making healthy food choices – and how great you'll feel, a week later, when the decisions you made are reflected on the scale or in your measurements. It'll feel more "worth it" than you can even imagine.

DINING OUT DO'S AND DON'TS

The great news about losing weight?
You're not alone!

DINING OUT DO'S AND DON'TS

You'll find that your Weight Watchers® meeting is a great place to pick up tips and hear about dining-out successes. And there are loads of other great resources for advice, including WeightWatchers.ca and Weight Watchers magazine. Here are some tips from these sources, as well as from Weight Watchers members, Leaders, and others.

DO your research.
Check out menus beforehand. If the restaurant is included in this book, use the *PointsPlus®* value listed. If the restaurant you expect to visit isn't included, ask if they'll fax you their menu, or check online.

DO use your weekly *PointsPlus* Allowance.
It's there to help, if needed, in situations exactly like these. Putting in gym time or going for a brisk walk will also help offset a little extra eating.

DO choose restaurants wisely.
Any restaurant will have options you can enjoy, but some may have fewer than others. Going out with friends? Voice your opinion before somebody else chooses a place, so you can steer the decision in the right direction.

DO set some limitations.
Decide on some guidelines before you go to a restaurant, and stick to them. For instance: Know before you go that you'll skip the all-inclusive menu and opt for à la carte selections.

DO go in with a plan.
Determine how much and what you would like to eat before you even leave for the restaurant.

DO decide what is most important to you.
If you have a favourite dessert at the restaurant you're planning to visit, order a lighter entrée and skip the appetizer. That way, you'll have room to enjoy the item that matters most.

DO watch out for key words indicating high-fat dishes.

Words like "battered," "breaded," "buttered," "creamed," "crispy," and "fried" are clear giveaways that the food item will most likely be high in fat and calories. Other words that translate into high-fat, high-calorie dishes: "au gratin," "scalloped," "hollandaise," "Parmigiana," and "scampi."

DO practise portion control.

Some restaurant portions can be two, three, even four times the "normal" size.

DO look for healthy key words.

Words that usually indicate healthier preparations include "au jus" (in its own juice), "baked," "boiled," "broiled," "grilled," "poached," "roasted," and "steamed."

DO start with a salad, fruit cup, or broth-based soup.

If you can, ask the waiter to bring it out before you even order your entrée. That way, you'll be less hungry when you make your main choice.

DO keep things in perspective.

Remember that what's on the menu at a favourite restaurant will still be there the next time you go. If you choose a low *PointsPlus* value option this time, know that you'll be able to plan for a higher one next time, if you choose to do so.

DO be aware of your "weaknesses."

If having the breadbasket on the table is making concentration on conversation difficult, ask the waiter not to put it on the table in the first place. Or if you're dining companions really want it, move it closer to them and out of your reach.

DINING OUT DO'S AND DON'TS

DO watch out for extras.

The average burger with ketchup, lettuce and tomato isn't so bad. But one with "the works" is usually loaded with extra calories and fat. Skip bacon, cheese, and mayo.

DO eat slowly.

It takes about 20 minutes for your body to recognize that it's full.

DO keep your calorie intake under control.

If you plan to have an alcoholic beverage, try alternating alcoholic beverages with non-caloric sodas, teas, or sparkling waters.

DON'T arrive starved.

Have a satisfying snack before you go, so you won't be overly hungry while you wait for your dinner.

A great choice: a 0 *PointsPlus*® value fruit or vegetable!

DO ask for a "doggy bag" before you even start eating.

This way you can start packing up your extras right away, and you won't be as inclined to pick at leftovers.

DON'T be afraid to ask for what you want.

You're paying good money for that meal, so feel comfortable saying: Can I get that without butter? grilled? with sauce on the side? Or, I'd like mixed greens instead of fries with my sandwich. Or, Can you substitute brown rice for white?

DON'T hesitate to ask for clarification.
If you don't know what a word means, or if you don't understand how a dish has been prepared, ask.

DON'T drink away your progress.
A drink with dinner may be fine, but too many margaritas may wreak havoc on your weight-loss efforts.

DON'T choose the jumbo size.
How about choosing the "small," or even the "children's" size?

DON'T think you have to clean your plate.
You paid for it. So you have to eat it, right? Wrong. When you feel satisfied, have the waiter take your plate away.

DON'T go top heavy.
Salad bars and garden salads grace menus across the country. But those extra toppings can sabotage your best efforts. Go light on croutons, grated cheese, and bacon. Opt instead for low-fat or nonfat dressings, and have them "on the side."

DON'T be too hard on yourself.
If you stray from your plan, tomorrow is a perfect day for getting back on track. And "later that day" works well, too!

For more dining out tips and ideas, ask your Weight Watchers® leader or visit WeightWatchers.ca.

Dining Out
A-Z Food List

DINING OUT A-Z FOOD LIST

▲ Power Foods	*PointsPlus®* value

A

Aburage (Japanese fried bean curd)

1 piece (15 g [1/2 oz])	1

Alcoholic beverages

86 proof, 1 jigger (45 ml [1 1/2 fl oz])	3
90 proof, 1 jigger (45 ml [1 1/2 fl oz])	4
94 proof, 1 jigger (45 ml [1 1/2 fl oz])	4
100 proof, 1 jigger (45 ml [1 1/2 fl oz])	5
cognac, 1 jigger (45 ml [1 1/2 fl oz])	4
creme de menthe, 1 jigger (45 ml [1 1/2 fl oz])	6
Kahlúa, 1 jigger (45 ml [1 1/2 fl oz])	6
liqueur, any type other than those listed here, 1 jigger (45 ml [1 1/2 fl oz])	6
liqueur, coffee with cream, 34 proof, 30 ml (1 fl oz)	3
liqueur, coffee without cream, 63 proof, 1 jigger (45 ml [1 1/2 fl oz])	5
liquor (bourbon, brandy, gin, rum, scotch, tequila, vodka, whiskey), 1 jigger (45 ml [1 1/2 fl oz])	4
mirin, 30 ml (1 fl oz)	1
sake, 125 ml (4 fl oz)	5
schnapps, any flavour, 1 jigger (45 ml [1 1/2 fl oz])	6

Alcoholic mixed drinks

Bay Breeze, 1 drink (165 ml [5 1/2 fl oz])	5
Bellini, 1 drink (175 ml [6 fl oz])	6
Black Russian, 1 drink (90 ml [3 fl oz])	8
Bloody Mary, 1 drink (150 ml [5 fl oz])	4
Brandy Alexander, 1 drink (90 ml [3 fl oz])	9
Cosmopolitan, 1 drink (100 ml [3 1/2 fl oz])	6
Daiquiri, 90 ml (3 fl oz)	4
Daiquiri, canned, 1 can (205 ml [6 3/4 fl oz])	9

Gimlet, gin, 1 drink (75 ml [2 1/2 fl oz])	4
Gimlet, vodka, 1 drink (75 ml [2 1/2 fl oz])	4
gin and tonic, 1 drink (175 ml [6 fl oz])	5
highball, made with sweetened mixer, 1 drink (175 ml [6 fl oz])	7
highball, made with unsweetened mixer, 1 drink (175 ml [6 fl oz])	4
Long Island Iced Tea, 1 drink (150 ml [5 fl oz])	8
Manhattan, dry, 1 drink (125 ml [4 fl oz])	10
Manhattan, perfect, 1 drink (125 ml [4 fl oz])	10
Manhattan, scotch, 1 drink (125 ml [4 fl oz])	10
Margarita, 1 drink (125 ml [4 fl oz])	9
Martini, 1 drink (75 ml [2 1/2 fl oz])	6
Martini, chocolate, 1 drink (75 ml [2 1/2 fl oz])	8
Martini, sour apple, 1 drink (90 ml [3 fl oz])	8
Mimosa, 1 drink (175 ml [6 fl oz])	4
Mojito, 1 drink (375 ml [12 fl oz])	7
Old Fashioned, 1 drink (60 ml [2 fl oz])	6
Piña Colada, 1 drink (175 ml [6 fl oz])	8
Piña Colada, canned, 1 can (205 ml [6.8 fl oz])	16
Rob Roy, 1 drink (125 ml [4 fl oz])	10
Sakatini, 1 drink (90 ml [3 fl oz])	7
sangria, 1 drink (125 ml [4 fl oz])	3
Screwdriver, 1 drink (175 ml [6 fl oz])	5
Singapore Sling, 1 drink (175 ml [6 fl oz])	6
Tom Collins, 1 drink (175 ml [6 fl oz])	4
Whiskey Sour, 1 drink (125 ml [4 fl oz])	6
White Russian, 1 drink (90 ml [3 fl oz])	8

▲ Power Foods	PointsPlus® value
Almond float	
250 ml (1 cup)	3
Aloo gobi	
250 ml (1 cup)	3
Aloo palak	
250 ml (1 cup)	4
Ambrosia	
125 ml (1/2 cup)	2
Apple	
baked, 1 large (200 g [7 oz])	9
candied, 1 large (275 g [9 oz])	14
caramel, 1 large (250 g [8 oz])	13
Apple brown Betty	
250 ml (1 cup)	6
Apple crisp	
175 ml (3/4 cup)	11
Apple kuchen	
215 g (7 1/2 oz)	12
Apple streusel	
125 ml (1/2 cup)	5
Arroz con pollo	
90 g (3 oz) chicken with 375 ml (1 1/2 cups) rice	15
Artichoke hearts	
marinated, 125 ml (1/2 cup)	4
Artichokes	
stuffed, 1 (225 g [7 3/4 oz])	15

B

	PointsPlus® value
Baba au rhum	
1 (95 g [3 1/4 oz])	10
Baba ganoush	
60 ml (1/4 cup)	3
Bacon	
Canadian-style, cooked, 1 slice (30 g [1 oz])	1
regular, cooked, crisp, 1 slice	1
regular, cooked, crisp, 3 slices	4

▲ Power Foods	PointsPlus® value
Bacon bits	
imitation, 5 ml (1 tsp)	0
Bagel	
any type other than those listed here, 1 small (7.5 cm [3"] diameter) or 1/2 large (11 cm [4 1/2"] diameter) or 60 g (2 oz)	4
Asiago cheese, restaurant-type, 1 large (135 g [4 1/2 oz])	9
cinnamon-raisin, 1 medium (110 g [3 3/4 oz])	7
egg, oat bran, onion, poppy, or sesame, 1 small (75 g [2 1/2 oz])	5
everything, restaurant-type, 1 large (125 g [4 oz])	9
mini, any type, 1 (6 cm [2 1/2"] diameter)	2
wheat, restaurant-type, 1 large (125 g [4 oz])	7
with cream cheese and lox, 1 large (185 g [6 1/2 oz])	14
Bagel chips	
regular or fat-free, 30 g (1 oz)	3
Baked Alaska	
5 cm (2") wedge or 1/12 of 22 cm (9") cake	6
Baklava	
1 piece (75 g [2 1/2 oz])	10
Banana split	
3 scoops (375 ml [1 1/2 cups]) ice cream, 1 banana, 45 ml (3 Tbsp) syrup, and 125 ml (1/2 cup) whipped cream	21
Bananas Foster	
2 scoops (250 ml [1 cup]) ice cream with 1/2 banana and 75 ml (1/3 cup) sauce (280 g [9 1/4 oz])	18
Beans	
▲ garbanzo (chick peas), cooked or canned, 125 ml (1/2 cup)	3

DINING OUT A-Z FOOD LIST

Power Foods	PointsPlus® value
▲ garbanzo (chick peas), cooked or canned, 250 ml (1 cup)	7
▲ kidney, cooked, 125 ml (1/2 cup)	3
Beans and franks	
250 ml (1 cup)	13
Beans, baked	
any type other than those listed here, 125 ml (1/2 cup)	5
deli, 125 ml (1/2 cup)	4
Beans, black, with rice	
250 ml (1 cup)	6
Beans, red, with rice	
250 ml (1 cup)	7
Beans, refried	
125 ml (1/2 cup)	4
Bear claw	
restaurant-type, 1 (125 g [4 oz])	11
Beef	
brisket, cooked, 90 g (3 oz)	9
brisket, lean, trimmed, cooked, 90 g (3 oz)	5
filet mignon, cooked, 1 small (125 g [4 oz])	10
filet mignon, cooked, 90 g (3 oz)	7
▲ filet mignon, trimmed, cooked, 1 small (125 g [4 oz])	5
▲ flank steak, trimmed, cooked, 1 slice (60 g [2 oz])	3
KC strip, cooked, 1 small (125 g [4 oz])	7
▲ KC strip, trimmed, cooked, 1 small (125 g [4 oz])	5
▲ KC strip, trimmed, cooked, 90 g (3 oz)	4
New York steak, cooked, 1 small (125 g [4 oz])	6
New York steak, trimmed, cooked, 90 g (3 oz)	4
porterhouse steak, cooked, 90 g (3 oz)	7

Power Foods	PointsPlus® value
porterhouse steak, trimmed, cooked, 90 g (3 oz)	6
rib eye, trimmed, cooked, 90 g (3 oz)	5
rib, large end, cooked, 90 g (3 oz)	7
rib, large end, trimmed, cooked, 90 g (3 oz)	7
rib, small end, trimmed, cooked, 90 g (3 oz)	5
rib, whole (ribs 6-12), cooked, 90 g (3 oz)	8
round, steak or roast, cooked, 90 g (3 oz)	5
▲ round, steak or roast, trimmed, cooked, 90 g (3 oz)	3
▲ rump roast, trimmed, cooked, 1 slice (60 g [2 oz])	2
▲ rump roast, trimmed, cooked, 90 g (3 oz)	3
shortribs, cooked, 90 g (3 oz)	11
shortribs, trimmed, cooked, 90 g (3 oz)	7
sirloin, cooked, 90 g (3 oz)	5
sirloin, trimmed, cooked, 1 slice (60 g [2 oz])	3
sirloin, trimmed, cooked, 90 g (3 oz)	4
skirt steak, cooked, 90 g (3 oz)	5
▲ steak, lean, cooked (round or loin cuts other than those listed here with all visible fat trimmed), 1 small (125 g [4 oz])	5
steak, regular, cooked, 1 small (125 g [4 oz])	10
strip sirloin, cooked, 1 small (125 g [4 oz])	7
strip sirloin, cooked, 90 g (3 oz)	5
▲ strip sirloin, trimmed, cooked, 1 small (125 g [4 oz])	5
▲ strip sirloin, trimmed, cooked, 90 g (3 oz)	3
T-bone steak, cooked, 1 small (125 g [4 oz])	9

▲ Power Foods	PointsPlus® value
T-bone steak, cooked, 90 g (3 oz)	7
T-bone steak, trimmed, cooked, 1 small (125 g [4 oz])	7
T-bone steak, trimmed, cooked, 90 g (3 oz)	5
tenderloin, cooked, 1 slice (60 g [2 oz])	5
tenderloin, cooked, 90 g (3 oz)	7
▲ tenderloin, trimmed, cooked, 1 slice (60 g [2 oz])	2
▲ tenderloin, trimmed, cooked, 90 g (3 oz)	4
Beef and broccoli	
250 ml (1 cup)	4
Beef Bourguignon	
250 ml (1 cup)	15
Beef, corned	
cooked, 90 g (3 oz)	6
Beef goulash	
250 ml (1 cup)	9
Beef, ground	
75% lean/25% fat (regular), cooked, 1 patty (90 g [3 oz])	5
80% lean/20% fat, cooked, 1 patty (90 g [3 oz])	6
85% lean/15% fat, cooked, 1 patty (90 g [3 oz])	5
90% lean/10% fat, cooked, 1 patty (125 ml [1/2 cup])	4
▲ 95% lean/5% fat, cooked, 1 patty (90 g [3 oz])	3
Beef masala	
250 ml (1 cup)	6
Beef Stroganoff with noodles	
250 ml (1 cup) stroganoff with 250 ml (1 cup) noodles	17
Beer	
light, 1 can or bottle (375 ml [12 fl oz])	4
regular, 1 can or bottle (375 ml [12 fl oz])	5

▲ Power Foods	PointsPlus® value
Beer, non-alcoholic	
1 can or bottle (375 ml [12 fl oz])	2
Beets	
▲ cooked, uncooked, or canned	0
pickled, 125 ml (1/2 cup)	2
Beignet	
1 (5 cm [2"] or 20 g [3/4 oz])	2
Berries	
▲ mixed	0
Beverage mix	
Daiquiri, 125 ml (1/2 cup)	5
Margarita, 125 ml (1/2 cup)	4
Piña Colada, 125 ml (1/2 cup)	3
sweet and sour, 125 ml (1/2 cup)	3
Whiskey Sour, bottled, 60 ml (2 fl oz)	2
Bhuna gosht	
250 ml (1 cup)	9
Bialy	
1 (90 g [3 oz])	7
Biryani	
chicken, 250 ml (1 cup)	11
lamb, 250 ml (1 cup)	15
Biscotti	
chocolate, 1 regular, 2 small, or 8 mini (30 g [1 oz])	4
plain or fat-free, 1 regular, 2 small, or 8 mini (30 g [1 oz])	3
Biscuits	
homemade, 1 small (5 cm [2"] diameter) or 1/2 large (45 g [1 1/2 oz])	3
Biscuits, breakfast	
egg on biscuit, fast food, 1	9
egg, and bacon on biscuit, fast food, 1	13
egg, and ham on biscuit, fast food, 1	12
egg, and sausage on biscuit, fast food, 1	15

DINING OUT A-Z FOOD LIST

▲ Power Foods	PointsPlus® value
egg, and steak on biscuit, fast food, 1	11
egg, cheese, and bacon on biscuit, fast food, 1	12
ham on biscuit, fast food, 1	11
steak on biscuit, fast food, 1	13
Bison (buffalo)	
▲ lean, all visible fat trimmed, cooked or uncooked, 90 g (3 oz)	3
▲ top sirloin, cooked, 125 g (4 oz)	5
Bistec de palomilla (Cuban fried steak)	
1 steak (170 g [6 oz])	11
Blackened chicken	
1 breast (90 g [3 oz])	7
Blackened fish	
1 fillet (170 g [6 oz])	12
Blackened steak	
170 g (6 oz)	17
Blanquette of veal	
250 ml (1 cup)	6
Blintz	
cheese, 1 (150 g [5 oz])	6
Borscht	
store-bought, 250 ml (1 cup)	2
Bouillabaisse	
500 ml (2 cups)	9
Bouillon or broth	
▲ prepared, any type, 250 ml (1 cup)	0
Bread	
any type, including cracked-wheat, French, Italian, mixed-grain, oat bran, oatmeal, pumpernickel, rice bran, rye, sourdough, Vienna, wheat, wheat bran, wheat germ, white, 1 slice (30 g [1 oz])	2
challah, 1 slice (12.5 cm x 7.5 cm x 2 cm [5" x 3" x 3/4"])	3

▲ Power Foods	PointsPlus® value
chapati, 1 piece (12.5 cm [5"] diameter)	3
cocktail (party-style), any type, 2 slices (20 g [3/4 oz])	1
egg, 1 slice (45 g [1 1/2 oz])	3
enjera, 1 (22 cm [9"] diameter)	2
Indian (Navajo) fry, 1 (12.5 cm [5"] diameter)	8
lefse, 1 (20-25 cm [8-10"] diameter)	6
naan, 1 piece (17 cm x 20 cm [7" x 8"] diameter)	5
pan Cubano, 1 (16 cm x 7.5 cm [6 1/2" x 3"])	10
Bread, banana	
with nuts, 1 slice (12.5 cm x 2 cm [5" x 3/4"]) or 75 g (2 1/2 oz)	6
without nuts, 1 slice (12.5 cm x 2 cm [5" x 3/4"]) or 65 g (2 1/4 oz)	6
Bread, Boston brown	
1 slice (9.5 cm x 1.25 cm [3 3/4" x 1/2"])	3
Bread, date-nut	
1 slice (12.5 cm x 1.25 cm [5" x 1/2"])	7
Bread, garlic	
fresh, 1 slice (45 g [1 1/2 oz])	6
Bread, Irish soda	
1/12 of an 20 cm (8") round loaf	8
Bread, jalapeño	
1 slice (45 g [1 1/2 oz])	3
Breadsticks	
any type other than soft, 1 long (18 cm x 1.25 cm [7 1/2" x 1/2"]) or 2 short (12.5 cm x 1.25 cm [5" x 1/2"])	1
soft, 1 (40 g [1 1/3 oz])	3
Brioche	
1 slice (30 g [1 oz])	3
Broccoli rice casserole	
250 ml (1 cup)	5

Power Foods	PointsPlus® value
Broth beverage	
beef with tomato juice, 250 ml (1 cup)	2
Broth or bouillon	
▲ prepared, any type, 250 ml (1 cup)	0
Brownie	
1 (5 cm [2"] square)	6
fast food, 1 (5 cm [2"] square)	7
walnut, restaurant-type, 1 (140 g [4 2/3 oz])	15
Bruschetta	
1 slice (90 g [3 oz])	3
Bubble and squeak	
250 ml (1 cup)	5
Bubble tea (milk tea)	
250 ml (1 cup)	2
Buffalo, water	
▲ cooked or uncooked, 30 g (1 oz)	1
Buffalo wings	
cooked, 3 (135 g [4 1/2 oz])	9
Bulgur	
▲ cooked, 250 ml (1 cup)	4
Burgoo	
250 ml (1 cup)	5
Burrito	
bean, 1 large (20 cm [8"])	10
bean, 1 small (170 g [6 oz])	7
bean and cheese, fast food, 2 pieces (185 g [6 1/2 oz])	10
bean and chili peppers, fast food, 2 pieces (200 g [7 oz])	11
bean and meat, fast food, 2 pieces (250 g [8 oz])	14
bean, cheese, and beef, fast food, 2 pieces (200 g [7 oz])	9
bean, cheese, and chili peppers, fast food, 2 pieces (375 g [12 oz])	18
bean, fast food, 1 piece (110 g [3 3/4 oz])	6

Power Foods	PointsPlus® value
beef and cheese, 1 large (20 cm [8"])	9
beef and cheese, 1 small (100 g [3 1/2 oz])	7
beef and chili peppers, fast food, 2 pieces (200 g [7 oz])	11
beef, cheese, and chili peppers, fast food, 2 pieces (320 g [10 3/4 oz])	17
beef, fast food, 2 pieces (225 g [7 3/4 oz])	14
chicken and cheese, 1 large (20 cm [8"])	8
chicken and cheese, 1 small (170 g [6 oz])	6
fruit, fast food, 1 small (75 g [2 1/2 oz])	6
vegetable, 1 (made with 15 cm [6"] tortilla)	6
Butter	
regular, 5 ml (1 tsp)	1
whipped, 5 ml (1 tsp)	1
Butter chicken	
250 ml (1 cup)	9

C

Power Foods	PointsPlus® value
Cabbage, stuffed	
2 (5 cm x 6 cm [2" x 2 1/2"])	7
Cake	
angel food, 1/16 of a 25 cm (10") tube	3
Benny, 1 piece (5 cm x 7.5 cm [2" x 3"])	4
carrot, restaurant-type, 1 piece (175 g [6 1/4 oz])	17
carrot, with cream cheese icing, 1/12 of a 22 cm (9") layer cake or 7.5 cm (3") square	18
coffee, 7.5 cm (3") square, or 1/12 of a 22 cm (9") tube	9
coffee, cheese, 1 piece (1/6 of a 500 g [16 oz] cake)	7

DINING OUT A-Z FOOD LIST

Cake (cont'd)

▲ Power Foods	*PointsPlus®* value
coffee, crème-filled, with chocolate frosting, 1/6 of a 580 g (19 oz) cake	8
coffee, fruit, 1 piece (50 g [1 3/4 oz])	4
corn, 2 (20 g [3/4 oz])	2
corn, sweet, 125 ml (1/2 cup)	10
double chocolate, restaurant-type, 1 piece (155 g [5 1/3 oz])	14
honey, 12.5 cm x 7.5 cm x 2.5 cm (5" x 3" x 1")	9
pineapple upside-down, 1/8 of a 25 cm (10") skillet cake	13
pound, 1 slice (12.5 cm x 7.5 cm x 1.5 cm [5" x 3" x 1"])	9
sponge, 1/12 of a 500 g (16 oz) cake	3
strawberry shortcake, 1/12 of a 22 cm (9") cake or 1 filled individual shortcake	8
white, without frosting, 1/12 of a 22 cm (9") diameter	7
with icing, 1/12 of a 22 cm (9") layer cake or 7.5 cm (3") square	14

Calamari

fried, 125 ml (1/2 cup)	11
▲ grilled, 125 ml (1/2 cup)	1

Calzone

ham and cheese, 1 (13 cm x 15 cm [5 1/4" x 6"])	15

Candy, chocolate

any type other than those listed here, 2 assorted pieces, 1/2 bar, 30 ml (2 Tbsp) or 30 g (1 oz) chips	4
any type other than those listed here, 250 ml (1 cup)	24
chips, semisweet, made with butter, 5 ml (1 tsp)	1
dark, 60-69% cacao solids, 1 square (30 g [1 oz])	4
dark, 70-85% cacao solids, 1 square (30 g [1 oz])	5

▲ Power Foods	*PointsPlus®* value
Candy, non-chocolate	
cotton, 45 g (1 1/2 oz)	5
taffy, 1 piece (15 g [1/2 oz])	2
Cannelloni	
cheese, with meat sauce, 2 shells with 125 ml (1/2 cup) sauce	22
cheese, with tomato sauce, 2 shells with 125 ml (1/2 cup) sauce	14
meat, with cream sauce, 2 shells with 125 ml (1/2 cup) sauce	19
meat, with tomato sauce, 2 shells with 125 ml (1/2 cup) sauce	15
spinach and cheese, with cream sauce, 2 shells with 125 ml (1/2 cup) sauce	17
spinach and cheese, with tomato sauce, 2 shells with 125 ml (1/2 cup) sauce	14
Cannoli	
1 (8.5 cm [3 1/2"])	10
Capon	
cooked, with skin, without bone, 30 g (1 oz)	2
Caponata (eggplant appetizer)	
250 ml (1 cup)	5
Cappuccino	
▲ made with fat-free milk, 1 small (250 ml [8 fl oz])	1
▲ made with fat-free milk, 1 tall (375 ml [12 fl oz])	2
▲ made with fat-free milk, 1 grande (500 ml [16 fl oz])	2
made with low-fat milk, 1 small (250 ml [8 fl oz])	2
made with low-fat milk, 1 tall (375 ml [12 fl oz])	3

▲ Power Foods	PointsPlus® value
made with low-fat milk, 1 grande (500 ml [16 fl oz])	3
made with whole milk, 1 small (250 ml [8 fl oz])	2
made with whole milk, 1 tall (375 ml [12 fl oz])	3
made with whole milk, 1 grande (500 ml [16 fl oz])	4
ready-made from machine, any flavour, 250 ml (1 cup)	2
Carne asada	
125 g (4 oz)	10
Carnitas	
250 ml (1 cup)	9
Carrots and parsnips	
250 ml (1 cup)	6
Cashew chicken	
90 g (3 oz) chicken with 75 ml (1/3 cup) sauce	7
Cassoulet	
250 ml (1 cup)	12
Catfish, channel, breaded and fried	
1 fillet (90 g [3 oz])	5
Cavatelli with sausage and broccoli	
250 ml (1 cup)	6
Caviar (fish roe)	
any type, 30 g (1 oz)	2
Cereal, hot	
▲ cream of rice, cooked, 250 ml (1 cup)	3
▲ cream of wheat, cooked, 250 ml (1 cup)	3
▲ farina, cooked, 250 ml (1 cup)	3
▲ grits, corn, cooked, 250 ml (1 cup)	5
▲ oatmeal, plain, cooked, 250 ml (1 cup)	4
Cereal, ready-to-eat	
any type other than those listed here, 250 ml (1 cup)	3

▲ Power Foods	PointsPlus® value
bran flakes, 175 ml (3/4 cup)	3
bran flakes, 250 ml (1 cup)	3
corn flakes, 250 ml (1 cup)	3
crispy rice, 250 ml (1 cup)	3
fortified, 250 ml (1 cup)	2
frosted, 250 ml (1 cup)	4
nuggets, 125 ml (1/2 cup)	6
puffed rice, 250 ml (1 cup)	1
puffed wheat, 250 ml (1 cup)	1
raisin bran, 175 ml (3/4 cup)	4
raisin bran, 250 ml (1 cup)	5
shredded wheat, 1 biscuit (20 g [3/4 oz])	2
Ceviche	
125 ml (1/2 cup)	2
Chalupa (pork and bean dish)	
250 ml (1 cup)	7
Champagne	
1 small glass (125 ml [4 fl oz])	3
Chana dal	
▲ 250 ml (1 cup)	5
Chana masala	
250 ml (1 cup)	9
Chao tom (shrimp mousse over sugar cane)	
4 pieces (100 g [3 1/2 oz])	2
Char shiu bao (roast pork bun)	
1 (60 g [2 oz])	5
Cheese, blue	
crumbled, 60 ml (1/4 cup) crumbled	3
Cheese, brie	
30 g (1 oz)	3
Cheese, camembert	
1 wedge (40 g [1 1/3 oz])	3
Cheese, Cheddar	
1 slice (30 g [1 oz])	3
Cheese, colby	
1 slice (30 g [1 oz])	3

▲ Power Foods	PointsPlus® value
Cheese, cottage	
regular (4%), plain, 250 ml (1 cup)	5
regular (4%), with fruit, 250 ml (1 cup)	6
Cheese, cream	
regular, 15 ml (1 Tbsp)	1
Cheese, feta	
crumbled, 5 ml (1 tsp)	0
crumbled, 15 ml (1 Tbsp)	1
crumbled, 60 ml (1/4 cup) or 40 g (1 1/3 oz)	3
crumbled, 250 ml (1 cup)	11
Cheese, fontina	
1 slice (30 g [1 oz])	3
Cheese fries	
restaurant-type, 265 g (8 2/3 oz)	18
Cheese, goat	
hard-type, 30 g (1 oz)	3
semisoft-type, 15 ml (1 Tbsp)	1
soft-type, 15 ml (1 Tbsp)	1
Cheese, gorgonzola	
30 g (1 oz)	3
Cheese, gouda	
30 g (1 oz)	3
Cheese, gruyere	
1 slice (30 g [1 oz])	3
Cheese, hard or semisoft	
regular, 1 slice (20 g [3/4 oz])	2
regular, 2.5 cm (1") cube, 60 ml (1/4 cup) shredded, or 45 ml (3 Tbsp) grated or 30 g (1 oz)	3
Cheese, Monterey Jack	
1 slice (30 g [1 oz])	3
Cheese, mozzarella	
fried, 2 slices (7 cm x 2.5 cm x 1.25 cm [2 3/4" x 1" x 1/2"] each)	10
Cheese, muenster	
1 slice (30 g [1 oz])	3
Cheese, Parmesan	
grated, 30 ml (2 Tbsp)	1
shredded, 15 ml (1 Tbsp)	1

▲ Power Foods	PointsPlus® value
Cheese, provolone	
regular, 1 slice (30 g [1 oz])	3
Cheese puffs	
hot, 2 (15 g [1/2 oz] each)	2
Cheese, soy	
regular, 1 slice (20 g [3/4 oz])	2
regular, 30 g (1 oz)	3
Cheese straws	
2 (5 cm [2"] long each)	2
Cheeseburger on bun	
double, fast food, 1	12
double, with bacon, fast food, 1	21
large, double, with condiments and vegetables, fast food, 1	19
large, fast food, 1	13
large, with bacon and condiments, fast food, 1	16
large, with condiments and vegetables, fast food, 1	13
large, with ham, condiments and vegetables, fast food, 1	20
plain, without mayonnaise, lettuce, and tomato, 1 (185 g [6 2/3 oz])	12
small, fast food, 1	8
small, with condiments and vegetables, fast food, 1	10
triple, plain, fast food, 1	21
Cheesecake	
any type, fast food, 1 piece (80 g [2 3/4 oz])	7
with fruit topping, 1/16 of a 25 cm (10") cake	12
without fruit topping, 1/16 of a 25 cm (10") cake	11
Cherries	
chocolate-covered, 2 (30 g [1 oz])	3
maraschino, 1	0
Chicken a la king	
250 ml (1 cup)	13
Chicken adobo	
1 thigh (125 g [4 oz])	6

Power Foods	PointsPlus® value
Chicken and broccoli	
250 ml (1 cup)	3
Chicken and dumplings	
cooked, with skin, 90 g (3 oz) chicken with 2 dumplings	9
cooked, without skin, 90 g (3 oz) chicken with 2 dumplings	8
Chicken and meatball fricassee	
500 ml (2 cups)	10
Chicken asopao	
250 ml (1 cup) with 1 piece chicken (290 g [10 oz])	9
Chicken breast	
barbecued, with skin and bone, 1 (135 g [4 1/2 oz])	7
cooked, with skin, without bone, 1 (90 g [3 oz])	4
fillet, grilled, 1 (90 g [3 oz])	3
five spice, 1 (135 g [4 1/2 oz])	7
fried, with skin and bone, 1 (135 g [4 1/2 oz])	11
roasted, with skin, without bone, 1/2 breast (100 g [3 1/2 oz])	5
▲ roasted, without skin and bone, 1/2 breast (90 g [3 oz])	3
▲ stewed, without skin and bone, 1/2 breast (95 g [3 1/3 oz])	3
Chicken breast on bun	
grilled, 1 (170 g [6 oz])	11
Chicken broiler or fryer	
roasted, with skin, without bone, 1 (300 g [10 1/2 oz])	18
Chicken cacciatore	
1/2 breast or 1 thigh and leg (185 g [6 1/2 oz])	11
Chicken Caesar wrap	
restaurant-type, 290 g (10 oz)	16
Chicken cordon bleu	
1 (190 g [6 3/4 oz])	10
Chicken cutlet	
pan-fried, 125 g (4 oz)	7

Power Foods	PointsPlus® value
Chicken, dark meat	
cooked, 1 slice or 125 ml (1/2 cup) cubed or shredded 60 g (2 oz)	2
cooked, 375 g (12 oz) cooked or (500 g [1 pound] uncooked)	15
Chicken drumstick	
barbecued, with skin and bone, 1 (45 g [1 1/2 oz])	3
cooked, with skin, without bone, 1 (60 g [2 oz])	3
cooked, with skin, without bone, 30 g (1 oz)	2
cooked, without skin and bone, 1 (30 g [1 oz])	2
fried, with skin and bone, 1 (45 g [1 1/2 oz])	5
fried, with skin and bone, fast food, 1 (60 g [2 oz])	5
fried, without skin and bone, 1 (45 g [1 1/2 oz])	2
Chicken hekka	
250 ml (1 cup)	7
Chicken in the pot	
without skin, 500 ml (2 cups)	12
Chicken jalfrezi	
250 ml (1 cup)	6
Chicken Kiev	
1 piece (10 cm x 20 cm [4" x 8"])	18
Chicken leg	
five spice with skin and bone, 1 thigh and drumstick (170 g [6 oz])	9
roasted, with skin and bone, 1 leg (95 g [3 1/3 oz])	4
roasted, with skin, without bone, 1 leg (125 g [4 oz])	7
Chicken long rice	
250 ml (1 cup)	5
Chicken marsala	
without bone, with sauce, 125 g (4 oz)	14

DINING OUT A-Z FOOD LIST

Power Foods	PointsPlus® value
Chicken mole	
250 ml (1 cup)	9
Chicken, nugget-style	
fried, 6 nuggets (5 cm x 2 cm [2" x 3/4"] each) or 75 g (2 1/2 oz)	8
fried, fast food, 6 nuggets (110 g [3 3/4 oz])	9
Chicken paprika	
1 breast or thigh with 125 ml (1/2 cup) sauce	8
Chicken parmigiana	
with sauce, 150 g (5 oz) with 125 ml (1/2 cup) sauce	11
without sauce, 160 g (5 1/2 oz)	8
Chicken pilaf (kotta pilafi)	
1 chicken breast with 250 ml (1 cup) pilaf	8
Chicken tenders	
restaurant-type, 90 g (3 oz)	5
Chicken tetrazzini	
375 ml (1 1/2 cups)	15
Chicken thigh	
barbecued, with skin and bone, 1 (90 g [3 oz])	6
cooked, with skin and bone, 1 (90 g [3 oz])	4
cooked, with skin, without bone, 1 (60 g [2 oz])	4
cooked, without skin and bone, 1 (60 g [2 oz])	3
cooked, without skin, with bone, 1 (90 g [3 oz])	3
fried, with skin and bone, 1 (90 g [3 oz])	8
fried, with skin, fast food, 1 (100 g [3 1/2 oz])	8
Chicken tikka	
125 g (4 oz)	5
Chicken wings	
cooked, with skin and bone, 1 (45 g [1 1/2 oz])	3

Power Foods	PointsPlus® value
fried, with skin, fast food, 1 (60 g [2 oz])	6
Chicken with cashews	
250 ml (1 cup)	11
Chile beef (neua pad prik)	
250 ml (1 cup)	7
Chili cheese dog	
restaurant-type, 1 (150 g [5 oz])	10
Chili con carne	
canned, 250 ml (1 cup)	7
fast food, 250 ml (1 cup)	7
homemade, 250 ml (1 cup)	9
Chili dog on roll	
1 (265 g [8 1/2 oz])	11
Chili fish (macher jhol)	
1 fillet (170 g [6 oz])	13
Chili rellenos	
beef and cheese, without sauce, 2 (215 g [7 1/2 oz])	19
Chimichanga	
beef, 1 (7.5 cm x 8.5 cm [3" x 3 1/2"])	12
beef and cheese, fast food, 1 (185 g [6 1/2 oz])	12
beef and red chili peppers, fast food, 1 (190 g [6 3/4 oz])	12
beef, cheese, and red chili peppers, fast food, 1 (180 g [6 1/3 oz])	10
beef, fast food, 1 (175 g [6 1/4 oz])	12
chicken, 1 (7.5 cm x 8.5 cm [3" x 3 1/2"])	10
Chitterlings	
cooked, 30 g (1 oz)	2
Chocolate mousse	
250 ml (1 cup)	25
Cholent	
250 ml (1 cup)	5
Chop suey	
beef, 250 ml (1 cup)	5
chicken, 250 ml (1 cup)	4
pork, 250 ml (1 cup)	5
vegetable, 250 ml (1 cup)	5

▲ Power Foods	PointsPlus® value
Chow fun	
beef, 250 ml (1 cup)	9
chicken, 250 ml (1 cup)	9
pork, 250 ml (1 cup)	9
shrimp, 250 ml (1 cup)	8
Chow mein	
beef, 250 ml (1 cup)	5
chicken, 250 ml (1 cup)	4
chicken subgum, 250 ml (1 cup)	4
pork, 250 ml (1 cup)	5
Chruscik	
1 (5 g [1/4 oz])	1
Chuleta	
1 pork chop (170 g [6 oz])	12
Chutney	
30 ml (2 Tbsp)	1
tamarind, 30 ml (2 Tbsp)	2
Cider	
apple, 125 ml (1/2 cup)	2
Cinnamon bun	
1 large	7
Cinnamon roll, mini	
fast food, 1 roll	3
Cioppino	
500 ml (2 cups)	13
Clams	
baked, 6 (75 g [2 1/2 oz])	7
breaded and fried, 20 (185 g [6 1/2 oz])	10
breaded and fried, fast food, 175 ml (3/4 cup)	12
Clams	
fried, 250 ml (1 cup)	11
Cobbler	
fruit, any type, 250 ml (1 cup)	13
Coconut rice	
Indian, 250 ml (1 cup)	6
Thai, 250 ml (1 cup)	10
Coconut shrimp	
4 jumbo (205 g [7 1/4 oz])	17

▲ Power Foods	PointsPlus® value
Coffee	
brewed, black, without sugar, regular or decaffeinated, 250 ml (1 cup)	0
Coffee, Irish	
175 ml (6 fl oz) with 30 ml (2 Tbsp) whipped cream	6
Coffee, Mexican	
175 ml (6 fl oz) with 30 ml (2 Tbsp) whipped cream	6
Colcannon	
250 ml (1 cup)	8
Coleslaw	
125 ml (1/2 cup)	4
Cookies	
amaretti, 1 (2.5 cm [1"] diameter)	3
bar, 1 (5 cm [2"] square)	3
Chinese almond, 2 (30 g [1 oz])	4
chocolate wafers, 2 (15 g [1/2 oz])	1
fig bar, 2 (30 g [1 oz])	3
fortune, 1 (5 g [1/4 oz])	1
fruit bar, 2 (30 g [1 oz])	3
fudge, cake-type, 1 (20 g [3/4 oz])	2
gingerbread, 1 (5 cm [2"] diameter)	2
gingersnaps, 2 (15 g [1/2 oz])	2
kringla, 2 (45 g [1 1/2 oz])	4
lace, 1 (5 g [1/4 oz])	1
ladyfingers, 1 large or 2 small (15 g [1/2 oz])	1
Mexican wedding, 2 (3.5 cm [1 1/2"] wide each)	2
molasses, 1 medium (15 g [1/2 oz])	2
rainbow, 1 medium (2.5 cm x 5 cm [1" x 2"])	3
rainbow, 1 small (3.5 cm [1 1/2"] diamond)	2
raisin, soft, 1 (15 g [1/2 oz])	2
rosettes, 2 (7.5 cm x 7.5 cm [3" x 3" each])	2

DINING OUT A-Z FOOD LIST

Cookies (cont'd)

▲ Power Foods	PointsPlus® value
rugalach, 1 (6 cm [2 1/2"] x 3 cm [1 1/4"])	3
sesame seed, 2 (5 cm [2"] long)	4
white macadamia nut, restaurant-type, 1 (50 g [1 3/4 oz])	7
Coq au vin	
500 ml (2 cups)	12
Coquilles St. Jacques	
2 shells (405 g [13 1/2 oz])	9
Corn	
▲ baby ears, 250 ml (1 cup)	1
cream-style, 250 ml (1 cup)	5
▲ kernels, cooked, 250 ml (1 cup)	4
Corn casserole	
125 ml (1/2 cup)	10
Corn dog	
fast food, 1 (170 g [6 oz])	12
1 (80 g [2 3/4 oz])	6
Corn on the cob	
▲ 1 ear (20 cm [8"] long)	4
▲ 1 ear (up to 17 cm [7"] long)	2
with butter, fast food, 1 ear (150 g [5 oz])	4
Corn on the grill	
with butter, 1 (125 g [4 oz])	6
Cornbread	
1 piece (5 cm [2"] square)	3
Mexican, 1/12 of a 25 cm (10") round or 95 g (3 1/3 oz)	8
Cornbread dressing	
250 ml (1 cup)	9
Cornish hen	
cooked, with skin, 1/2 (135 g [4 1/2 oz])	9
▲ cooked, without skin, 1/2 (110 g [3 3/4 oz])	3
Couscous	
cooked, 250 ml (1 cup)	4
▲ whole-wheat, cooked, 250 ml (1 cup)	5

▲ Power Foods	PointsPlus® value
Crab cakes	
blue, 1 (60 g [2 oz])	2
fast food, 1 (60 g [2 oz])	4
2 (65 g [2 1/4 oz] each or 7.5 cm [3"] round)	5
Crab, deviled	
125 ml (1/2 cup)	4
Crab puffs	
6 (45 g [1 1/2"] rounds)	5
Crab rangoon	
1 large (130 g [4 1/4 oz]) or 5 mini	5
Crackers	
lavash, 1/4 of a 25 cm (10") cracker	7
oyster, 20 (20 g [3/4 oz] or 125 ml [1/2 cup])	3
oyster, 250 ml (1 cup)	5
rice, 8 (15 g [1/2 oz])	1
rye, wafers, plain or seasoned, 1 (30 g [1 oz])	2
saltines, 4	1
saltines, 6	2
saltines, fat-free, low-sodium, 6	3
wheat, regular, 15 g (1/2 oz)	2
whole-wheat, 15 g (1/2 oz)	2
Crawfish pie	
1/8 of a 22 cm (9") pie	14
Cream	
clotted (English double devon cream), 30 ml (2 Tbsp)	4
half and half, 30 ml (2 Tbsp)	1
light, 30 ml (2 Tbsp)	2
Cream puff	
1 (60 g [2 oz])	9
Cream, sour	
regular, 15 ml (1 Tbsp)	1
Cream, whipped	
aerosol, 60 ml (1/4 cup)	1
fresh, unsweetened, 60 ml (1/4 cup)	3
Creamed chipped beef	
250 ml (1 cup)	12

Power Foods	PointsPlus® value
Creamer	
fat-free, liquid or powder, flavoured, 30 ml (2 Tbsp)	1
▲ fat-free, liquid or powder, plain, 15 ml (1 Tbsp)	0
▲ fat-free, liquid or powder, plain, 60 ml (1/4 cup)	1
nondairy, liquid, plain or flavoured, 30 ml (2 Tbsp)	1
nondairy, powder, plain or flavoured, 15 ml (1 Tbsp)	1
Crème brûlée	
175 ml (3/4 cup)	12
Crème caramel	
250 ml (1 cup)	8
Crème fraiche	
30 ml (2 Tbsp)	3
Creole	
chicken, without rice, 250 ml (1 cup)	7
shrimp, without rice, 250 ml (1 cup)	5
Crêpes	
chicken, 2 (290 g [10 oz])	12
plain, 1 (15 cm [6"] diameter)	2
seafood, 2 (330 g [11 oz])	12
Suzette, 2 (140 g [4 3/4 oz])	11
Vietnamese (banh xeo), 1 (20 cm x 17 cm [8" x 3"] or 200 g [7 oz])	17
Crispbreads	
5 crackers (20 g [3/4 oz])	2
Croissant	
apple, 1 medium (60 g [2 oz])	4
butter, 1 medium (60 g [2 oz])	6
cheese, 1 medium (60 g [2 oz])	6
chocolate-filled, 1 (12.5 cm [5"] long)	7
egg and cheese, fast food, 1 (135 g [4 1/2 oz])	10
egg, cheese, and bacon, fast food, 1 (135 g [4 1/2 oz])	11
egg, cheese, and ham, fast food, 1 (155 cm [5 1/4 oz])	13

Power Foods	PointsPlus® value
egg, cheese, and sausage, fast food, 1 (165 g [5 3/4 oz])	14
plain, 1 (12.5 cm [5"] long)	6
Croquettes	
beef, 2 (75 g [2 1/2 oz] each)	10
chicken, 2 (75 g [2 1/2 oz] each)	9
Croutons	
plain, 250 ml (1 cup)	3
seasoned, 250 ml (1 cup)	5
Cruller	
French, glazed, 1 (7.5 cm [3"] diameter)	5
glazed, 1 (10 cm [4"] diameter)	7
glazed, 1 long (13 cm [5 1/4"] x 6 cm [2 1/2"] x 3.5 cm [1 1/2"] high)	9
plain, 1 (60 g [2 oz])	6
Crumpet	
1 (7.5 cm [3"] diameter)	4
Curry	
African, fish, 125 ml (1/2 cup)	6
African, shrimp, 125 ml (1/2 cup)	7
beef, 250 ml (1 cup)	11
Bengali, fish, 1 fillet (135 g [4 1/2 oz]) with 250 ml (1 cup) vegetables	11
chicken, 250 ml (1 cup)	10
egg, 250 ml (1 cup)	2
goat, 125 g (4 oz)	6
▲ chicken (gaeng kheow wan gai), 250 ml (1 cup)	8
Japanese, 250 ml (1 cup)	5
lamb, 250 ml (1 cup)	11
Massaman beef, 250 ml (1 cup)	21
panang, with beef, 250 ml (1 cup)	14
panang, with chicken, 250 ml (1 cup)	13
panang, with pork, 250 ml (1 cup)	15
Vietnamese chicken, 250 ml (1 cup)	9
Custard	
250 ml (1 cup)	9

▲ Power Foods	PointsPlus® value

D

Danish pastry

cheese, 1 (10.5 cm [4 1/4"] diameter)	7
cheese, fast food, 1 (90 g [3 oz])	10
cinnamon, 1 (10.5 cm [4 1/4"] diameter)	7
cinnamon, fast food, 1 (90 g [3 oz])	10
fruit, 1 (10.5 cm [4 1/4"] diameter)	7
fruit, fast food, 1 (90 g [3 oz])	9
nut, 1 (10.5 cm [4 1/4"] diameter)	8

Dhansak

| 250 ml (1 cup) | 7 |

Dim sum

bean curd roll with shrimp and vegetables, 1 (12.5 cm [5"] long x 5 cm [2"] wide)	3
bean curd roll with vegetables, 1 (12.5 cm [5"] long x 3.5 cm [1 1/2"] wide)	2
sesame seed balls, 1 (7.5 cm x 7.5 cm [3" x 3"])	7

Dip

any type other than those listed here, 30 ml (2 Tbsp)	2
artichoke, baked, 60 ml (1/4 cup)	6
Mexican 7-layer, 125 ml (1/2 cup)	4
spinach, 60 ml (1/4 cup)	5
spinach-artichoke, restaurant-type, 60 g (2 oz)	3

Dolma

| 4 (95 g [3 1/4 oz]) | 5 |

Donair

| 125 g (4 oz) meat with onion, tomato, and 30 ml (2 Tbsp) sauce | 16 |

Doro wat

| 250 ml (1 cup) | 7 |

Doughnut holes

| yeast, glazed, 2 (30 g [1 oz]) | 3 |

▲ Power Foods	PointsPlus® value

Doughnuts

any type other than those listed here, store-bought, 1 (60 g [2 oz])	6
cake-type, plain, 1 (8.5 cm [3 1/2"] diameter)	6
cake-type, wheat, sugared or glazed, 1 (8.5 cm [3 1/2"] diameter)	6
cake-type, white, sugared or glazed, 1 (8.5 cm [3 1/2"] diameter)	7
cake-type, with icing, 1 (8.5 cm [3 1/2"] diameter)	7
malasadas (Portuguese doughnuts), 1 (7.5 x 5 cm [3" x 2"])	3
with crème filling, 1 (8.5 cm x 6 cm [3 1/2" x 2 1/2"] oval)	9
yeast, glazed, 1 (10 cm [4"] diameter)	7
yeast, with jelly filling, 1 (8.5 cm x 6 cm [3 1/2" x 2 1/2"] oval)	8

Dressing, salad, creamy

| regular, 30 ml (2 Tbsp) | 4 |

Dressing, salad, French

| regular, 15 ml (1 Tbsp) | 2 |

Dressing, salad, ginger

| 30 ml (2 Tbsp) | 2 |

Dressing, salad, Italian-type (other than creamy Italian)

fat-free, 30 ml (2 Tbsp)	1
low-fat, 15 ml (1 Tbsp)	0
reduced-calorie, 30 ml (2 Tbsp)	1
regular, 30 ml (2 Tbsp)	2

Dressing, salad, mayonnaise-type

| regular, 15 ml (1 Tbsp) | 2 |

Dressing, salad, Russian

| regular, 15 ml (1 Tbsp) | 2 |

Dressing, salad, sesame seed

| regular, 15 ml (1 Tbsp) | 2 |

Dressing, salad, Thousand Island

| 15 ml (1 Tbsp) | 1 |

Duck

| domestic, cooked, with skin, 1/4 duck (150 g [5 oz]) | 13 |

▲ Power Foods	PointsPlus® value
domestic, cooked, without skin, 1/4 duck (125 g [4 oz])	6
domestic, cooked, without skin, 60 g (2 oz)	3
Duck a l'orange	
1/4 duck with 30 ml (2 Tbsp) sauce	15
Duck with fruit sauce	
1/4 duck with skin and 125 ml (1/2 cup) sauce	16
Duck, tea smoked	
60 g (2 oz)	3
Dumpling	
beef or pork, fried, 4 (185 g [6 1/2 oz])	7
beef or pork, steamed, 4 (165 g [5 3/4 oz])	7
chicken, fried, 4 (185 g [6 1/2 oz])	5
chicken, steamed, 4 (165 g [5 3/4 oz])	5
kroppkakor (potato), boiled, 1 (5 cm [2"] wide)	3
kroppkakor (potato), fried, 1 (5 cm [2"] wide)	4
potato, 6 (2.5 cm [1"] diameter)	3
shrimp, fried, 4 (185 g [6 1/2 oz])	5
shrimp, steamed, 4 (165 g [5 3/4 oz])	5
vegetarian, fried, 4 (8.5 cm [3 1/2"] x 5 cm [2"] wide)	4
vegetarian, steamed, 4 (8.5 cm [3 1/2"] x 5 cm [2"] wide)	4

E

▲ Power Foods	PointsPlus® value
Éclair	
1 (155 cm [5 1/4 oz])	11
Edamame	
▲ in pods, 250 ml (1 cup)	3
▲ shelled, 125 ml (1/2 cup)	3
Egg, deviled	
2 stuffed halves	4
Egg foo yung	
beef, 1 (7.5 cm [3"] diameter)	4
chicken, 1 (7.5 cm [3"] diameter)	4

▲ Power Foods	PointsPlus® value
pork, 1 (7.5 cm [3"] diameter)	5
shrimp, 1 (7.5 cm [3"] diameter)	4
Egg, fried	
2 large	5
Egg roll	
beef, 1 (11 cm [4 1/2"] long)	6
chicken, 1 (11 cm [4 1/2"] long)	5
pork, 1 (11 cm [4 1/2"] long)	6
shrimp, 1 (11 cm [4 1/2"] long)	4
Egg, scrambled	
2 or 125 ml (1/2 cup)	5
Egg, whole	
▲ hard-boiled, 1 medium	2
▲ poached, 1 large	2
Eggplant	
breaded and fried, 2 slices (7.5 cm [3"] diameter)	3
Eggplant parmigiana	
with sauce, 1 piece (7.5 cm x 10 cm [3" x 4"]) with 125 ml (1/2 cup) Italian tomato sauce	14
without sauce, 1 piece (7.5 cm x 10 cm [3" x 4"])	11
Eggs Benedict	
2 English muffin halves with 2 eggs and 60 ml (1/4 cup) Hollandaise sauce	17
Empanadas	
2 (7.5 cm [3"] diameter)	6
Enchilada de camarones	
250 ml (1 cup)	5
Enchiladas	
beef, 2 (300 g [10 1/2] oz)	13
cheese, 2 (26 g [8 1/2] oz)	12
cheese and beef, fast food, 1 (190 g [6 3/4 oz])	9
cheese, fast food, 1 (165 g [5 3/4 oz])	9
chicken, 2 (300 g [10 1/2] oz)	11
pork, 2 (300 g [10 1/2] oz)	13
sour cream, 1 (160 g [5 1/2 oz])	9

DINING OUT A-Z FOOD LIST

▲ Power Foods	*PointsPlus®* value
Enchirito	
cheese, beef, and beans, fast food, 1 (190 g [6 3/4 oz])	9
Escargots	
6 snails with 30 ml (2 Tbsp) butter	6
Étouffée	
crawfish, 250 ml (1 cup)	9
shrimp, 250 ml (1 cup)	10

F

▲	*PointsPlus®* value
Fadge (potato bread)	
1 piece (95 g [3 1/4 oz])	2
Fajitas	
beef, 2 (275 g [9 oz])	13
chicken, 2 (26 g [8 1/2 oz])	10
pork, 2 (300 g [10 1/2] oz)	14
shrimp, 2 (275 g [9 oz])	10
vegetarian, 1 (160 g [5 1/2 oz])	6
Falafel in pita	
1 large pita with 4 falafel patties	13
Falafel patties	
4 (5 cm [2"] diameter each)	8
Fattoush	
500 ml (2 cups)	7
Fettuccine Alfredo	
250 ml (1 cup)	17
Fish	
▲ bass, striped, cooked, 1 fillet (170 g [6 oz])	5
▲ bluefish, cooked, 1 fillet (170 g [6 oz])	6
▲ carp, cooked, 1 fillet (170 g [6 oz])	7
▲ catfish, cooked, 1 fillet (170 g [6 oz])	6
▲ cod, cooked, 1 fillet (90 g [3 oz])	2
eel, cooked, 30 g (1 oz)	2
▲ flounder, cooked, 1 fillet (170 g [6 oz])	4
▲ grouper, cooked, 1 fillet (170 g [6 oz])	4

▲ Power Foods	*PointsPlus®* value
▲ haddock, cooked, 1 fillet (170 g [6 oz])	4
▲ haddock, smoked, 30 g (1 oz)	1
▲ halibut, cooked, 1 fillet or steak (170 g [6 oz])	5
herring, cooked, 30 g (1 oz)	1
lox, 30 g (1 oz)	1
mackerel, 1 fillet (170 g [6 oz])	8
▲ mahi mahi (dolphinfish), cooked, 1 fillet (170 g [6 oz])	4
▲ monkfish, cooked, 90 g (3 oz)	2
▲ orange roughy, cooked, 90 g (3 oz)	2
▲ perch, cooked, 1 fillet (170 g [6 oz])	4
▲ pike, cooked, 1 fillet (170 g [6 oz])	4
▲ pollack, cooked, 1 fillet (170 g [6 oz])	4
pompano, cooked, 1 fillet (170 g [6 oz])	9
▲ rockfish, cooked, 1 fillet (170 g [6 oz])	5
sablefish, cooked, 1/2 fillet (150 g [5 oz])	10
sablefish, smoked, 30 g (1 oz)	2
▲ salmon, Atlantic wild, cooked, 1/2 fillet (160 g [5 1/2 oz])	7
▲ salmon, canned in water, drained, 125 ml (1/2 cup)	4
salmon, farm-raised, cooked, 1 fillet (170 g [6 oz])	9
salmon, smoked, 30 g (1 oz)	1
▲ sea bass, cooked, 1 fillet (100 g [3 1/2 oz])	3
▲ snapper, cooked, 1 fillet (170 g [6 oz])	5
▲ sole, cooked, 1 fillet (170 g [6 oz])	4
▲ swordfish, cooked, 1 fillet or steak (170 g [6 oz])	6
▲ tilapia, cooked, 90 g (3 oz)	2
▲ trout, cooked, 1 fillet (170 g [6 oz])	8
▲ trout, rainbow, cooked, 1 fillet (170 g [6 oz])	6
tuna, canned in oil, drained, 125 ml (1/2 cup) or 125 g (4 oz)	5

▲ Power Foods	PointsPlus® value
▲ tuna, canned in water, drained, 125 ml (1/2 cup) or 125 g (4 oz)	3
▲ tuna, cooked, 1 fillet or steak (170 g [6 oz])	5
▲ whitefish, cooked, 1 fillet (160 g [5 1/2 oz])	6
▲ whitefish, smoked, 60 g (2 oz)	1
▲ whiting, cooked, 170 g (6 oz)	4
▲ yellowtail, cooked, 1/2 fillet (150 g [5 oz])	7

Fish amandine

1 fillet (250 g [8 oz])	13

Fish and brewis

250 ml (1 cup)	14

Fish and chips

150 g (5 oz) fish fillet with 20 chips (French fries)	17

Fish fillet

battered or breaded, fried, fast food, 1 fillet (95 g [3 1/4 oz])	6
fillet, grilled, with lemon pepper, 2 (9.5 cm [3 3/4 oz])	2
fried, breaded with flour, 1 (170 g [6 oz])	13
fried, without flour, 1 (170 g [6 oz])	14
grilled, with garlic butter, 1 (110 g [3 3/4 oz])	3

Fish sticks

breaded, 4 (75 g [2 1/2 oz])	5

Fish, stuffed

baked, 190 g (6 3/4 oz)	9

Fish Veronique

1 fillet (170 g [6 oz])	12

Flan

175 ml (3/4 cup)	9

Flanken

2 slices (125 g [4 oz])	8

Flatbreads

20 g (3/4 oz)	1

Flauta

beef, 1 (15 cm x 3 cm [6" x 1 1/4"])	12

▲ Power Foods	PointsPlus® value
chicken, 1 (15 cm x 3 cm [6" x 1 1/4"])	11
pork, 1 (15 cm x 3 cm [6" x 1 1/4"])	11

Focaccia

1/4 of a 25 cm (10") diameter	7

Fondue, cheese

125 ml (1/2 cup) fondue with 60 g (2 oz) bread	12

Frankfurter

beef or pork, regular, 1 (12.5 cm [5"] long x 2.25 cm [7/8"] diameter)	5

Frankfurter on roll

plain, 1 (125 g [4 oz])	8
plain, fast food, 1 (100 g [3 1/2 oz])	7
with chili, fast food, 1 (125 g [4 oz])	8

Frankfurter roll or bun

regular, 1 (60 g [2 oz])	4

French fries

20 (11 cm [4 1/2"] long or 160 g [5 1/2 oz])	11
fast food, 1 small serving	7
fast food, 1 medium serving	11
fast food, 1 extra large serving	14

French toast

2 slices (135g [4 1/2 oz])	8
with butter, fast food, 2 slices (140 g [4 3/4 oz])	10

French toast sticks

fast food, 5 pieces (150 g [5 oz])	13

Frijoles, with cheese

fast food, 250 ml (1 cup)	5

Fritters

apple, restaurant-type, 1 (125 g [4 oz])	12
conch, 2 (50 g [1 3/4 oz])	3
corn, 3 (6 cm x 5 cm [2 1/2" x 2]" each)	6
vegetable, 250 ml (1 cup)	12

DINING OUT A-Z FOOD LIST

▲ Power Foods / *PointsPlus®* value

Frog legs

fried, 2 (30 g [1 oz]) — 4

Fromage frais (soft cheese with fruit)

30 g (1 oz) — 3

Fruit and yogourt parfait

restaurant-type, 265 g (8 1/2 oz) — 6

Fruit compote

125 ml (1/2 cup) — 4

Fruit cup

▲ restaurant-type — 0

Fudge

with or without nuts, 1 piece
(2.5 cm x 5 cm [1" x 2"]) or 30 g (1 oz) — 3

G

Gefilte fish

1 piece (45 g [1 1/2 oz]) — 1

Gelatin desserts

prepared from dry mix,
sweetened with sugar, 125 ml
(1/2 cup) — 2

Gelatin-fruit mold

125 ml (1/2 cup) — 3

General Tso's chicken

250 ml (1 cup) — 17

Ginger chicken

250 ml (1 cup) — 8

Ginger fish

250 ml (1 cup) — 9

Gingerbread

1/9 of an 20 cm (8") square pan — 7

Gnocchi

cheese, 250 ml (1 cup) — 12

potato, 250 ml (1 cup) — 5

spinach, 250 ml (1 cup) — 13

Goat masala

250 ml (1 cup) — 6

Goose

cooked, with skin, without bone,
60 g (2 oz) — 4

cooked, without skin and bone,
60 g (2 oz) — 3

Gordita

beef, 1 (7.5 cm [3"] diameter) — 11

Gosht shaha korma

250 ml (1 cup) — 15

Gravy

brown, 60 ml (1/4 cup) — 3

cream, 60 ml (1/4 cup) — 4

giblet, 60 ml (1/4 cup) — 2

sausage, 60 ml (1/4 cup) — 4

Green rice

250 ml (1 cup) — 7

Greens

cooked, seasoned with bacon
or salt pork, 250 ml (1 cup) — 4

Guacamole

60 ml (1/4 cup) — 2

Gumbo

chicken, 250 ml (1 cup) — 7

seafood, 250 ml (1 cup) — 6

Gyoza

3 (35 g [1 1/4 oz]) — 3

Gyro

1 (330 g [11 oz]) — 16

H

Halvah

1 piece (5 cm x 4.5 cm x
2.5 cm [2" x 1 3/4" x 1"]) — 6

Ham

▲ canned, extra lean (approximately
5% fat), 30 g (1 oz) — 1

▲ cooked, lean, 1 slice or 125 ml
(1/2 cup) cubed or shredded,
60 g (2 oz) — 2

▲ Power Foods	PointsPlus® value
cooked, regular, 1 slice or 1 25 ml (1/2 cup) cubed or shredded, 60 g (2 oz)	3
Ham, glazed with pineapple	
125 g (4 oz) ham with 1/2 pineapple slice	7
Ham patty	
grilled, 1 (60 g [2 oz])	6
Hamantaschen	
1 piece (7.5 cm [3"] diameter)	3
Hamburger on bun	
double patty, plain, fast food, 1 (170 g [6 oz])	14
double patty, with condiments, fast food, 1 (215 g [7 1/2 oz])	15
plain, without mayonnaise, lettuce, and tomato, 90 g (3 oz) cooked hamburger on 45 g (1 1/2 oz) bun	10
single patty, plain, fast food, 1 (140 g [4 3/4 oz])	11
single patty, with condiments, fast food, 1 (170 g [6 oz])	12
small, plain, fast food, 1 (90 g [3 oz])	7
small, with condiments, fast food, 1 (125 g [4 oz])	7
triple patty, with condiments, fast food, 1 (275 g [9 oz])	18
regular, 1 (60 g [2 oz])	4
Haroset	
60 ml (1/4 cup)	1
Haupia (coconut pudding)	
5 cm (2") square	3
Herring	
chopped, 60 ml (1/4 cup)	4
kippered, boneless, 30 g (1 oz)	2
pickled, 60 ml (1/4 cup)	2
Hibachi	
chicken, 250 ml (1 cup)	8
shrimp, 250 ml (1 cup)	6

▲ Power Foods	PointsPlus® value
steak, 250 ml (1 cup)	10
vegetables, 250 ml (1 cup)	5
Honey	
15 ml (1 Tbsp)	2
Honeybun	
glazed, 1 (10 cm x 7.5 cm [4" x 3"] oval)	7
Hot cross buns	
1 (65 g [2 1/4 oz])	6
Hot dog	
beef or pork, regular, 1 (12.5 cm [5"] long x 2.25 cm [7/8"]" diameter) or 60 g (2 oz)	5
Hot dog on roll	
plain, 1 (125 g [4 oz])	8
plain, fast food, 1 (100 g [3 1/2 oz])	7
with chili, fast food, 1 (125 g [4 oz])	8
Hot dog roll or bun	
regular, 1 (60 g [2 oz])	4
Huevos rancheros	
2 eggs on 2 tortillas	16
Huli huli chicken	
breast, with skin and bone, 1 (205 g [7 1/4 oz])	13
drumstick, with skin and bone, 1 (60 g [2 oz])	3
thigh, with skin and bone, 1 (90 g [3 oz])	5
Hummus	
60 ml (1/4 cup)	4
Hunan beef	
250 ml (1 cup)	10
Hungarian goulash	
250 ml (1 cup)	9
Hush puppies	
2 (65 g [2 1/4 oz])	5
fast food, 5 pieces (80 g [2 3/4 oz])	7

DINING OUT A-Z FOOD LIST

I

Ice cream

fat-free, sweetened with sugar, 1 scoop or 125 ml (1/2 cup)	2
light, sweetened with sugar, 1 scoop or 125 ml (1/2 cup)	3
premium, 1 scoop or 125 ml (1/2 cup)	8
regular, 1 scoop or 125 ml (1/2 cup)	4
vanilla, rich, 1 scoop or 125 ml (1/2 cup)	5

Ice cream cone only

cake or wafer-type, 1 large (30 g [1 oz])	3
plain or sugar, 1 small (10 g [1/3 oz])	1

Ice cream, fried

125 ml (1/2 cup)	12

Ice cream soda

375 ml (12 fl oz)	11

Ice cream, soft-serve

French vanilla, 125 ml (1/2 cup)	5

Ice cream sundae

any type, 1 large (185 g [6 1/2 oz])	13
any type, 1 scoop (125 ml [1/2 cup]) ice cream with syrup, nuts, and whipped topping (135 g [4 1/2 oz])	9
caramel, fast food, 1 (160 g [5 1/2 oz])	8
hot fudge, fast food, 1 (160 g [5 1/2 oz])	8
strawberry, fast food, 1 (160 g [5 1/2 oz])	7

Ice cream sundae on a cone

1 (100 g [3 1/2 oz])	9

Ices

fruit, 125 ml (1/2 cup)	4
Italian, restaurant-type, 125 ml (1/2 cup)	2

Imperial roll

1 (11 cm [4 1/2"] long)	5

Italian casserole (ground beef, pasta and cheese over rolls)

1/8 of a 25 cm (10") round casserole	15

J

Jalapeño poppers

1 (45 g [1 1/2 oz])	4

Jam

regular or reduced-sugar, 15 ml (1 Tbsp)	1

Jamaican rice and peas

250 ml (1 cup)	8

Jambalaya

chicken, with rice, 375 ml (1 1/2 cups)	11
fish, with rice, 375 ml (1 1/2 cups)	11

JapChae

beef, 250 ml (1 cup)	8
chicken, 250 ml (1 cup)	9
pork, 250 ml (1 cup)	9

Jelly

15 ml (1 Tbsp)	1

Jerk chicken breast

without skin, 1 large breast (165 g [5 3/4 oz])	5

Johnny cake

1 piece (6 cm [2 1/2"] square)	5

Juice

apple, 125 ml (1/2 cup)	2
grapefruit, 125 ml (1/2 cup)	1
orange, fresh, 250 ml (1 cup)	3

K

Kabobs

beef, 2 skewers (135 g [4 1/2 oz])	8
chicken, 2 skewers (135 g [4 1/2 oz])	5
fish, 2 skewers (135 g [4 1/2 oz])	5
lamb, 2 skewers (135 g [4 1/2 oz])	8

▲ Power Foods	PointsPlus® value
Kahlua pig	
90 g (3 oz)	4
Kasha (buckwheat groats)	
▲ cooked, 250 ml (1 cup)	4
Kasha varnishkes	
250 ml (1 cup)	7
Kashmiri (lamb meatballs)	
6 (100 g [3 1/2 oz])	11
Kataifi	
1 piece (5 cm [2"] long)	7
Katsu	
ahi, 2 slices (11 cm [4 1/2"] x 1.25 cm [1/2"] x 2 cm [3/4"] thick)	6
chicken, 2 slices (11 cm [4 1/2"] x 1.25 cm [1/2"] x 2 cm [3/4"] thick)	6
pork, 2 slices (11 cm [4 1/2"] x 1.25 cm [1/2"] x 2 cm [3/4"] thick)	7
Ketchup	
15 ml (1 Tbsp)	0
60 ml (1/4 cup)	2
Kheer	
125 ml (1/2 cup)	7
Kibbe	
baked, 3 pieces (3.5 cm [1 1/2"] squares)	3
Kielbasa	
30 g (1 oz)	2
Kim chee	
▲ 125 ml (1/2 cup)	0
King ranch chicken casserole	
250 ml (1 cup)	9
Kishke	
1 small piece (20 g [3/4 oz])	2
Knish	
potato, 1 (8.5 cm [3 1/2"] square)	7
Kofta (vegetable balls without sauce)	
2 balls (90 g [3 oz])	6
Kofta, malai (vegetable balls in cream sauce)	
2 balls with 125 ml (1/2 cup) sauce	10

▲ Power Foods	PointsPlus® value
Kolache	
fruit-filled, 1 (7.5 cm [3"] diameter)	5
without filling, 1 (7.5 cm [3"] diameter)	4
Korean barbecue beef	
125 g (4 oz)	7
Korean barbecue chicken thighs	
1 (150 g [5 oz])	12
Korean barbecue short ribs	
125 g (4 oz)	8
Korma	
chicken, 250 ml (1 cup)	15
lamb, 250 ml (1 cup)	16
vegetable, 250 ml (1 cup)	12
Kreplach	
boiled, 2 pieces (10 cm x 7.5 cm x 7.5 cm [4" x 3" x 3"] each)	6
fried, 2 pieces (10 cm x 7.5 cm x 7.5 cm [4" x 3" x 3"] each)	8
Kugel	
lukschen (noodle), with fruit, 1 piece (7.5 cm x 8 cm [3" x 3 1/4"])	9
lukschen (noodle), without fruit, 1 piece (7.5 cm x 8 cm [3" x 3 1/4"])	6
Kugel	
potato, 1 piece (7.5 cm x 8 cm [3" x 3 1/4"])	5
Kung pao	
beef, 250 ml (1 cup)	12
chicken, 250 ml (1 cup)	9
pork, 250 ml (1 cup)	11
shrimp, 250 ml (1 cup)	10

L

	PointsPlus® value
Lamb	
leg, cooked, 1 slice (60 g [2 oz])	3
leg, cooked, 90 g (3 oz)	5
leg, trimmed, cooked, 1 slice (60 g [2 oz])	3
leg, trimmed, cooked, 90 g (3 oz)	5

DINING OUT A-Z FOOD LIST

Lamb (cont'd)

▲ Power Foods	PointsPlus® value
loin, cooked, 1 slice (60 g [2 oz])	4
loin, cooked, 90 g (3 oz)	6
loin, trimmed, cooked, 1 slice (60 g [2 oz])	3
loin, trimmed, cooked, 90 g (3 oz)	4
rib, cooked, 90 g (3 oz)	8
shoulder, cooked, 1 slice (60 g [2 oz])	5
shoulder, cooked, 90 g (3 oz)	7
Lamb, ground	
cooked, 125 ml (1/2 cup) or 60 g (2 oz)	4
Lamb masala	
250 ml (1 cup)	7
Lasagna	
cheese, with tomato sauce, 1 piece (290 g [10 oz])	9
chicken, 250 ml (1 cup)	7
vegetable, 250 ml (1 cup)	8
vegetarian, with cheese, 1 piece (290 g [10 oz])	12
vegetarian, with cheese and spinach, 1 piece (300 g [10 1/2 oz])	10
with meat, 10 cm x 6 cm (4" x 2 1/2") or 250 ml (1 cup)	7
with meat sauce, 250 ml (1 cup)	7
Latte	
▲ made with fat-free milk, 1 small (250 ml [8 fl oz])	2
▲ made with fat-free milk, 1 tall (375 ml [12 fl oz])	3
▲ made with fat-free milk, 1 grande (500 ml [16 fl oz])	4
made with low-fat milk, 1 small (250 ml [8 fl oz])	3
made with low-fat milk, 1 tall (375 ml [12 fl oz])	4
made with low-fat milk, 1 grande (500 ml [16 fl oz])	5
made with whole milk, 1 small (250 ml [8 fl oz])	3

▲ Power Foods	PointsPlus® value
made with whole milk, 1 tall (375 ml [12 fl oz])	5
made with whole milk, 1 grande (500 ml [16 fl oz])	7
Lau lau (pork and fish in taro or spinach leaves)	
1 (215 g [7 1/2 oz])	8
Lechon asado (roast pork)	
90 g (3 oz)	4
Lemon grass chicken	
250 ml (1 cup)	9
Lemonade	
fresh or prepared from concentrate or powder, 250 ml (1 cup)	3
Lettuce wrap	
beef, 2 (13.5 cm [5"] long x 7.5cm [3"] wide each)	5
chicken, 2 (13.5 cm [5"] long x 7.5 cm [3"] wide each)	4
Limeade	
250 ml (1 cup)	3
Linguine with red clam sauce	
250 ml (1 cup) linguine with 125 ml (1/2 cup) sauce	8
Linguine with white clam sauce	
250 ml (1 cup) linguine with 125 ml (1/2 cup) sauce	10
Liver	
▲ beef, cooked, 1 slice or 125 ml (1/2 cup) or 60 g (2 oz)	2
chicken, cooked, 125 ml (1/2 cup) or 60 g (2 oz)	2
chopped, 60 ml (1/4 cup)	5
lamb, pan-fried, 90 g (3 oz)	5
turkey, cooked, 30 g (1 oz)	1
veal, pan-fried, 90 g (3 oz)	4
Liver with bacon	
2 slices (125 g [4 oz]) with 2 slices bacon	11

Power Foods	PointsPlus® value
Liver with onions	
2 slices (125 g [4 oz]) with 125 ml (1/2 cup) onions	8
Lo mein	
beef, 250 ml (1 cup)	10
chicken, 250 ml (1 cup)	9
pork, 250 ml (1 cup)	9
shrimp, 250 ml (1 cup)	9
vegetable, 250 ml (1 cup)	8
Lobster Cantonese	
250 ml (1 cup)	9
Lobster Newburg	
250 ml (1 cup)	14
Lobster thermidor	
250 ml (1 cup)	14
Lomi lomi salmon	
125 ml (1/2 cup)	2
Lumpia (Filipino spring rolls)	
1 (11 cm x 2.5 cm x 3.5 cm [4 1/2" x 1" x 1 1/2"])	6

M

Power Foods	PointsPlus® value
Macaroni	
regular, cooked, 250 ml (1 cup)	5
▲ whole-wheat, cooked, 250 ml (1 cup)	5
Macaroni and cheese	
250 ml (1 cup)	10
Bahamian, 250 ml (1 cup)	9
Malanga	
▲ cooked, 1 large (200 g [7 oz])	5
▲ cooked, 175 ml (3/4 cup)	4
Manapua with char shiu filling	
1 (95 g [3 1/4 oz])	6
Mandelbrot	
1 slice (7.5 cm x 5 cm x 1.25 cm [3" x 2" x 1/2"])	5
Mango lassi	
250 ml (1 cup)	3

Power Foods	PointsPlus® value
Manicotti	
with meat sauce, 2 pieces with 125 ml (1/2 cup) sauce	16
with tomato sauce, 2 pieces with 125 ml (1/2 cup) sauce	13
Margarine	
regular, 5 ml (1 tsp)	1
Margarine-butter blend	
5 ml (1 tsp)	1
Marmalade	
regular, 15 ml (1 Tbsp)	1
Masala dosa	
with filling, 1 (15 cm [6"] diameter with 75 ml [1/3 cup] potato filling)	13
without filling, 1 (15 cm [6"] diameter)	12
Matzo	
any variety, 1 board (30 g [1 oz])	3
Matzo brie	
1/4 of a 25 cm (10") round or 250 ml (1 cup)	5
Mayonnaise	
regular, 5 ml (1 tsp)	1
Meat loaf	
1 slice (1.75 cm [5/8"] thick)	6
Meatballs	
with sauce, 2 meatballs and 125 ml (1/2 cup) Italian tomato sauce	13
without sauce, 2 (3 cm [1 1/4"] each)	10
Melba toast	
any variety, 4 slices or 6 rounds (20 g [3/4 oz])	2
Milk	
chocolate, low-fat, 250 ml (1 cup)	4
chocolate, regular, 250 ml (1 cup)	6
low-fat or light (1/2% or 1%), 250 ml (1 cup)	3
reduced-fat (2%), 250 ml (1 cup)	3
whole, 250 ml (1 cup)	4

DINING OUT A-Z FOOD LIST

Power Foods	PointsPlus® value
Mochi	
butter, 1 piece (5 cm [2"] square)	7
1 piece (5 cm [2"] square)	2
Mole poblano	
60 ml (1/4 cup)	5
Mongolian beef	
250 ml (1 cup)	8
Moo goo gai pan	
250 ml (1 cup)	7
Moo shoo	
chicken, 125 ml (1/2 cup) with 2 pancakes	8
pork, 125 ml (1/2 cup) with 2 pancakes	9
tofu, 125 ml (1/2 cup) with 2 pancakes	8
Moussaka	
1 piece (7.5 cm x 10 cm [3" x 4"])	12
Muffin	
any type other than those listed here, 1 large (7.5 cm [3"] diameter)	8
any type, fast food, 1 (130 g [4 1/4 oz])	11
banana walnut, restaurant-type, 1 muffin (150 g [5 oz])	15
blueberry, reduced-fat, restaurant-type, 1 muffin (150 g [5 oz])	11
chocolate chip, restaurant-type, 1 muffin (150 g [5 oz])	14
corn, restaurant-type, 1 muffin (150 g [5 oz])	13
cranberry orange, restaurant-type, 1 muffin (150 g [5 oz])	12
mini, any type, 1 (3 cm [1 1/4"] diameter or 15 g [1/2 oz])	1
oat bran, 1 (6 cm [2 1/2"] diameter x 5.5 cm [2 1/4"])	4
pumpkin, restaurant-type, 1 muffin (150 g [5 oz])	12

Power Foods	PointsPlus® value
Muffin, breakfast	
butter on English muffin, fast food, 1 (65 g [2 1/4 oz])	5
cheese and sausage on English muffin, fast food, 1 (125 g [4 oz])	11
egg, cheese, and Canadian bacon on English muffin, fast food, 1 (140 g [4 3/4 oz])	8
egg, cheese, and sausage on English muffin, fast food, 1 (165 g [5 3/4 oz])	13
Muffin, English	
any type other than those listed here, 1 (60 g [2 oz])	3
cinnamon-raisin, 1 (60 g [2 oz])	4
Muffuletta	
1 (335 g [11 1/4 oz])	22
Mun doo	
fried, 4 (185 g [6 1/2 oz])	5
steamed, 4 (165 g [5 3/4 oz])	5
Mung dal	
250 ml (1 cup)	6
Mushrooms, marinated	
125 ml (1/2 cup)	3
Mushrooms, stuffed	
4 (80 g [2 3/4 oz])	4
Mussels Mariniere	
4 mussels with 45 ml (3 Tbsp) sauce	5
Mustard, prepared	
any type other than honey, 15 ml (1 Tbsp)	0
honey, 15 ml (1 Tbsp)	1
honey, 5 ml (1 tsp)	0
Musubi, spam	
1 (8.5 cm x 5 cm x 2.5 cm [3 1/2" x 2" x 1"])	7
Mutter paneer	
250 ml (1 cup)	13

▲ Power Foods	PointsPlus® value

N

Nachos

beef, 4 (265 g [8 1/2 oz])	14
cheese, 4 (90 g [3 oz])	9
cheese and bean, 4 (185 g [6 1/2 oz])	10
cheese and jalapeño peppers, fast food, 6-8 nachos	17
cheese, beans, ground beef, and peppers, fast food, 6-8 nachos (275 g [9 oz])	16
cheese, fast food, 6-8 nachos (125 g [4 oz])	9
chicken, 4 (265 g [8 1/2 oz])	13
with cheese sauce, 125 ml (1/2 cup) tortilla chips with 60 ml (1/4 cup) sauce	6
with cinnamon sugar, fast food, 6-8 nachos (110 g [3 3/4 oz])	17

Nam Prik

| 15 ml (1 Tbsp) | 1 |

Napoleon

| 1 piece (11 cm x 5 cm x 3.5 cm [4 1/2" x 2" x 1 1/2"]) | 15 |

Natto

| 250 ml (1 cup) | 10 |

Nebeyaki udon

| 500 ml (2 cups) | 7 |

Nikujaga

| 250 ml (1 cup) | 14 |

Noodles, cellophane

| cooked, 250 ml (1 cup) | 5 |

Noodles, drunken

| 250 ml (1 cup) | 6 |

Noodles, fried

| 250 ml (1 cup) | 8 |

Noodles, Japanese, soba

| cooked, 250 ml (1 cup) | 3 |
| with sauce, 250 ml (1 cup) | 12 |

▲ Power Foods	PointsPlus® value

Noodles, Japanese, somen

| cooked, 250 ml (1 cup) | 6 |

Noodles, Oriental (bean thread)

| cooked, 250 ml (1 cup) | 6 |

Noodles, rice

| cooked, 250 ml (1 cup) | 5 |

Nuoc cham

| 15 ml (1 Tbsp) | 0 |

Nuts, mixed

dry roasted, 250 ml (1 cup)	23
oil roasted, 250 ml (1 cup)	25
shelled, 30 g (1 oz)	5

O

Oil

| olive, 5 ml (1 tsp) | 1 |

Okonmiyaki, without sauce and mayonnaise (Japanese style pizza)

| 1 (20 cm [8"] diameter) | 9 |

Okra

| fried, 250 ml (1 cup) | 10 |

Olives

| 6 large or 10 small (30 g [1 oz]) | 1 |

Omelette

cheese, 1 (2-egg)	8
ham and cheese, 1 (2-egg)	9
ham and cheese, restaurant-type, 1 (285 g [9 1/2 oz])	15
herb, 1 (2-egg)	6
plain, 1 (2-egg)	6
vegetable, 1 (2-egg)	8
vegetable, restaurant-type, 1 (365 g [11 3/4 oz])	15

Onion, blooming

| 1/4 of a 40 cm (16") diameter onion | 6 |

Onion rings

| fast food, 8-9 rings | 8 |
| fried, 4 (10 cm [4"] diameter each) | 7 |

▲ Power Foods	PointsPlus® value
Orange chicken	
250 ml (1 cup)	14
Osso bucco	
170 g (6 oz) veal with 60 ml (1/4 cup) sauce	12
Oyster pie	
1/8 of a 22 cm (9") pie	10
Oysters	
battered or breaded and fried, fast food, 6 (150 g [5 oz])	10
fried, 10 (155 g [5 1/4 oz])	8
Oysters Rockefeller	
4 (60 g [2 oz])	3

P

▲ Power Foods	PointsPlus® value
Pad Thai (rice noodles with chicken and shrimp)	
250 ml (1 cup)	10
Paella	
250 ml (1 cup)	9
Pajun (Korean (Green) onion and shrimp pancake)	
1 (15-20 cm [6-8"] diameter)	9
Pakora, vegetable	
1 (5 cm x 7.5 cm [2" x 3"] or 50 g [1 3/4 oz])	4
Palak paneer	
250 ml (1 cup)	15
Palak vada (vegetable dumpling)	
fried, 1 (6 cm [2 1/2"] x 3.5 cm [1 1/2"])	5
steamed, 1 (6 cm [2 1/2"] x 3.5 cm [1 1/2"])	3
Pancakes	
buttermilk, restaurant-type, 2 (170 g [6 oz])	13
with butter and syrup, fast food, 2 (250 g [8 oz])	14
without butter and syrup, fast food, 1 serving (155 g [5 1/4 oz])	11

▲ Power Foods	PointsPlus® value
Pancakes, Chinese	
1 (30 g [1 oz])	2
Pancakes, scallion	
1 (12.5 cm [5"] diameter)	7
Pancit canton (sautéed egg noodles)	
250 ml (1 cup)	6
Paneer, fried	
30 g (1 oz)	3
250 ml (1 cup)	6
Panettone	
1/12 of a 22 cm (9") tube or 45 g (1 1/2 oz)	7
Panini	
chicken, 1 (250 g [8 oz])	13
ham and cheese, 1 (215 g [7 1/2 oz])	13
turkey, restaurant-type, 1 (300 g [10 1/2 oz])	19
vegetable, 1 (390 g [13 oz])	12
Paprikash	
375 ml (1 1/2 cups) chicken mixture with 125 ml (1/2 cup) sauce	10
Paratha	
10 cm (4") triangle	4
Pasta	
regular, cooked, 250 ml (1 cup)	5
▲ whole-wheat, cooked, 250 ml (1 cup)	4
Pasta e fagioli	
250 ml (1 cup)	6
Pasta primavera	
with marinara sauce, 250 ml (1 cup) pasta with 175 ml (3/4 cup) sauce	7
with cream sauce, 250 ml (1 cup) pasta with 175 ml (3/4 cup) sauce	14
Pasta with garlic and oil	
250 ml (1 cup)	8
Pastitsio	
1 piece (8 cm x 7.5 cm [3 1/4" x 3"])	14
Pastrami	
beef, extra lean, 1 slice (30 g [1 oz])	1

▲ Power Foods	*PointsPlus®* value
Pâté	
liver, 1 slice (10.5 cm x 3.5 cm x 1.25 cm [4 1/4" x 1 1/2" x 1/2"])	3
Peach melba	
125 ml (1/2 cup) ice cream with 2 peach halves and raspberry sauce	9
Peanuts	
dry roasted, 250 ml (1 cup)	24
oil roasted, 250 ml (1 cup)	23
shelled, 15 ml (1 Tbsp)	2
shelled, 40 (30 g [1 oz])	5
Pear	
poached, 1 pear with 30 ml (2 Tbsp) whipped cream	7
Peas	
▲ chick (garbanzo beans), cooked or canned, 125 ml (1/2 cup)	3
▲ chick (garbanzo beans), cooked or canned, 250 ml (1 cup)	7
Peas, Bahamian style	
with rice, 250 ml (1 cup)	9
Peking duck	
60 g (2 oz) duck with 1 piece duck skin and 3 pancakes	11
Penne a la vodka	
250 ml (1 cup) pasta with 125 ml (1/2 cup) sauce	9
Pepper steak	
170 g (6 oz)	14
Chinese, 250 ml (1 cup)	5
Pepper, stuffed	
with beef and rice, 1 (225 g [7 3/4 oz])	9
Petit fours	
2 (4.5 cm x 3.5 cm x 2.5 cm [1 3/4" x 1 1/2" x 1"] each)	6
Petite marmite	
500 ml (2 cups)	8
Pheasant	
cooked, 30 g (1 oz)	2

▲ Power Foods	*PointsPlus®* value
Picadillo	
250 ml (1 cup)	11
Pickles	
sweet, 1 medium (7 cm [2 3/4"] long) or 1 large (7.5 cm [3"] long)	1
sweet, 1 small	0
sweet, 30 g (1 oz)	1
▲ unsweetened	0
Pico de gallo	
▲ fresh or canned, without added sugar or oil	0
Pie, dessert	
any type other than those listed here, fruit, one-crust, 1/8 of 22 cm (9") diameter	8
any type other than those listed here, fruit, two-crust, 1/8 of 22 cm (9") diameter	11
chiffon, 1/8 of a 22 cm (9") one-crust pie	10
cream, with fruit, 1/8 of a 22 cm (9") one-crust pie	11
cream, without fruit, 1/8 of a 22 cm (9") one-crust pie	10
custard, 1/8 of a 22 cm (9") one-crust pie	9
fried, fruit, 1 (12.5 cm x 9.5 cm [5" x 3 3/4"])	11
fruit, fast food, 1 (8.5 cm [3 1/2"])	9
individual, 1 (12.5 cm x 9.5 cm [5" x 3 3/4"])	11
key lime, 1/8 of a 22 cm (9") one-crust pie	14
meringue, any type other than those listed here, 1/8 of 22 cm (9") diameter	12
mincemeat, with meat, 1/8 of a 22 cm (9") two-crust pie	13
mincemeat, without meat, 1/8 of a 22 cm (9") two-crust pie	16
rhubarb, 1/8 of a 22 cm (9") two-crust pie	13

▲ Power Foods	PointsPlus® value
Pierogies	
cabbage, 2 (8.5 cm [3 1/2"] each)	8
cheese, 2 (8.5 cm [3 1/2"] each)	8
meat, 2 (8.5 cm [3 1/2"] each)	9
potato, 2 (8.5 cm [3 1/2"] each)	8
Pigeon (squab)	
without skin and bone, cooked, 30 g (1 oz)	1
Pita	
white or whole-wheat, 1 large (60 g [2 oz])	4
white or whole-wheat, 1 small (30 g [1 oz])	2
Pizza bagel	
mini, any type, 4 (125 g [4 oz])	5
Pizza, deep dish, one-meat topping, restaurant-type	
1 small slice (1/8 of a 30 cm [12"] or 1/12 of a 40 cm [16"] pie)	8
1 large slice (1/8 of a 40-45 cm [16-18"] pie)	13
Pizza, fast food, single serving	
cheese, 1 (265 g [8 1/2 oz])	15
Pizza, thin crust, cheese, restaurant-type	
1 large slice (1/8 of a 40-45 cm [16-18"] pie)	7
Pizza, thin crust, cheese, restaurant-type	
1 small slice (1/8 of a 30 cm [12"] or 1/12 of a 40 cm [16"] pie)	5
Pizza, thin crust, one-meat topping, restaurant-type	
1 small slice (1/8 of a 30 cm [12"] or 1/12 of a 40 cm [16"] pie)	5
1 large slice (1/8 of a 40-45 cm [16-18"] pie)	8
Plantain	
baked or boiled, 250 ml (1 cup)	5
fried, 250 ml (1 cup)	5

▲ Power Foods	PointsPlus® value
Plátanos maduros (fried sweet plantains)	
250 ml (1 cup)	5
Poi	
▲ 125 ml (1/2 cup) or 125 g (4 oz)	4
Poke, ahi or tako	
125 ml (1/2 cup)	2
Polenta	
cooked, 125 ml (1/2 cup)	3
Popcorn	
buttered, popped, 750 ml (3 cups)	6
movie, without butter, 750 ml (3 cups)	4
▲ plain, air-popped, 750 ml (3 cups)	2
plain, oil-popped, 750 ml (3 cups)	4
Popovers	
2 (7.5 cm [3"] diameter or 45 g [1 1/2 oz] each)	4
Pork	
backribs, cooked, 90 g (3 oz)	8
centre loin, cooked, 1 slice (60 g [2 oz])	3
centre loin, cooked, 90 g (3 oz)	4
▲ centre loin, trimmed, cooked, 1 slice (60 g [2 oz])	2
▲ centre loin, trimmed, cooked, 90 g (3 oz)	4
▲ chop, trimmed, cooked, without bone, 90 g (3 oz)	3
country-style ribs, cooked, 90 g (3 oz)	6
leg cooked, 90 g (3 oz)	6
leg, cooked, 1 slice (60 g [2 oz])	4
leg, trimmed, cooked, 1 slice (60 g [2 oz])	3
leg, trimmed, cooked, 90 g (3 oz)	4
loin, centre rib, cooked, 90 g (3 oz)	5
loin, cooked, 1 slice (60 g [2 oz])	4
loin, cooked, 90 g (3 oz)	5
loin, trimmed, cooked, 1 slice (60 g [2 oz])	3

▲ Power Foods	PointsPlus® value
loin, trimmed, cooked, 90 g (3 oz)	4
shoulder, cooked, 1 slice (60 g [2 oz])	4
shoulder, cooked, 90 g (3 oz)	6
shoulder, trimmed, cooked, 1 slice (60 g [2 oz])	3
shoulder, trimmed, cooked, 90 g (3 oz)	4
sirloin, cooked, 1 slice (60 g [2 oz])	3
sirloin, cooked, 90 g (3 oz)	5
▲ sirloin, trimmed, cooked, 1 slice (60 g [2 oz])	3
▲ sirloin, trimmed, cooked, 90 g (3 oz)	4
spareribs, without bone, cooked, 90 g (3 oz)	8
▲ tenderloin, trimmed, cooked, 1 slice (60 g [2 oz])	2
▲ tenderloin, trimmed, cooked, 250 ml (1 cup)	4
▲ tenderloin, trimmed, cooked, 90 g (3 oz)	3
top loin, cooked, 1 slice (60 g [2 oz])	3
top loin, cooked, 90 g (3 oz)	4
▲ top loin, trimmed, cooked, 1 slice (60 g [2 oz])	2
▲ top loin, trimmed, cooked, 90 g (3 oz)	3
Pork and broccoli	
250 ml (1 cup)	4
Pork, barbecue	
250 ml (1 cup)	9
Pork, Chinese roast	
250 ml (1 cup)	6
Pork, ground	
cooked, 90 g (3 oz)	7
Pork with cashews	
250 ml (1 cup)	12
Portuguese sweet bread	
1/8 loaf (90 g [3 oz])	7
Pot pie	
any type, fast food, 1 (420 g [14 oz])	22

▲ Power Foods	PointsPlus® value
Potato latkes	
2 (8.5 cm [3 1/2"] diameter)	7
Potato pancakes	
1 (95 g [3 1/4 oz])	2
Potato skins	
with cheese, bacon and sour cream, 2 (200 g [7 oz])	10
2 (125 g [4 oz])	6
Potatoes, au gratin	
250 ml (1 cup)	14
Potatoes, baked	
▲ plain, 1 large (200 g [7 oz])	5
▲ plain, 1 medium (160 g [5 1/2 oz])	4
▲ plain, 1 small (90 g [3 oz])	2
stuffed with bacon and cheese, 1 (285 g [9 2/3 oz])	13
stuffed with cheese, 1 (160 g [5 1/2 oz])	5
stuffed with sour cream and chives, 1 (160 g [5 1/2 oz])	5
stuffed with vegetables and cheese, 1 (400 g [13 1/3 oz])	12
with vegetables and cheese, fast food, 1 (390 g [13 oz])	11
Potatoes, hash brown	
fast food, 125 ml (1/2 cup)	4
250 ml (1 cup)	8
Potatoes, home-fried	
250 ml (1 cup)	6
Potatoes, mashed	
garlic, 125 ml (1/2 cup)	5
125 ml (1/2 cup)	3
Potatoes, O'Brien	
250 ml (1 cup)	4
Potatoes, red	
▲ cooked, 1 small (4.5 cm-6 cm [1 3/4-2 1/2"] or 150 g [5 oz])	3
▲ cooked, 1 medium (6-8 cm [2 1/2-3 1/4"] or 170 g [6 oz])	4

Potatoes, red (cont'd)

▲ Power Foods	PointsPlus® value
▲ cooked, 1 large (7.5-10.5 cm [3-4 1/4"] diameter or 300 g [10 1/2 oz])	7
▲ cooked, 125 ml (1/2 cup)	2
Potatoes, scalloped	
125 ml (1/2 cup)	5
Potatoes, sweet	
candied, 125 ml (1/2 cup)	5
▲ cooked, 1 large (12.5 cm [5"] long or 250 ml [1 cup] or 200 g [7 oz])	4
▲ cooked, 1 medium (135 g [4 1/2 oz])	3
▲ cooked, 1 small (90 g [3 oz])	2
Potatoes, white	
▲ cooked, 1 small (4.5 cm-6 cm [1 3/4-2 1/2"] or 150 g [5 oz])	3
▲ cooked, 1 medium (6-8 cm [2 1/2-3 1/4"] or 170 g [6 oz])	4
▲ cooked, 1 large (7.5-10.5 cm [3-4 1/4"] diameter or 300 g [10 1/2 oz])	7
▲ cooked, 125 ml (1/2 cup)	2
Poutine	
20 French fries with 60 g (2 oz) cheese and 125 ml (1/2 cup) sauce	19
Preserves	
15 ml (1 Tbsp)	1
Pretzels	
regular or whole-wheat, 30 g (1 oz)	3
sticks, 45 (2 g [3/4 oz])	2
twists, 15 small or 7 regular or 20 g (3/4 oz)	2
Profiterole	
1 small (30 g [1 oz])	3
Pudding, any flavour	
any type other than those listed here, 250 ml (1 cup)	8
Pudding, banana	
250 ml (1 cup)	9
Pudding, bread	
250 ml (1 cup)	16

▲ Power Foods	PointsPlus® value
Pudding, Indian	
250 ml (1 cup)	8
Pudding, plum	
125 ml (1/2 cup) with 15 ml (1 Tbsp) sauce	11
Pudding, rice	
250 ml (1 cup)	10
Pudding, tapioca	
Thai, 125 ml (1/2 cup)	4
250 ml (1 cup)	6
Pumpkin bread	
1 slice (2 cm [3/4"] thick)	8
Puris	
1 (10 cm [4"] diameter)	3

Q

Quail	
cooked, 30 g (1 oz)	2
cooked, 90 g (3 oz)	5
Quenelles	
8 (6 cm x 3.5 cm x 2 cm [2 1/2" x 1 1/2" x 3/4"])	12
Quesadilla	
beef, 1/2 of 170 g (6") diameter	7
cheese, 1/2 of 170 g (6") diameter	6
chicken, 1/2 of 170 g (6") diameter	7
vegetable, 1/2 of 170 g (6") diameter	7
Quiche	
vegetable, 1/8 of a 22 cm (9") pie	9
Quiche Lorraine	
1/8 of a 22 cm (9") pie	11

R

Raita	
125 ml (1/2 cup)	2
Rajmah	
250 ml (1 cup)	8

DINING OUT A-Z FOOD LIST

Power Foods	PointsPlus® value
Ratatouille	
250 ml (1 cup)	5
Ravioli	
cheese, with tomato sauce, 8 pieces or 250 ml (1 cup) with 125 ml (1/2 cup) sauce	19
cheese, without sauce, 8 pieces or 250 ml (1 cup)	16
meat, with tomato sauce, 8 pieces or 250 ml (1 cup) with 125 ml (1/2 cup) sauce	17
meat, without sauce, 8 pieces or 250 ml (1 cup)	14
Red snapper Veracruz	
170 g (6 oz) cooked fillet with 175 ml (3/4 cup) sauce	12
Relish	
any type, 5 ml (1 tsp)	0
pickle, hot dog, 15 ml (1 Tbsp)	0
pickle, sweet, 15 ml (1 Tbsp)	1
Rice (crisp) and marshmallow treat	
restaurant-type, 100 g (3 1/2 oz)	11
Rice, brown	
cooked, 250 ml (1 cup)	5
Rice, Cuban	
250 ml (1 cup)	6
Rice, fried	
kho-phat (Thai fried rice), 250 ml (1 cup)	9
plain, 250 ml (1 cup)	10
with beef, 250 ml (1 cup)	10
with chicken, 250 ml (1 cup)	10
with pork, 250 ml (1 cup)	10
with shrimp, 250 ml (1 cup)	9
Rice pilaf	
250 ml (1 cup)	7
Rice, Spanish	
250 ml (1 cup)	7
Rice, sushi	
cooked, 125 ml (1/2 cup)	3

Power Foods	PointsPlus® value
Rice, white	
cooked, 250 ml (1 cup)	5
Rice, wild	
cooked, 250 ml (1 cup)	4
Rice, with pigeon peas (arroz con gandules)	
250 ml (1 cup)	8
Risotto	
125 ml (1/2 cup)	6
Rocky mountain oysters	
2 slices (30 g [1 oz] each)	10
Rogan josh	
250 ml (1 cup)	11
Rolls, dinner	
any type, 1 (60 g [2 oz])	5
egg, 1 (6 cm [2 1/2"] diameter)	3
oat bran, 1 (35 g [1 1/4 oz])	2
rye, 1 large (8.5-10 cm [3 1/2-4"] diameter)	3
wheat, 1 (30 g [1 oz])	2
whole-wheat, 1 (45 g [1 1/2 oz])	3
Rolls, French	
1 (35 g [1 1/4 oz])	3
Rolls, hard	
1 (60 g [2 oz])	4
Rolls, Kaiser	
restaurant-type, 1 (60 g [2 oz])	4
Ropa vieja	
250 ml (1 cup)	9
Runza	
1 (160 g [5 1/2 oz])	10

S

Saag gosht	
250 ml (1 cup)	7
Saag paneer	
250 ml (1 cup)	8

▲ Power Foods	PointsPlus® value
Sachertorte	
1/16 of a 22 cm (9") cake	9
Saganaki	
1 piece (2.5 cm [1"] x 5 cm [2"] x 1.25 cm [1/2"] thick)	6
Saimin	
250 ml (1 cup)	5
Salad	
Caesar, 750 ml (3 cups)	7
carrot and raisin, 125 ml (1/2 cup)	8
chef's, fast food, 1 (345 g [11 1/2 oz])	6
chef's, with dressing, 1 L (4 cups)	8
chef's, without dressing, 1 L (4 cups)	6
chicken, 125 ml (1/2 cup)	6
chicken macaroni, 250 ml (1 cup)	7
chicken, Oriental, 500 ml (2 cups)	8
cobb, without dressing, 750 ml (3 cups)	11
conch, 250 ml (1 cup)	3
egg, 125 ml (1/2 cup)	8
garden, restaurant-type, 1 (170 g [6 oz])	3
Greek, with dressing, 750 ml (3 cups)	10
Greek, without dressing, 750 ml (3 cups)	3
green papaya, with pork and shrimp, 250 ml (1 cup)	4
green papaya, without meat, 2 lettuce leaves filled with salad	2
grilled chicken Caesar, restaurant-type, 185 g (6 1/2 oz)	8
grilled chicken, without dressing, fast food, 1 (380 g [12 1/4 oz])	5
lobster, 125 ml (1/2 cup)	4
macaroni, 125 ml (1/2 cup)	7
▲ mixed greens	0
Niçoise, with dressing, 1 L (4 cups)	20

▲ Power Foods	PointsPlus® value
Niçoise, without dressing, 1 L (4 cups)	9
pasta, 125 ml (1/2 cup)	4
potato, 125 ml (1/2 cup)	8
potato macaroni, 125 ml (1/2 cup)	10
potato, German, 125 ml (1/2 cup)	2
potato, hot, with ham, 250 ml (1 cup)	8
seaweed, 125 ml (1/2 cup)	1
shrimp, 125 ml (1/2 cup)	3
▲ side, without dressing, fast food, 1	0
southwestern grilled chicken, restaurant-type, 1 (395 g [13 1/4 oz])	7
spinach, with dressing, 500 ml (2 cups)	7
taco, with chili con carne, fast food, 375 ml (1 1/2 cups)	7
taco, with shell, without dressing, fast food, 1	18
taco, without shell, without dressing, fast food, 1	10
Thai beef, 250 ml (1 cup)	15
Thai chicken, 250 ml (1 cup)	12
Thai seafood, 500 ml (2 cups)	11
three-bean, 125 ml (1/2 cup)	5
tomato and mozzarella, without dressing, 2 large tomato slices with 60 g (2 oz) cheese	5
▲ tossed	0
tuna, 125 ml (1/2 cup)	8
tuna macaroni, 250 ml (1 cup)	6
turkey cobb, restaurant-type, 1 (335 g [11 1/4 oz])	10
turkey macaroni, 250 ml (1 cup)	6
vegetable, with cheese and egg, without dressing, fast food, 375 ml (1 1/2 cups)	3
vegetable, with chicken, without dressing, fast food, 375 ml (1 1/2 cups)	2
vegetable, with pasta and seafood, without dressing, fast food, 375 ml (1 1/2 cups)	10

▲ Power Foods	PointsPlus® value
vegetable, with shrimp, without dressing, fast food, 375 ml (1 1/2 cups)	3
vegetable, with turkey, ham and cheese, without dressing, fast food, 375 ml (1 1/2 cups)	7
Waldorf, 125 ml (1/2 cup)	6
yogourt and cucumber, 125 ml (1/2 cup)	1
Salisbury steak	
170 g (6 oz)	12
Salsa	
▲ black bean and corn, 125 ml (1/2 cup)	2
▲ fat-free	0
▲ peach, 30 ml (2 Tbsp)	0
▲ peach, 125 ml (1/2 cup)	1
pineapple, 30 ml (2 Tbsp)	0
pineapple, 125 ml (1/2 cup)	1
Samosa	
1 (6 cm [2 1/2"] x 6 cm [2 1/2"] x 7.5 cm [3"] triangle)	3
Sandwich	
bacon, lettuce, and tomato, restaurant-type, 1 (280 g [9 1/4 oz])	18
chicken fillet, plain, fast food, 1 (185 g [6 1/2 oz])	14
chicken fillet, with cheese, fast food, 1 (250 g [8 oz])	17
chicken salad on regular bread, 1 (155 cm [5 1/4 oz])	10
chicken, fried, fast food, 1 (205 g [7 1/4 oz])	12
club, 1 (270 g [8 3/4 oz])	17
croque-monsieur, 1 (185 g [6 1/2 oz])	12
Cuban, 1/2 (16 m x 7.5 cm x 10 cm [6 1/2" x 3" x 4"])	12
egg and cheese, fast food, 1 (155 cm [5 1/4 oz])	9
egg salad, 1 (170 g [6 oz])	12

▲ Power Foods	PointsPlus® value
fish and cheese, fried, fast food, 1 (185 g [6 1/2 oz])	14
fish with tartar sauce, fast food, 1 (160 g [5 1/2 oz])	12
grilled cheese with bacon, 1 (140 g [4 3/4 oz])	17
grilled cheese, restaurant-type, 1 (125 g [4 oz])	14
grilled chicken, fast food, 1 (190 g [6 3/4 oz])	10
grilled ham and cheese, restaurant-type, 1 (150 g [5 oz])	15
grinder, 1 (80 g [2 3/4 oz])	6
ham and cheese, 1 (125 g [4 oz])	10
ham and cheese, fast food, 1 (155 cm [5 1/4 oz])	9
ham and cheese, restaurant-type, 1 (275 g [9 oz])	9
ham, egg, and cheese, fast food, 1 (150 g [5 oz])	9
hero, 1 (335 g [11 1/4 oz])	6
hoagie, 1 (80 g [2 3/4 oz])	6
lobster roll, 1 (130 g [4 1/4 oz])	6
lobster salad, 1 (135 g [4 1/2 oz])	8
Monte Cristo, 1 (110 g [3 3/4 oz])	7
peanut butter and jelly, 1 (95 g [3 1/4 oz)	9
peanut butter and jelly, restaurant-type, 1 (130 g [4 1/4 oz])	11
Philly cheese steak, 1 (275 g [9 oz])	14
po' boy (poor boy), 1 (80 g [2 3/4 oz])	6
po' boy, oyster, 1 (270 g [8 3/4 oz])	19
po' boy, shrimp, 1 (270 g [8 3/4 oz])	20
Reuben, 1 (250 g [8 oz])	18
roast beef, 1 (215 g [7 1/2 oz])	9
roast beef with cheese, fast food, 1 (170 g [6 oz])	12
roast beef, open-face, with gravy, 1 (165 g [5 3/4 oz])	9
roast beef, plain, fast food, 1 (150 g [5 oz])	9

DINING OUT A-Z FOOD LIST

Power Foods	PointsPlus® value	Power Foods	PointsPlus® value
shrimp salad, 1 (135 g [4 1/2 oz])	8	chili, red, 60 ml (1/4 cup)	1
steak, fast food, 1 (200 g [7 oz])	12	chili, sriracha, 5 ml (1 tsp)	0
submarine, 1 (80 g [2 3/4 oz])	6	clam, red, 125 ml (1/2 cup)	3
submarine with cold cuts, fast food, 1 (250 g [8 oz])	12	clam, white, 125 ml (1/2 cup)	5
submarine with roast beef, fast food, 1 (215 g [7 1/2 oz])	11	curry, Hawaiian-style, 60 ml (1/4 cup)	5
submarine with tuna salad, fast food, 1 (275 g [9 oz])	16	donair, 30 ml (2 Tbsp)	2
		duck, 15 ml (1 Tbsp)	1
toasted cheese, 1 (110 g [3 3/4 oz])	9	hoisin, 5 ml (1 tsp)	0
tuna melt, 1 (165 g [5 3/4 oz])	10	hollandaise, 60 ml (1/4 cup)	8
tuna salad, 1 (175 g [6 1/4 oz])	11	horseradish, 15 ml (1 Tbsp)	0
turkey, 1 (125 g [4 oz])	7	hot dog, 60 ml (1/4 cup)	2
Sashimi		hot, any type, 5 ml (1 tsp)	0
any type except salmon or mackerel, 4 pieces (60 g [2 oz])	1	kung pao, 30 ml (2 Tbsp)	2
		marinara, 125 ml (1/2 cup)	3
mackerel, 4 pieces (60 g [2 oz])	4	meat, 125 ml (1/2 cup)	5
salmon, 4 pieces (60 g [2 oz])	2	mornay, 60 ml (1/4 cup)	4
Satay		oyster, 5 ml (1 tsp)	0
beef, with peanut sauce, 2 skewers with 60 ml (1/4 cup) sauce	12	peanut satay, 15 ml (1 Tbsp)	1
		peanut, spicy, 30 ml (2 Tbsp)	4
beef, without peanut sauce, 2 skewers (90 g [3 oz])	5	pepper, 5 ml (1 tsp)	0
		pesto, 30 ml (2 Tbsp)	4
chicken, with peanut sauce, 2 skewers with 60 ml (1/4 cup) sauce	12	plum, 15 ml (1 Tbsp)	2
		puttanesca, 125 ml (1/2 cup)	12
		remoulade, 30 ml (2 Tbsp)	4
chicken, without peanut sauce, 2 skewers (90 g [3 oz])	3	shoyu (soy), 15 ml (1 Tbsp)	0
Sauce		shoyu (soy), low-sodium, 15 ml (1 Tbsp)	0
Alfredo, regular, 125 ml (1/2 cup)	10	sofrito, 60 ml (1/4 cup)	4
barbecue, 15 ml (1 Tbsp)	0	soy (shoyu), 15 ml (1 Tbsp)	0
barbecue, 60 ml (1/4 cup)	1	soy (shoyu), low-sodium, 15 ml (1 Tbsp)	0
béarnaise, 60 ml (1/4 cup)	8	Spanish, 125 ml (1/2 cup)	3
black bean, 5 ml (1 tsp)	0	steak, 15 ml (1 Tbsp)	0
Bolognese meat, 125 ml (1/2 cup)	6	taco, 15 ml (1 Tbsp)	0
brown, Chinese, 60 ml (1/4 cup)	1	tahini, 30 ml (2 Tbsp)	5
cheese, 60 ml (1/4 cup)	2	tamari, 15 ml (1 Tbsp)	0
chili, green, 60 ml (1/4 cup)	0	tartar, 15 ml (1 Tbsp)	2
chili, red, 15 ml (1 Tbsp)	0		

▲ Power Foods	PointsPlus® value
teriyaki, 15 ml (1 Tbsp)	0
tomato, Italian, 125 ml (1/2 cup)	3
tzatziki, 125 ml (1/2 cup)	2
Vietnamese spring roll dipping, 30 ml (2 Tbsp)	0
wine, 60 ml (1/4 cup)	3
Worcestershire, 15 ml (1 Tbsp)	0
Sauerbraten	
90 g (3 oz) beef with 30 ml (2 Tbsp) gravy	6
Sauerkraut	
▲ bottled or canned	0
Sausage	
andouille, 60 g (2 oz)	3
beef and pork, cooked, 1 link or patty (30 g [1 oz])	3
beef, cooked, 30 g (1 oz)	2
blood pudding (blood sausage), 30 g (1 oz)	3
chicken, cooked, 45 g (1 1/2 oz)	1
chorizo, 1 link (13.5 cm [5 1/2"] long or 110 g [3 1/2 oz])	12
Italian pork, cooked, 1 link (70 g [2 1/3 oz])	6
patty, restaurant-type, 1 patty (45 g [1 1/2 oz])	4
Sausage	
Polish, 30 g (1 oz)	3
pork and beef, smoked link, 1 (10 cm x 2.75 cm [4" x 1 1/8"] diameter)	6
pork, cooked, 1 patty (30 g [1 oz])	3
pork, smoked link, 1 (10 cm x 2.75 cm [4" x 1 1/8"] diameter)	6
summer, beef and pork (huringer, cervelat), 30 g (1 oz)	3
Sausage biscuit	
fast food, 1 (135 g [4 1/2 oz])	13
Sausage in brioche	
1 slice (5 cm [2"] thick)	16

▲ Power Foods	PointsPlus® value
Sausage on a roll	
plain, 1 (155 cm [5 1/4 oz])	10
Scallops, fried	
20 small (100 g [3 1/2 oz])	6
breaded, fast food, 6 pieces (150 g [5 oz])	11
Schaum torte	
with whipped cream, 1/10 of a 25 cm (10") pan	9
without whipped cream, 1/10 of a 25 cm (10") pan	4
Schmaltz (chicken fat)	
15 ml (1 Tbsp)	3
Scone	
1 small (45 g [1 1/2 oz])	4
1 regular (75 g [2 1/2 oz])	7
blueberry, restaurant-type, 1 (130 g [4 1/4 oz])	12
chocolate, cinnamon, or raspberry, restaurant-type, 1 (130 g [4 1/4 oz])	13
cranberry or orange, restaurant-type, 1 (130 g [4 1/4 oz])	11
Scrapple	
1 slice (11 cm [4 1/2"] x 2 cm [3/4"] x 1 cm [3/8"] thick) or 60 g (2 oz)	3
Seafood cakes (haw mok thalay)	
175 ml (3/4 cup)	9
Seeds	
caraway, flax, poppy, sesame, sunflower, 15 ml (1 Tbsp)	1
caraway, flax, poppy, sesame, sunflower, 5 ml (1 tsp)	0
Sesame chicken	
250 ml (1 cup)	10
Sesame noodles	
250 ml (1 cup)	7
Shabu shabu	
125 ml (4 oz) beef, 60 g (2 oz) tofu, and 375 ml (1 1/2 cups) vegetables	10

Power Foods	PointsPlus® value
Shake	
milk, any flavour, fast food, 1 large (500 ml [16 fl oz])	16
milk, any flavour, fast food, 1 medium (375 ml [12 fl oz])	12
Shark, batter-dipped and fried	
90 g (3 oz)	5
Shawarma	
chicken, 125 ml (1/2 cup)	7
chicken, without skin and bone, 1 thigh (60 g [2 oz])	5
Shellfish	
▲ clams, cooked, 125 ml (1/2 cup) or 60 g (2 oz)	2
conch, cracked, 1 (15 cm [6"] long x 7.5 cm [3"])	10
▲ crab, imitation (surimi), 125 ml (1/2 cup) or 90 g (3 oz)	2
▲ crabmeat, cooked, 125 ml (1/2 cup) or 60 g (2 oz)	1
▲ crabmeat, lump, 90 g (3 oz)	2
▲ crayfish, cooked, 16 or 125 ml (1/2 cup) or 60 g (2 oz)	1
cuttlefish, cooked, 90 g (3 oz)	3
▲ lobster, cooked, 1/2 cup (75 g [2 1/2 oz])	2
▲ lobster, cooked, 60 g (2 oz)	1
▲ lobster, imitation (surimi), 125 ml (1/2 cup) or 90 g (3 oz)	2
lobster, spiny, cooked, 1 (165 g [5 3/4 oz])	5
▲ mussels, cooked, 125 ml (1/2 cup) or 60 g (2 oz)	2
▲ oysters, cooked, 125 ml (1/2 cup)	2
▲ oysters, cooked or uncooked, 6 medium (60 g [2 oz])	1
▲ scallops, cooked, 4 large or 10 small (60 g [2 oz])	2
▲ scallops, cooked, 90 g (3 oz)	2
▲ shrimp, cooked, 60 g (2 oz)	1
▲ squid, cooked, 90 g (3 oz)	2

Power Foods	PointsPlus® value
Shepherd's pie	
250 ml (1 cup)	10
Sherbet	
125 ml (1/2 cup)	3
Shish kabob	
lamb, 2 small skewers (140 g [4 3/4 oz])	8
Shoyu chicken	
1 thigh (90 g [3 oz])	6
Shrimp	
breaded and fried, fast food, 6-8 shrimp (165 g [5 3/4 oz])	12
broiled, stuffed, 6 large (170 g [6 oz])	18
Shrimp and broccoli	
250 ml (1 cup)	3
Shrimp, barbecued	
4 large shrimp with 60 ml (1/4 cup) sauce	11
Shrimp Cantonese	
250 ml (1 cup)	9
Shrimp, fried	
10 (150 g [5 oz])	9
stuffed, 6 large (285 g [9 1/2 oz])	11
Shrimp puffs	
6 (45 g [1 1/2"] rounds)	5
Shrimp remoulade	
6 small shrimp with 60 ml (1/4 cup) remoulade sauce	9
Shrimp scampi	
9 medium (100 g [3 1/2 oz])	10
Shrimp toast	
1 piece (30 g [1 oz])	3
Shumai	
fried, 2 (5 cm [2"] diameter)	3
steamed, 2 (5 cm [2"] diameter)	3
Sloppy Joe	
1 (170 g [6 oz])	9
Smoothie	
250 ml (1 cup)	4

Power Foods	PointsPlus® value
Snow cone	
1 (250 ml [8 fl oz])	3
Soft drink, diet	
any flavour, 375 ml (12 fl oz)	0
Soft drink, sweetened with sugar	
any flavour other than those listed here, sweetened with sugar, 375 ml (12 fl oz)	4
cream, 375 ml (12 fl oz)	5
ginger ale, 375 ml (12 fl oz)	3
grape, 375 ml (12 fl oz)	5
orange, 375 ml (12 fl oz)	5
tonic water, 1 bottle (330 ml [11 fl oz])	3
Soft drink, unsweetened	
club soda, 375 ml (12 fl oz)	0
seltzer, plain or flavoured, 375 ml (12 fl oz)	0
Sopaipillas	
2 (10 cm x 7.5 cm [4" x 3"] each)	3
Sorbet, any flavour	
1 scoop or 125 ml (1/2 cup)	2
Soufflé	
cheese, 250 ml (1 cup)	5
fruit, 125 ml (1/2 cup)	4
Soup	
asparagus crab, 250 ml (1 cup)	2
avgolemono, 250 ml (1 cup)	4
black bean, 250 ml (1 cup)	2
broccoli cheese, 250 ml (1 cup)	7
cabbage, 250 ml (1 cup)	2
Cheddar cheese, 250 ml (1 cup)	10
cherry, 250 ml (1 cup)	8
chicken enchilada, 250 ml (1 cup)	6
chicken noodle, 250 ml (1 cup)	3
chicken, with matzo balls, 250 ml (1 cup) soup with 2 (3.5 cm [1 1/2"]) matzo balls	3
chicken, with tortilla strips and shredded cheese, 250 ml (1 cup)	5

Power Foods	PointsPlus® value
chicken, without matzo balls (broth only), 250 ml (1 cup)	0
clam chowder, Manhattan, 250 ml (1 cup)	5
clam chowder, New England, 250 ml (1 cup)	5
cream of broccoli, 250 ml (1 cup)	7
cream of mushroom, 250 ml (1 cup)	9
cream of potato, 250 ml (1 cup)	3
cream of tomato, 250 ml (1 cup)	5
▲ egg drop, 250 ml (1 cup)	1
French onion au gratin, 250 ml (1 cup)	8
gazpacho, 250 ml (1 cup)	4
hot and sour, 250 ml (1 cup)	3
hot and spicy chicken, 250 ml (1 cup)	4
Italian wedding, 250 ml (1 cup)	5
knefla, 250 ml (1 cup)	7
lentil, 250 ml (1 cup)	4
lobster bisque, 250 ml (1 cup)	4
minestrone, 250 ml (1 cup)	5
miso, 250 ml (1 cup)	2
mulligatawny, 250 ml (1 cup)	7
mushroom barley, 250 ml (1 cup)	4
oxtail, 250 ml (1 cup)	2
oxtail, Hawaiian-style, 250 ml (1 cup)	7
pigeon pea and dumpling, 375 ml (1 1/2 cups)	9
Portuguese bean, 250 ml (1 cup)	6
pozole (pork and hominy), 250 ml (1 cup)	5
sambhar (Indian lentil), 250 ml (1 cup)	3
Scotch broth, 250 ml (1 cup)	6
shark fin, 250 ml (1 cup)	3
split pea, 250 ml (1 cup)	4
suimono, 250 ml (1 cup)	2
Thai chicken coconut, 250 ml (1 cup)	10
tomato, 250 ml (1 cup)	3
tortilla, 250 ml (1 cup)	7
turtle, 250 ml (1 cup)	3

DINING OUT A-Z FOOD LIST

Power Foods	PointsPlus® value
vegetable, 250 ml (1 cup)	3
vichyssoise, 250 ml (1 cup)	3
Vietnamese beef noodle, 250 ml (1 cup)	2
wonton, 250 ml (1 cup) with 4 wontons	5
yogourt and cucumber, 250 ml (1 cup)	3
Souse, chicken	
1 leg and 1 thigh with skin (135 g [4 1/2 oz])	8
Souvlaki, chicken	
1 large or 2 small skewers (135 g [4 1/2 oz])	5
in pita bread, 1 (185 g [6 1/2 oz])	8
Souvlaki, lamb	
1 large or 2 small skewers (140 g [4 3/4 oz])	8
in pita bread, 1 (185 g [6 1/2 oz])	9
Spaetzle	
125 ml (1/2 cup)	6
Spaghetti	
regular, cooked, 250 ml (1 cup)	5
spinach, cooked, 250 ml (1 cup)	4
▲ whole-wheat, cooked, 250 ml (1 cup)	4
Spaghetti bolognese	
250 ml (1 cup) spaghetti with 125 ml (1/2 cup) sauce	12
Spaghetti carbonara	
250 ml (1 cup)	13
Spaghetti with marinara sauce	
250 ml (1 cup) spaghetti with 125 ml (1/2 cup) sauce	8
Spaghetti with meat sauce	
250 ml (1 cup) spaghetti with 125 ml (1/2 cup) sauce	11
with meatballs, 250 ml (1 cup) spaghetti with 125 ml (1/2 cup) sauce and 2 meatballs	18
Spanakopita	
1 (7.5 cm [3"]) square or 250 ml (1 cup)	9

Power Foods	PointsPlus® value
Spareribs, barbecued	
4 (10 cm [4"] long)	9
6 (175 g [6 1/4 oz])	13
Chinese, 2 (10 cm [4"] long)	4
Spoon bread	
125 ml (1/2 cup)	5
Spring roll	
beef or pork, 1 (11 cm [4 1/2"] long)	6
chicken, 1 (11 cm [4 1/2"] long)	5
shrimp, 1 (11 cm [4 1/2"] long)	4
Thai, 1 (10 cm [4"] long)	5
Vietnamese, fresh, 1 (50 g [1 3/4 oz])	2
Vietnamese, fried, 1 (10 cm [4"] long)	5
Sprinkles	
any type, 15 ml (1 Tbsp)	0
Spumoni	
125 ml (1/2 cup)	7
Squab (pigeon)	
▲ without skin and bone, cooked, 30 g (1 oz)	1
Squid, fried	
90 g (3 oz)	4
Steak au poivre	
170 g (6 oz) with 15 ml (1 Tbsp) sauce	13
Steak, chicken-fried	
with cream gravy, 170 g (6 oz) with 60 ml (1/4 cup) cream gravy	18
without gravy, 170 g (6 oz)	14
Stew	
bean and lentil (dal maharani), 250 ml (1 cup)	6
beef, 250 ml (1 cup)	7
Brunswick, 375 ml (1 1/2 cups)	7
carne guisado (Cuban beef stew), 250 ml (1 cup)	7
Irish brown, 250 ml (1 cup)	8
lamb, 250 ml (1 cup)	6
menudo (beef tripe and hominy stew), 250 ml (1 cup)	7

▲ Power Foods	PointsPlus® value
Sticky rice with mango	
250 ml (1 cup) sliced mangoes with 125 ml (1/2 cup) sticky rice	11
Stir-fry	
beef, with garlic or black bean sauce, 250 ml (1 cup)	8
broccoli, 250 ml (1 cup)	4
bulgogi (beef), 250 ml (1 cup)	5
chicken, with garlic or black bean sauce, 250 ml (1 cup)	8
▲ mung beans, sprouted, 250 ml (1 cup)	2
pad si-iew (beef with noodles), 250 ml (1 cup)	7
pork, with garlic or black bean sauce, 250 ml (1 cup)	9
shrimp, with garlic or black bean sauce, 250 ml (1 cup)	7
vegetables with beef, 250 ml (1 cup)	4
vegetables with chicken, 250 ml (1 cup)	3
vegetables with pork, 250 ml (1 cup)	4
vegetables, with oil or sauce, 250 ml (1 cup)	4
▲ vegetables, without sauce, 250 ml (1 cup)	1
Stromboli	
1 slice (2.5 cm [1"] thick or 60 g [2 oz])	5
Strudel, any type	
1 piece (13.5 cm x 5 cm [5 1/2" x 2"])	12
Succotash	
▲ cooked, 250 ml (1 cup)	6
Sugar, brown	
light or dark, packed, 5 ml (1 tsp)	0
light or dark, packed, 15 ml (1 Tbsp)	1
Sugar, white	
15 ml (1 Tbsp)	1
Sukiyaki with sauce	
500 ml (2 cups) with 60 ml (1/4 cup) sauce	15

▲ Power Foods	PointsPlus® value
Summer squash casserole	
250 ml (1 cup)	9
Sunomono	
125 ml (1/2 cup)	0
Surimi, crab or lobster	
▲ flake- or chunk-style, 125 ml (1/2 cup) or 90 g (3 oz)	2
Sushi	
Alaskan roll, 2 pieces (2.5 cm [1"] high x 4.5 cm [1 3/4"] diameter)	3
California roll, 4 large pieces (2.5 cm [1"] high x 4.5 cm [1 3/4"] diameter) or 30 g (1 oz) each	4
cone, 1	3
inari, 1	3
kappa maki (cucumber roll), 4 medium pieces (3.5 cm [1 1/2"] diameter x 2 cm [3/4"] thick)	3
kappa maki (cucumber roll), 6 small pieces (2.5 cm [1"] diameter x 2.5 cm [1"] thick)	3
maki (vegetables and rice rolled with seaweed), 4 medium pieces (3.5 cm [1 1/2"] diameter x 2 cm [3/4"] thick)	3
maki (vegetables and rice rolled with seaweed), 6 small pieces (2.5 cm [1"] diameter x 2.5 cm [1"] thick)	3
nigiri (sliced uncooked fish over rice), 4 medium pieces (3.5 cm [1 1/2"] diameter x 2 cm [3/4"] thick)	3
nigiri (sliced uncooked fish over rice), 6 small pieces (2.5 cm [1"] diameter x 2.5 cm [1"] thick)	3
nigiri uni (sea urchin), 4 medium pieces (5 cm [2"] long x 2 cm [3/4"] wide)	3

DINING OUT A-Z FOOD LIST

▲ Power Foods	*PointsPlus®* value	▲ Power Foods	*PointsPlus®* value
nigiri, albacore (white tuna), 4 medium pieces (5 cm [2"] long x 2 cm [3/4"] wide)	3	nigiri, suzuki (sea bass), 4 medium pieces (5 cm [2"] long x 2 cm [3/4"] wide)	3
nigiri, amaebi (sweet shrimp), 4 medium pieces (5 cm [2"] long x 2 cm [3/4"] wide)	3	nigiri, suzume, 4 medium pieces (5 cm [2"] long x 2 cm [3/4"] wide)	3
nigiri, conch, 4 medium pieces (5 cm [2"] long x 2 cm [3/4"] wide)	3	nigiri, tai (red snapper), 4 medium pieces (5 cm [2"] long x 2 cm [3/4"] wide)	3
nigiri, ebi (cooked shrimp), 4 medium pieces (5 cm [2"] long x 2 cm [3/4"] wide)	3	nigiri, tairagai (scallops), 4 medium pieces (5 cm [2"] long x 2 cm [3/4"] wide)	3
nigiri, hamachi (yellow tail), 4 medium pieces (5 cm [2"] long x 2 cm [3/4"] wide)	3	nigiri, tako (octopus), 4 medium pieces (5 cm [2"] long x 2 cm [3/4"] wide)	3
nigiri, hirame (fluke), 4 medium pieces (5 cm [2"] long x 2 cm [3/4"] wide)	3	nigiri, tobiko (flying fish roe), 4 medium pieces (5 cm [2"] long x 2 cm [3/4"] wide)	3
nigiri, hokigai (surf clam), 4 medium pieces (5 cm [2"] long x 2 cm [3/4"] wide)	3	nigiri, unagi (fresh water eel), 4 medium pieces (5 cm [2"] long x 2 cm [3/4"] wide)	3
nigiri, ika (squid), 4 medium pieces (5 cm [2"] long x 2 cm [3/4"] wide)	3	nori maki (uncooked fish and rice rolled with seaweed), 4 medium pieces (3.5 cm [1 1/2"] diameter x 2 cm [3/4"] thick)	3
nigiri, ikura (salmon roe), 4 medium pieces (5 cm [2"] long x 2 cm [3/4"] wide)	3	nori maki (uncooked fish and rice rolled with seaweed), 6 small pieces (2.5 cm [1"] diameter x 2.5 cm [1"] thick)	3
nigiri, kani (crab), 4 medium pieces (5 cm [2"] long x 2 cm [3/4"] wide)	3	Philadelphia roll, 2 large pieces (2.5 cm [1"] high x 4.5 cm [1 3/4"] diameter)	3
nigiri, maguro (tuna), 4 medium pieces (5 cm [2"] long x 2 cm [3/4"] wide)	3	rainbow roll, 4 medium pieces (3.5 cm [1 1/2"] diameter x 2 cm [3/4"] thick)	3
nigiri, masago (smelt roe), 4 medium pieces (5 cm [2"] long x 2 cm [3/4"] wide)	3	rainbow roll, 6 small pieces (2.5 cm [1"] diameter x 2.5 cm [1"] thick)	3
nigiri, saba (mackerel), 4 medium pieces (5 cm [2"] long x 2 cm [3/4"] wide)	3	spider roll, 6 pieces (5 cm [2"] diameter x 2.5 cm [1"] thick)	10
nigiri, sake (fresh salmon), 4 medium pieces (5 cm [2"] long x 2 cm [3/4"] wide)	3	tamago-yaki (omelette roll), 2 pieces (2 cm [3/4"] wide)	3
nigiri, smoked salmon, 4 medium pieces (5 cm [2"] long x 2 cm [3/4"] wide)	3	tempura roll, shrimp, 6 pieces (3.5 cm [1 1/2"] diameter x 2.5 cm [1"] thick)	10

▲ Power Foods   *PointsPlus®* value

tempura roll, vegetable, 6 pieces (3.5 cm [1 1/2"] diameter x 2.5 cm [1"] thick)	5
tuna roll, 4 medium pieces (3.5 cm [1 1/2"] diameter x 2 cm [3/4"] thick))	3
tuna roll, 6 small pieces (2.5 cm [1"] diameter x 2.5 cm [1"] thick)	3
tuna roll, spicy, 6 pieces (5 cm [2"] diameter x 2.5 cm [1"] thick)	7
unagi maki, 4 medium pieces (3.5 cm [1 1/2"] diameter x 2 cm [3/4"] thick)	3
unagi maki, 6 small pieces (2.5 cm [1"] diameter x 2.5 cm [1"] thick)	3
uni maki, 4 medium pieces (3.5 cm [1 1/2"] diameter x 2 cm [3/4"] thick)	3
uni maki, 6 small pieces (2.5 cm [1"] diameter x 2.5 cm [1"] thick)	3
yellow tail roll, 4 medium pieces (3.5 cm [1 1/2"] diameter x 2 cm [3/4"] thick)	3
yellow tail roll, 6 small pieces (2.5 cm [1"] diameter x 2.5 cm [1"] thick)	3

Swedish meatballs

6 (2.5 cm [1"] diameter)	10

Sweet and sour

beef, 250 ml (1 cup)	13
chicken, 250 ml (1 cup)	11
pork, 250 ml (1 cup)	13
shrimp, 250 ml (1 cup)	11

Sweet potato pie

1/8 of a 22 cm (9") pie	11

Sweet roll

1 large (125 g [4 oz])	6
cheese, 1 (65 g [2 1/4 oz])	7

Sweetbreads

▲ cooked, 30 g (1 oz)	1

Syrup

chocolate, 15 ml (1 Tbsp)	1
chocolate fudge, 30 ml (2 Tbsp)	4
maple, 15 ml (1 Tbsp)	1
pancake, regular, 15 ml (1 Tbsp)	1
pancake, with butter, 15 ml (1 Tbsp)	2
table blend, 15 ml (1 Tbsp)	2

Szechuan pork hotpot

250 ml (1 cup)	6

T

Tabouli

125 ml (1/2 cup)	6

Taco

beef, 1 (100 g [3 1/2 oz])	6
breakfast, 1 (100 g [3 1/2 oz])	5
chicken, 1 (100 g [3 1/2 oz])	5
fish, 1 (130 g [4 1/4 oz])	5
hard, fast food, 1 (90 g [3 oz])	4
pork, 1 (100 g [3 1/2 oz])	5
soft, fast food, 1 (100 g [3 1/2 oz])	4

Tamale pie

250 ml (1 cup)	12

Tamales

2 (10 cm x 5 cm [4" x 2"])	10

Tandoori chicken

breast, without skin, 1 piece (135 g [4 1/2 oz])	4
thigh, without skin, 1 piece (90 g [3 oz])	4

Tandoori fish

175 ml (3/4 cup)	5

Tandoori shrimp

175 ml (3/4 cup)	3

▲ Power Foods	*PointsPlus®* value
Taquitos	
beef, 1 (13.5 cm [5 1/2"] x 3.5 cm [1 1/2"])	5
chicken, 1 (13.5 cm [5 1/2"] x 3.5 cm [1 1/2"])	3
Tarte aux fruits	
1/8 of 22 cm (9") tart	11
individual, 1 (10 cm [4"])	15
Tea	
decaffeinated or regular, hot or iced, sweetened with sugar, 250 ml (1 cup)	2
decaffeinated or regular, hot or iced, without sugar, 250 ml (1 cup)	0
herb, chamomile, brewed, 250 ml (1 cup)	0
Tempeh (fermented soybean cake)	
60 ml (1/4 cup) or 45 g (1 1/2 oz)	2
Tempura	
shrimp, 4 jumbo (110 g [3 3/4 oz])	13
vegetable, 250 ml (1 cup)	8
Teppan yaki (mixed grill of beef, chicken, shrimp and vegetables)	
375 ml (1 1/2 cups)	12
Teriyaki	
beef, 2 slices (125 g [4 oz])	7
chicken, 2 slices (125 g [4 oz])	6
fish other than salmon, 125 g (4 oz)	6
salmon, 125 g (4 oz)	7
tofu, 250 ml (1 cup)	4
Thai chicken with basil	
without skin and bone, 1 breast (90 g [3 oz])	5
Thai coffee or tea	
250 ml (1 cup)	9
Thai crisp noodles	
250 ml (1 cup)	9
Thai grilled beef (nuea nam tok)	
125 ml (1/2 cup) on lettuce leaves	6

▲ Power Foods	*PointsPlus®* value
Tirami-su	
restaurant-type, 1 slice (140 g [4 3/4 oz])	12
Tofu, fried	
agadashi, 3.5 cm x 5 cm (1 1/2" x 2")	7
1 piece (15 g [1/2 oz])	1
Tofu, frozen	
125 ml (1/2 cup)	6
Tom yum kung	
250 ml (1 cup)	2
Tomatoes	
▲ dried, not packed in oil, 1 medium	0
dried, packed in oil, drained, 1 medium	0
Tomatoes, green, fried	
2 slices (3.5 cm [1 1/2"] thick)	5
Tonkatsu	
beef, 175 ml (3/4 cup)	7
chicken, 175 ml (3/4 cup)	7
pork, 175 ml (3/4 cup)	9
Topping	
butterscotch, 30 ml (2 Tbsp)	3
caramel, regular or fat-free, 30 ml (2 Tbsp)	3
fruit, 15 ml (1 Tbsp)	2
fudge, regular, 15 ml (1 Tbsp)	2
nuts in syrup, 30 ml (2 Tbsp)	5
Topping, whipped	
dairy or nondairy, aerosol or frozen, 60 ml (1/4 cup)	1
dairy or nondairy, light or fat-free, aerosol or frozen, 30 ml (2 Tbsp)	0
dairy or nondairy, light or fat-free, aerosol or frozen, 75 ml (1/3 cup)	1
Tortellini	
cheese, without sauce, 150 ml (2/3 cup)	4
meat, without sauce, 150 ml (2/3 cup)	4

▲ Power Foods	*PointsPlus®* value
Tortiere (French Canadian meat pie)	
1/8 of a 22 cm (9") pie	10
Tortilla, corn	
2 small (10 cm [4"] diameter) or 30 g (1 oz)	2
1 medium (15 cm [6"] diameter or 30 g [1 oz])	2
1/2 large (290 g [10"] diameter or 30 g (1 oz)	2
Tortilla, flour	
2 small (10 cm [4"] diameter) or 30 g (1 oz)	2
1 medium (15 cm [6"] diameter or 30 g [1 oz])	2
1/2 large (290 g [10"] diameter) or 30 g (1 oz)	2
1 extra large (125 g [4 oz])	9
Tortilla, wheat	
burrito-size, 1 large (25 cm [10"])	2
Tortilla, whole-wheat	
1 medium (17 cm [7"] diameter)	2
Tortoni	
75 g (2 1/2 oz)	7
Tostada	
beans and cheese, fast food, 1 (150 g [5 oz])	6
beans, beef, and cheese, fast food, 1 (250 g [8 oz])	9
beef, 1 (255 g [8 1/4 oz])	11
beef and cheese, fast food, 1 (165 g [5 3/4 oz])	8
chicken, 1 (255 g [8 1/4 oz])	10
guacamole, fast food, 2 (280 g [9 1/4 oz])	10
Trifle	
250 ml (1 cup)	6
Tripe, beef	
▲ cooked, 30 g (1 oz)	1
Tuna noodle casserole	
250 ml (1 cup)	10

▲ Power Foods	*PointsPlus®* value
Turkey	
deli-sliced, 1 slice (20 g [3/4 oz])	0
deli-sliced, 30 g (1 oz)	1
Turkey breast	
cooked, with skin, 1 slice (60 g [2 oz])	3
Turkey, dark meat	
cooked, with skin, 250 ml (1 cup) chopped or diced or 150 g (5 oz)	8
cooked, without skin, 1 slice or 125 ml (1/2 cup) cubed or shredded 60 g (2 oz)	2
Turkey, ground	
93% lean/7% fat, cooked, 1 patty (90 g [3 oz])	4
regular, cooked, 1 patty (90 g [3 oz])	5
Turkey leg	
cooked, with skin and bone, 1 (625 g [1 1/4 pounds])	28
cooked, with skin, without bone, 1 slice (60 g [2 oz])	3
Turkey, light meat	
cooked, with skin, 250 ml (1 cup)	7
▲ cooked, without skin, 1 slice or 125 ml (1/2 cup) cubed or shredded 60 g (2 oz)	2
Turkey roast	
seasoned, light and dark meat, 250 ml (1 cup)	5
Turkey tetrazzini	
375 ml (1 1/2 cups)	15
Turkey thigh	
cooked, with skin, without bone, 1 slice (60 g [2 oz])	3
Turkey wing	
cooked, with skin and bone, 1 (185 g [6 1/2 oz])	11
Turnover	
fruit, any type, 1 (7.5 x 3.5 cm [3" x 1 1/2"])	6

DINING OUT A-Z FOOD LIST

▲ Power Foods	PointsPlus® value
Turnover	
fruit, any type, fast food, 1 (125 g [4 oz])	9
Twice-cooked pork	
250 ml (1 cup)	10
Tzimmes, vegetable	
175 ml (3/4 cup)	4

U

▲ Power Foods	PointsPlus® value
Urad dal (split matpe beans without skin)	
250 ml (1 cup)	5

V

▲ Power Foods	PointsPlus® value
Veal, breast	
cooked, 90 g (3 oz)	6
trimmed, cooked, 90 g (3 oz)	4
Veal cutlet, breaded	
fried, 125 g (4 oz)	9
Veal, leg	
cooked, 90 g (3 oz)	4
trimmed, cooked, 90 g (3 oz)	4
Veal, loin	
cooked, 90 g (3 oz)	6
▲ trimmed, cooked, 90 g (3 oz)	4
Veal marsala	
125 g (4 oz) veal with sauce	12
Veal parmigiana	
with sauce, 150 g (5 oz) veal with 125 ml (1/2 cup) tomato sauce	13
without sauce, 160 g (5 1/2 oz)	10
Veal piccata	
2 slices (125 g [4 oz])	10
Veal, rib	
cooked, 90 g (3 oz)	5
trimmed, cooked, 90 g (3 oz)	4
Veal scaloppine	
2 pieces (135 g [4 1/2 oz])	9

▲ Power Foods	PointsPlus® value
Veal, shank	
cooked, 90 g (3 oz)	4
cooked, 90 g (3 oz)	4
▲ trimmed, cooked, 90 g (3 oz)	3
Veal, shoulder	
cooked, 90 g (3 oz)	5
trimmed, cooked, 90 g (3 oz)	4
Veal, sirloin	
cooked, 1 slice or 125 ml (1/2 cup) or 60 g (2 oz)	3
cooked, 90 g (3 oz)	5
▲ trimmed, cooked, 90 g (3 oz)	3
Veal with peppers	
150 g (5 oz)	11
Vegetable pulao	
250 ml (1 cup)	4
Vegetables	
creamed, except cream-style corn, 250 ml (1 cup)	2
fried, 250 ml (1 cup)	4
sautéed, 250 ml (1 cup)	7
Vegetables, Chinese	
with beef, 250 ml (1 cup)	7
with chicken, 250 ml (1 cup)	5
with peas, prepared with oil, 250 ml (1 cup)	5
▲ with peas, prepared without oil, 250 ml (1 cup)	2
with pork, 250 ml (1 cup)	7
with shrimp, 250 ml (1 cup)	5
with tofu, 250 ml (1 cup)	4
Vegetarian breakfast sausage	
link, 2 (45 g [1 1/2 oz])	3
patty, 1 (40 g [1 1/3 oz])	2
Vegetarian breakfast strips	
4 (30 g [1 oz])	3
Vegetarian burger on bun, restaurant-type	
1 (215 g [7 1/2 oz])	12

▲ Power Foods	PointsPlus® value
Venison	
▲ cooked, 30 g (1 oz)	1
Vietnamese beef balls (thit bo vien)	
6 (45 g [1 1/2 oz])	2
Vindaloo	
chicken, 250 ml (1 cup)	9
lamb, 250 ml (1 cup)	16
pork, 250 ml (1 cup)	10
Vitello tonnato	
2 slices veal (125 g [4 oz]) with 125 ml (1/2 cup) sauce	16

W

▲ Power Foods	PointsPlus® value
Waffle	
any type, 1 (17 cm [7"] square)	6
Wiener schnitzel	
1 slice (90 g [3 oz])	10
Wine	
any type other than those listed here, 1 small glass (125 ml [4 fl oz])	3
dessert, dry, 60 ml (2 fl oz)	3
dessert, sweet, 60 ml (2 fl oz)	3
light, 1 small glass (125 ml [4 fl oz])	2
sherry, dry or sweet, 125 ml (1/2 cup)	6
Wine cooler	
1 (250 ml [8 fl oz])	4
Wine, non-alcoholic	
1 small glass (125 ml [4 fl oz])	0
Wine spritzer	
1 (250 ml [8 fl oz])	4
Wontons	
boiled, 6 (175 g [6 oz])	6
fried, 6 (125 g [4 oz])	12

Y

▲ Power Foods	PointsPlus® value
Yaki-soba	
beef, 125 ml (1/2 cup) noodles with 125 ml (1/2 cup) beef and vegetables	5

▲ Power Foods	PointsPlus® value
chicken, 125 ml (1/2 cup) noodles with 125 ml (1/2 cup) chicken and vegetables	5
pork, 125 ml (1/2 cup) noodles with 125 ml (1/2 cup) pork and vegetables	5
Yakitori	
1 skewer (215 g [7 1/2 oz])	6
Yam	
▲ cooked, 1 large (12.5 cm [5"] long or 200 g [7 oz])	6
▲ cooked, 250 ml (1 cup)	4
Yogourt, frozen	
fat-free, no sugar added, 1 scoop or 125 ml (1/2 cup)	3
fat-free, sweetened with sugar, 1 scoop or 125 ml (1/2 cup)	3
low-fat, 1 scoop or 125 ml (1/2 cup)	3
Yorkshire pudding	
1 piece (10 cm [4"] square)	7
Yosenabe	
500 ml (2 cups)	5

Z

▲ Power Foods	PointsPlus® value
Zabaglione	
125 ml (1/2 cup)	4
Zeppole	
1 (10 cm [4"] diameter)	7
Ziti, baked	
with meat, 250 ml (1 cup)	10
without meat, 250 ml (1 cup)	7
Zucchini bread	
1 slice (2 cm [3/4"] thick)	6
Zuppa di pesce	
500 ml (2 cups)	11
Zuppa Inglese	
1/16 of a 25 cm (10") cake	9

Ethnic & Regional Favourites

ETHNIC & REGIONAL FAVORITES

AFRICAN

Bread

enjera, 1 (22 cm (9") diameter)	2

Curry

African, fish, 125 ml (1/2 cup)	6
African, shrimp, 125 ml (1/2 cup)	7

BRITISH/IRISH

Beef, corned

cooked, 90 g (3 oz)	6

Bread, Irish soda

1/12 of an 20 cm (8") round loaf	8

Bubble and squeak

250 ml (1 cup)	5

Burgoo

250 ml (1 cup)	5

Carrots and parsnips

250 ml (1 cup)	6

Coffee, Irish

175 ml (6 fl oz) with 30 ml (2 Tbsp) whipped cream	6

Colcannon

250 ml (1 cup)	8

Cream

clotted (English double devon cream), 30 ml (2 Tbsp)	4

Crumpet

1 (7.5 cm [3"] diameter)	4

Fadge (potato bread)

1 piece (95 g [3 1/4 oz])	2

Fish and chips

150 g (5 oz) fish fillet with 20 chips (French fries)	17

Popovers

2 (7.5 cm [3"] diameter or 45 g [1 1/2 oz] each)	4

Pudding, plum

125 ml (1/2 cup) with 15 ml (1 Tbsp) sauce	11

Sauce

Worcestershire, 15 ml (1 Tbsp)	0

Scone

1 small (45 g [1 1/2 oz])	4
1 regular (75 g [2 1/2 oz])	7
blueberry, restaurant-type, 1 (130 g [4 1/4 oz])	12
chocolate, cinnamon, or raspberry, restaurant-type, 1 (130 g [4 1/4 oz])	13
cranberry or orange, restaurant-type, 1 (130 g [4 1/4 oz])	11

Stew

Irish brown, 250 ml (1 cup)	8
lamb, 250 ml (1 cup)	6

Trifle

250 ml (1 cup)	6

Yorkshire pudding

1 piece (10 cm [4"] square)	7

CAJUN/CREOLE

Bananas Foster

2 scoops (250 ml [1 cup]) ice cream with 1/2 banana and 75 ml (1/3 cup) sauce (280 g [9 1/4 oz])	18

Beans, red, with rice

250 ml (1 cup)	7

Beignet

1 (5 cm [2"] or 20 g [3/4 oz])	2

Blackened chicken

1 breast (90 g [3 oz])	7

Blackened fish

1 fillet (170 g [6 oz])	12

Blackened steak

170 g (6 oz)	17

ETHNIC & REGIONAL FAVORITES

▲ Power Foods	*PointsPlus®* value
Crawfish pie	
1/8 of a 22 cm (9") pie	14
Creole	
chicken, without rice, 250 ml (1 cup)	7
shrimp, without rice, 250 ml (1 cup)	5
Étouffée	
crawfish, 250 ml (1 cup)	9
shrimp, 250 ml (1 cup)	10
Green rice	
250 ml (1 cup)	7
Gumbo	
chicken, 250 ml (1 cup)	7
seafood, 250 ml (1 cup)	6
Jambalaya	
chicken, with rice, 375 ml (1 1/2 cups)	11
fish, with rice, 375 ml (1 1/2 cups)	11
Muffuletta	
1 (335 g [11 1/4 oz])	22
Oyster pie	
1/8 of a 22 cm (9") pie	10
Pudding, bread	
250 ml (1 cup)	16
Sandwich	
po' boy (poor boy), 1 (80 g [2 3/4 oz])	6
po' boy, oyster, 1 (270 g [8 3/4 oz])	19
po' boy, shrimp, 1 (270 g [8 3/4 oz])	20
Sauce	
remoulade, 30 ml (2 Tbsp)	4
Sausage	
andouille, 60 g (2 oz)	3
Shrimp remoulade	
6 small shrimp with 60 ml (1/4 cup) remoulade sauce	9
Soup	
turtle, 250 ml (1 cup)	3

▲ Power Foods	*PointsPlus®* value

CANADIAN, BAKERY

Bear claw	
restaurant-type, 1 (125 g [4 oz])	11
Bread, banana	
with nuts, 1 slice (12.5 cm x 2 cm [5" x 3/4"]) or 75 g (2 1/2 oz)	6
without nuts, 1 slice (12.5 cm x 2 cm [5" x 3/4"]) or 65 g (2 1/4 oz)	6
Bread, Boston brown	
1 slice (9.5 cm x 1.25 cm [3 3/4" x 1/2"])	3
Bread, date-nut	
1 slice (12.5 cm x 1.25 cm [5" x 1/2"])	7
Brownie	
1 (5 cm [2"] square)	6
Cake	
angel food, 1/16 of a 25 cm (10") tube	3
carrot, restaurant-type, 1 piece (175 g [6 1/4 oz])	17
carrot, with cream cheese icing, 1/12 of a 22 cm (9") layer cake or 7.5 cm (3") square	18
coffee, 7.5 cm (3") square, or 1/12 of a 22 cm (9") tube	9
coffee, cheese, 1 piece (1/6 of a 500 g [16 oz] cake)	7
coffee, crème-filled, with chocolate frosting, 1/6 of a 580 g (19 oz) cake	8
coffee, fruit, 1 piece (50 g [1 3/4 oz])	4
double chocolate, restaurant-type, 1 piece (155 g [5 1/3 oz])	14
honey, 12.5 cm x 7.5 cm x 2.5 cm (5" x 3" x 1")	9
pineapple upside-down, 1/8 of a 25 cm (10") skillet cake	13
pound, 1 slice (12.5 cm x 7.5 cm x 1.5 cm [5" x 3" x 1"])	9

ETHNIC & REGIONAL FAVOURITES

Power Foods	PointsPlus® value
sponge, 1/12 of a 500 g (16 oz) cake	3
strawberry shortcake, 1/12 of a 22 cm (9") cake or 1 filled individual shortcake	8
white, without frosting, 1/12 of a 22 cm (9") diameter	7
with icing, 1/12 of a 22 cm (9") layer cake or 7.5 cm (3") square	14
Cheesecake	
with fruit topping, 1/16 of a 25 cm (10") cake	12
without fruit topping, 1/16 of a 25 cm (10") cake	11
Cinnamon bun	
1 large	7
Cobbler	
fruit, any type, 250 ml (1 cup)	13
Cookies	
bar, 1 (5 cm [2"] square)	3
chocolate wafers, 2 (15 g [1/2 oz])	1
fudge, cake-type, 1 (20 g [3/4 oz])	2
gingerbread, 1 (5 cm [2"] diameter)	2
gingersnaps, 2 (15 g [1/2 oz])	2
lace, 1 (5 g [1/4 oz])	1
ladyfingers, 1 large or 2 small (15 g [1/2 oz])	1
molasses, 1 medium (15 g [1/2 oz])	2
rainbow, 1 medium (2.5 cm x 5 cm [1" x 2"])	3
rainbow, 1 small (3.5 cm [1 1/2"] diamond)	2
raisin, soft, 1 (15 g [1/2 oz])	2
white macadamia nut, restaurant-type, 1 (50 g [1 3/4 oz])	7
Danish pastry	
cheese, 1 (10.5 cm [4 1/4"] diameter)	7
cinnamon, 1 (10.5 cm [4 1/4"] diameter)	7
fruit, 1 (10.5 cm [4 1/4"] diameter)	7
nut, 1 (10.5 cm [4 1/4"] diameter)	8

Power Foods	PointsPlus® value
Doughnuts	
any type other than those listed here, store-bought, 1 (60 g [2 oz])	6
cake-type, plain, 1 (8.5 cm [3 1/2"] diameter)	6
cake-type, wheat, sugared or glazed, 1 (8.5 cm [3 1/2"] diameter)	6
cake-type, white, sugared or glazed, 1 (8.5 cm [3 1/2"] diameter)	7
cake-type, with icing, 1 (8.5 cm [3 1/2"] diameter)	7
with crème filling, 1 (8.5 cm x 6 cm [3 1/2" x 2 1/2"] oval)	9
yeast, glazed, 1 (10 cm [4"] diameter)	7
yeast, with jelly filling, 1 (8.5 cm x 6 cm [3 1/2" x 2 1/2"] oval)	8
Fudge	
with or without nuts, 1 piece (2.5 cm x 5 cm [1" x 2"]) or 30 g (1 oz)	3
Gingerbread	
1/9 of an 20 cm (8") square pan	7
Honeybun	
glazed, 1 (10 cm x 7.5 cm [4" x 3"] oval)	7
Hot cross buns	
1 (65 g [2 1/4 oz])	6
Muffin	
any type other than those listed here, 1 large (7.5 cm [3"] diameter)	8
banana walnut, restaurant-type, 1 muffin (150 g [5 oz])	15
blueberry, reduced-fat, restaurant-type, 1 muffin (150 g [5 oz])	11
chocolate chip, restaurant-type, 1 muffin (150 g [5 oz])	14
corn, restaurant-type, 1 muffin (150 g [5 oz])	13
cranberry orange, restaurant-type, 1 muffin (150 g [5 oz])	12
mini, any type, 1 (3 cm [1 1/4"] diameter or 15 g [1/2 oz])	1

Power Foods	PointsPlus® value
oat bran, 1 (6 cm [2 1/2"] diameter x 5.5 cm [2 1/4"])	4
pumpkin, restaurant-type, 1 muffin (150 g [5 oz])	12
Pie, dessert	
any type other than those listed here, fruit, one-crust, 1/8 of 22 cm (9") diameter	8
any type other than those listed here, fruit, two-crust, 1/8 of 22 cm (9") diameter	11
chiffon, 1/8 of a 22 cm (9") one-crust pie	10
cream, with fruit, 1/8 of a 22 cm (9") one-crust pie	11
cream, without fruit, 1/8 of a 22 cm (9") one-crust pie	10
custard, 1/8 of a 22 cm (9") one-crust pie	9
fried, fruit, 1 (12.5 cm x 9.5 cm [5" x 3 3/4"])	11
individual, 1 (12.5 cm x 9.5 cm [5" x 3 3/4"])	11
key lime, 1/8 of a 22 cm (9") one-crust pie	14
meringue, any type other than those listed here, 1/8 of 22 cm (9") diameter	12
mincemeat, with meat, 1/8 of a 22 cm (9") two-crust pie	13
mincemeat, without meat, 1/8 of a 22 cm (9") two-crust pie	16
rhubarb, 1/8 of a 22 cm (9") two-crust pie	13
Pumpkin bread	
1 slice (2 cm [3/4"] thick)	8
Sweet roll	
1 large (125 g [4 oz])	6
cheese, 1 (65 g [2 1/4 oz])	7
Turnover	
fruit, any type, 1 (7.5 x 3.5 cm [3" x 1 1/2"])	6

CANADIAN, BAR/PUB

Power Foods	PointsPlus® value
Alcoholic beverages	
86 proof, 1 jigger (45 ml [1 1/2 fl oz])	3
90 proof, 1 jigger (45 ml [1 1/2 fl oz])	4
94 proof, 1 jigger (45 ml [1 1/2 fl oz])	4
100 proof, 1 jigger (45 ml [1 1/2 fl oz])	5
cognac, 1 jigger (45 ml [1 1/2 fl oz])	4
creme de menthe, 1 jigger (45 ml [1 1/2 fl oz])	6
Kahlúa, 1 jigger (45 ml [1 1/2 fl oz])	6
liqueur, any type other than those listed here, 1 jigger (45 ml [1 1/2 fl oz])	6
liqueur, coffee with cream, 34 proof, 30 ml (1 fl oz)	3
liqueur, coffee without cream, 63 proof, 1 jigger (45 ml [1 1/2 fl oz])	5
liquor (bourbon, brandy, gin, rum, scotch, tequila, vodka, whiskey), 1 jigger (45 ml [1 1/2 fl oz])	4
mirin, 30 ml (1 fl oz)	1
sake, 125 ml (4 fl oz)	5
schnapps, any flavour, 1 jigger (45 ml [1 1/2 fl oz])	6
Alcoholic mixed drinks	
Bay Breeze, 1 drink (165 ml [5 1/2 fl oz])	5
Bellini, 1 drink (175 ml [6 fl oz])	6
Black Russian, 1 drink (90 ml [3 fl oz])	8
Bloody Mary, 1 drink (150 ml [5 fl oz])	4
Brandy Alexander, 1 drink (90 ml [3 fl oz])	9
Cosmopolitan, 1 drink (100 ml [3 1/2 fl oz])	6
Daiquiri, 90 ml (3 fl oz)	4
Daiquiri, canned, 1 can (205 ml [6 3/4 fl oz])	9
Gimlet, gin, 1 drink (75 ml [2 1/2 fl oz])	4

ETHNIC & REGIONAL FAVOURITES

Canadian, Bar/Pub, Alcoholic mixed drinks (cont'd)

▲ Power Foods	PointsPlus® value
Gimlet, vodka, 1 drink (75 ml [2 1/2 fl oz])	4
gin and tonic, 1 drink (175 ml [6 fl oz])	5
highball, made with sweetened mixer, 1 drink (175 ml [6 fl oz])	7
highball, made with unsweetened mixer, 1 drink (175 ml [6 fl oz])	4
Long Island Iced Tea, 1 drink (150 ml [5 fl oz])	8
Manhattan, dry, 1 drink (125 ml [4 fl oz])	10
Manhattan, perfect, 1 drink (125 ml [4 fl oz])	10
Manhattan, scotch, 1 drink (125 ml [4 fl oz])	10
Margarita, 1 drink (125 ml [4 fl oz])	9
Martini, 1 drink (75 ml [2 1/2 fl oz])	6
Martini, chocolate, 1 drink (75 ml [2 1/2 fl oz])	8
Martini, sour apple, 1 drink (90 ml [3 fl oz])	8
Mimosa, 1 drink (175 ml [6 fl oz])	4
Mojito, 1 drink (375 ml [12 fl oz])	7
Old Fashioned, 1 drink (60 ml [2 fl oz])	6
Piña Colada, 1 drink (175 ml [6 fl oz])	8
Piña Colada, canned, 1 can (205 ml [6.8 fl oz])	16
Rob Roy, 1 drink (125 ml [4 fl oz])	10
Sakatini, 1 drink (90 ml [3 fl oz])	7
sangria, 1 drink (125 ml [4 fl oz])	3
Screwdriver, 1 drink (175 ml [6 fl oz])	5
Singapore Sling, 1 drink (175 ml [6 fl oz])	6
Tom Collins, 1 drink (175 ml [6 fl oz])	4
Whiskey Sour, 1 drink (125 ml [4 fl oz])	6
White Russian, 1 drink (90 ml [3 fl oz])	8

▲ Power Foods	PointsPlus® value
Beer	
light, 1 can or bottle (375 ml [12 fl oz])	4
regular, 1 can or bottle (375 ml [12 fl oz])	5
Beer, non-alcoholic	
1 can or bottle (375 ml [12 fl oz])	2
Beverage mix	
Daiquiri, 125 ml (1/2 cup)	5
Margarita, 125 ml (1/2 cup)	4
Piña Colada, 125 ml (1/2 cup)	3
sweet and sour, 125 ml (1/2 cup)	3
Whiskey Sour, bottled, 60 ml (2 fl oz)	2
Buffalo wings	
cooked, 3 (135 g [4 1/2 oz])	9
Champagne	
1 small glass (125 ml [4 fl oz])	3
Cherries	
maraschino, 1	0
Nuts, mixed	
dry roasted, 250 ml (1 cup)	23
oil roasted, 250 ml (1 cup)	25
shelled, 30 g (1 oz)	5
Peanuts	
dry roasted, 250 ml (1 cup)	24
oil roasted, 250 ml (1 cup)	23
shelled, 15 ml (1 Tbsp)	2
shelled, 40 (30 g [1 oz])	5
Pretzels	
regular or whole-wheat, 30 g (1 oz)	3
sticks, 45 (2 g [3/4 oz])	2
twists, 15 small or 7 regular or 20 g (3/4 oz)	2
Soft drink, unsweetened	
club soda, 375 ml (12 fl oz)	0
seltzer, plain or flavoured, 375 ml (12 fl oz)	0
Soft drink, sweetened with sugar	
tonic water, 1 bottle (330 ml [11 fl oz])	3

ETHNIC & REGIONAL FAVOURITES

Power Foods	PointsPlus® value
Wine	
any type other than those listed here, 1 small glass (125 ml [4 fl oz])	3
dessert, dry, 60 ml (2 fl oz)	3
dessert, sweet, 60 ml (2 fl oz)	3
light, 1 small glass (125 ml [4 fl oz])	2
Wine cooler	
1 (250 ml [8 fl oz])	4
Wine spritzer	
1 (250 ml [8 fl oz])	4
Wine, non-alcoholic	
1 small glass (125 ml [4 fl oz])	0

CANADIAN, BARBECUE

Power Foods	PointsPlus® value
Beans, baked	
any type other than those listed here, 125 ml (1/2 cup)	5
Beef	
brisket, cooked, 90 g (3 oz)	9
brisket, lean, trimmed, cooked, 90 g (3 oz)	5
rib, large end, cooked, 90 g (3 oz)	7
rib, large end, trimmed, cooked, 90 g (3 oz)	7
rib, small end, trimmed, cooked, 90 g (3 oz)	5
rib, whole (ribs 6-12), cooked, 90 g (3 oz)	8
shortribs, cooked, 90 g (3 oz)	11
shortribs, trimmed, cooked, 90 g (3 oz)	7
Chicken breast	
barbecued, with skin and bone, 1 (135 g [4 1/2 oz])	7
fillet, grilled, 1 (90 g [3 oz])	3
Chicken drumstick	
barbecued, with skin and bone, 1 (45 g [1 1/2 oz])	3

Power Foods	PointsPlus® value
Chicken thigh	
barbecued, with skin and bone, 1 (90 g [3 oz])	6
Corn on the cob	
▲ 1 ear (up to 17 cm [7"] long)	2
▲ 1 ear (20 cm [8"] long)	4
Corn on the grill	
with butter, 1 (125 g [4 oz])	6
Ham patty	
grilled, 1 (60 g [2 oz])	6
Hibachi	
chichen, 250 ml (1 cup)	8
shrimp, 250 ml (1 cup)	6
steak, 250 ml (1 cup)	10
vegetables, 250 ml (1 cup)	5
Kabobs	
beef, 2 skewers (135 g [4 1/2 oz])	8
chicken, 2 skewers (135 g [4 1/2 oz])	5
fish, 2 skewers (135 g [4 1/2 oz])	5
lamb, 2 skewers (135 g [4 1/2 oz])	8
Pork	
backribs, cooked, 90 g (3 oz)	8
country-style ribs, cooked, 90 g (3 oz)	6
spareribs, without bone, cooked, 90 g (3 oz)	8
Pork, barbecue	
250 ml (1 cup)	9
Sauce	
barbecue, 15 ml (1 Tbsp)	0
barbecue, 60 ml (1/4 cup)	1
Shrimp, barbecued	
4 large shrimp with 60 ml (1/4 cup) sauce	11
Spareribs, barbecued	
4 (10 cm [4"] long)	9
6 (175 g [6 1/4 oz])	13

ETHNIC & REGIONAL FAVOURITES

▲ Power Foods | *PointsPlus®* value

CANADIAN, DINER

Apple

baked, 1 large (200 g [7 oz]) — 9

Bacon

regular, cooked, crisp, 1 slice — 1

regular, cooked, crisp, 3 slices — 4

Brownie

walnut, restaurant-type, 1 (140 g [4 2/3 oz]) — 15

Cereal, hot

▲ cream of rice, cooked, 250 ml (1 cup) — 3

▲ cream of wheat, cooked, 250 ml (1 cup) — 3

▲ farina, cooked, 250 ml (1 cup) — 3

▲ oatmeal, plain, cooked, 250 ml (1 cup) — 4

Cereal, ready-to-eat

any type other than those listed here, 250 ml (1 cup) — 3

bran flakes, 175 ml (3/4 cup) — 3

bran flakes, 250 ml (1 cup) — 3

corn flakes, 250 ml (1 cup) — 3

crispy rice, 250 ml (1 cup) — 3

fortified, 250 ml (1 cup) — 2

frosted, 250 ml (1 cup) — 4

nuggets, 125 ml (1/2 cup) — 6

puffed rice, 250 ml (1 cup) — 1

puffed wheat, 250 ml (1 cup) — 1

raisin bran, 175 ml (3/4 cup) — 4

raisin bran, 250 ml (1 cup) — 5

shredded wheat, 1 biscuit (20 g [3/4 oz]) — 2

Cheese, Cheddar

1 slice (30 g [1 oz]) — 3

Cheese, cream

regular, 15 ml (1 Tbsp) — 1

Cheese fries

restaurant-type, 265 g (8 2/3 oz) — 18

Cheese, hard or semisoft

regular, 1 slice (20 g [3/4 oz]) — 2

Cheeseburger on bun

plain, without mayonnaise, lettuce, and tomato, 1 (185 g [6 2/3 oz]) — 12

Chicken Caesar wrap

restaurant-type, 290 g (10 oz) — 16

Chicken tenders

restaurant-type, 90 g (3 oz) — 5

Chili cheese dog

restaurant-type, 1 (150 g [5 oz]) — 10

Coleslaw

125 ml (1/2 cup) — 4

Crackers

oyster, 20 (20 g [3/4 oz] or 125 ml [1/2 cup]) — 3

oyster, 250 ml (1 cup) — 5

saltines, 4 — 1

saltines, 6 — 2

saltines, fat-free, low-sodium, 6 — 3

Dip

spinach-artichoke, restaurant-type, 60 g (2 oz) — 3

Egg, fried

2 large — 5

Egg, scrambled

2 or 125 ml (1/2 cup) — 5

Egg, whole

▲ poached, 1 large — 2

Fish

▲ salmon, canned in water, drained, 125 ml (1/2 cup) — 4

tuna, canned in oil, drained, 125 ml (1/2 cup) or 125 g (4 oz) — 5

▲ tuna, canned in water, drained, 125 ml (1/2 cup) or 125 g (4 oz) — 3

▲ Power Foods	PointsPlus® value
Fish and brewis	
250 ml (1 cup)	14
French fries	
20 (11 cm [4 1/2"] long or 160 g [5 1/2 oz])	11
French toast	
2 slices (135g [4 1/2 oz])	8
Fruit and yogourt parfait	
restaurant-type, 265 g (8 1/2 oz)	6
Fruit cup	
▲ restaurant-type	0
Hamburger on bun	
plain, without mayonnaise, lettuce, and tomato, 90 g (3 oz) cooked hamburger on 45 g (1 1/2 oz) bun	10
Jam	
regular or reduced-sugar, 15 ml (1 Tbsp)	1
Jelly	
15 ml (1 Tbsp)	1
Juice	
apple, 125 ml (1/2 cup)	2
grapefruit, 125 ml (1/2 cup)	1
orange, fresh, 250 ml (1 cup)	3
Meat loaf	
1 slice (1.75 cm [5/8"] thick)	6
Muffin, English	
any type other than those listed here, 1 (60 g [2 oz])	3
cinnamon-raisin, 1 (60 g [2 oz])	4
Omelette	
cheese, 1 (2-egg)	8
ham and cheese, 1 (2-egg)	9
ham and cheese, restaurant-type, 1 (285 g [9 1/2 oz])	15
herb, 1 (2-egg)	6
plain, 1 (2-egg)	6
vegetable, 1 (2-egg)	8

▲ Power Foods	PointsPlus® value
vegetable, restaurant-type, 1 (365 g [11 3/4 oz])	15
Onion rings	
fried, 4 (10 cm [4"] diameter each)	7
Pancakes	
buttermilk, restaurant-type, 2 (170 g [6 oz])	13
Potatoes, hash brown	
250 ml (1 cup)	8
Potatoes, home-fried	
250 ml (1 cup)	6
Preserves	
15 ml (1 Tbsp)	1
Pudding, any flavour	
any type other than those listed here, 250 ml (1 cup)	8
Pudding, banana	
250 ml (1 cup)	9
Pudding, tapioca	
250 ml (1 cup)	6
Salad	
chef's, with dressing, 1 L (4 cups)	8
chef's, without dressing, 1 L (4 cups)	6
chicken, 125 ml (1/2 cup)	6
egg, 125 ml (1/2 cup)	8
garden, restaurant-type, 1 (170 g [6 oz])	3
grilled chicken Caesar, restaurant-type, 185 g (6 1/2 oz)	8
lobster, 125 ml (1/2 cup)	4
macaroni, 125 ml (1/2 cup)	7
potato, 125 ml (1/2 cup)	8
shrimp, 125 ml (1/2 cup)	3
spinach, with dressing, 500 ml (2 cups)	7
southwestern grilled chicken, restaurant-type, 1 (395 g [13 1/4 oz])	7
tuna, 125 ml (1/2 cup)	8
turkey cobb, restaurant-type, 1 (335 g [11 1/4 oz])	10

ETHNIC & REGIONAL FAVOURITES

Canadian, Diner (cont'd)

▲ Power Foods	*PointsPlus®* value
Sandwich	
bacon, lettuce, and tomato, restaurant-type, 1 (280 g [9 1/4 oz])	18
chicken salad on regular bread, 1 (155 cm [5 1/4 oz])	10
club, 1 (270 g [8 3/4 oz])	17
egg salad, 1 (170 g [6 oz])	12
grilled cheese with bacon, 1 (140 g [4 3/4 oz])	17
grilled cheese, restaurant-type, 1 (125 g [4 oz])	14
grilled ham and cheese, restaurant-type, 1 (150 g [5 oz])	15
grinder, 1 (80 g [2 3/4 oz])	6
ham and cheese, 1 (125 g [4 oz])	10
ham and cheese, restaurant-type, 1 (275 g [9 oz])	9
hero, 1 (335 g [11 1/4 oz])	6
hoagie, 1 (80 g [2 3/4 oz])	6
Monte Cristo, 1 (110 g [3 3/4 oz])	7
peanut butter and jelly, restaurant-type, 1 (130 g [4 1/4 oz])	11
Reuben, 1 (250 g [8 oz])	18
roast beef, open-face, 1 (215 g [7 1/2 oz])	9
roast beef, open-face, with gravy, 1 (165 g [5 3/4 oz])	9
shrimp salad, 1 (135 g [4 1/2 oz])	8
tuna melt, 1 (165 g [5 3/4 oz])	10
tuna salad, 1 (175 g [6 1/4 oz])	11
turkey, 1 (125 g [4 oz])	7
Soft drink, diet	
any flavour, 375 ml (12 fl oz)	0
Soft drink, sweetened with sugar	
any flavour other than those listed here, sweetened with sugar, 375 ml (12 fl oz)	4
cream, 375 ml (12 fl oz)	5
ginger ale, 375 ml (12 fl oz)	3
grape, 375 ml (12 fl oz)	5
orange, 375 ml (12 fl oz)	5

▲ Power Foods	*PointsPlus®* value
Soup	
broccoli cheese, 250 ml (1 cup)	7
Cheddar cheese, 250 ml (1 cup)	10
chicken noodle, 250 ml (1 cup)	3
clam chowder, Manhattan, 250 ml (1 cup)	5
clam chowder, New England, 250 ml (1 cup)	5
cream of broccoli, 250 ml (1 cup)	7
cream of mushroom, 250 ml (1 cup)	9
cream of potato, 250 ml (1 cup)	3
cream of tomato, 250 ml (1 cup)	5
tomato, 250 ml (1 cup)	3
vegetable, 250 ml (1 cup)	3
Syrup	
maple, 15 ml (1 Tbsp)	1
pancake, regular, 15 ml (1 Tbsp)	1
pancake, with butter, 15 ml (1 Tbsp)	2
Tortiere (French Canadian meat pie)	
1/8 of a 22 cm (9") pie	10
Waffle	
any type, 1 (17 cm [7"] square)	6

CANADIAN, FAST FOOD

Biscuits, breakfast	
egg on biscuit, 1	9
egg, and bacon on biscuit, 1	13
egg, and ham on biscuit, 1	12
egg, and sausage on biscuit, 1	15
egg, and steak on biscuit, 1	11
egg, cheese, and bacon on biscuit, 1	12
ham on biscuit, 1	11
steak on biscuit, 1	13
Brownie	
1 (5 cm [2"] square)	7
Burrito	
bean and cheese, 2 pieces (185 g [6 1/2 oz])	10

▲ Power Foods	PointsPlus® value
bean and chili peppers, 2 pieces (200 g [7 oz])	11
bean and meat, 2 pieces (250 g [8 oz])	14
bean, cheese, and beef, 2 pieces (200 g [7 oz])	9
bean, cheese, and chili peppers, 2 pieces (375 g [12 oz])	18
bean, 1 piece (110 g [3 3/4 oz])	6
beef and chili peppers, 2 pieces (200 g [7 oz])	11
beef, cheese, and chili peppers, 2 pieces (320 g [10 3/4 oz])	17
beef, 2 pieces (225 g [7 3/4 oz])	14
fruit, 1 small (75 g [2 1/2 oz])	6
Cheeseburger on bun	
double, 1	12
double, with bacon, 1	21
large, double, with condiments and vegetables, 1	19
large, 1	13
large, with bacon and condiments, 1	16
large, with condiments and vegetables, 1	13
large, with ham, condiments and vegetables, 1	20
small, 1	8
small, with condiments and vegetables, 1	10
triple, plain, 1	21
Cheesecake	
any type, 1 piece (80 g [2 3/4 oz])	7
Chicken drumstick	
fried, with skin and bone, 1 (60 g [2 oz])	5
Chicken thigh	
fried, with skin, 1 (100 g [3 1/2 oz])	8
Chicken, nugget-style	
fried, 6 nuggets (110 g [3 3/4 oz])	9

▲ Power Foods	PointsPlus® value
Chicken wings	
fried, with skin, 1 (60 g [2 oz])	6
Chili con carne	
250 ml (1 cup)	7
Chimichanga	
beef and cheese, 1 (185 g [6 1/2 oz])	12
beef and red chili peppers, 1 (190 g [6 3/4 oz])	12
beef, cheese, and red chili peppers, 1 (180 g [6 1/3 oz])	10
beef, 1 (175 g [6 1/4 oz])	12
Cinnamon roll, mini	
1 roll	3
Clams	
breaded and fried, 175 ml (3/4 cup)	12
Corn dog	
1 (170 g [6 oz])	12
Corn on the cob	
with butter, 1 ear (150 g [5 oz])	4
Crab cakes	
1 (60 g [2 oz])	4
Croissant	
egg and cheese, 1 (135 g [4 1/2 oz])	10
egg, cheese, and bacon, 1 (135 g [4 1/2 oz])	11
egg, cheese, and ham, 1 (155 cm [5 1/4 oz])	13
egg, cheese, and sausage, 1 (165 g [5 3/4 oz])	14
Danish pastry	
cheese, 1 (90 g [3 oz])	10
cinnamon, 1 (90 g [3 oz])	10
fruit, 1 (90 g [3 oz])	9
Donair	
125 g (4 oz) meat with onion, tomato, and 30 ml (2 Tbsp) sauce	16
Enchiladas	
cheese and beef, 1 (190 g [6 3/4 oz])	9
cheese, 1 (165 g [5 3/4 oz])	9

ETHNIC & REGIONAL FAVOURITES

Power Foods	PointsPlus® value
Enchirito	
cheese, beef, and beans, 1 (190 g [6 3/4 oz])	9
Fish fillet	
battered or breaded, fried, 1 fillet (95 g [3 1/4 oz])	6
Frankfurter on roll	
plain, 1 (100 g [3 1/2 oz])	7
with chili, 1 (125 g [4 oz])	8
French fries	
1 small serving	7
1 medium serving	11
1 extra large serving	14
French toast	
with butter, 2 slices (140 g [4 3/4 oz])	10
French toast sticks	
5 pieces (150 g [5 oz])	13
Frijoles, with cheese	
250 ml (1 cup)	5
Hamburger on bun	
double patty, plain, 1 (170 g [6 oz])	14
double patty, with condiments, 1 (215 g [7 1/2 oz])	15
single patty, plain, 1 (140 g [4 3/4 oz])	11
single patty, with condiments, 1 (170 g [6 oz])	12
small, plain, 1 (90 g [3 oz])	7
small, with condiments, 1 (125 g [4 oz])	7
triple patty, with condiments, 1 (275 g [9 oz])	18
Hot dog on roll	
plain, 1 (100 g [3 1/2 oz])	7
with chili, 1 (125 g [4 oz])	8
Hush puppies	
5 pieces (80 g [2 3/4 oz])	7
Ice cream sundae	
caramel, 1 (160 g [5 1/2 oz])	8
hot fudge, 1 (160 g [5 1/2 oz])	8
strawberry, 1 (160 g [5 1/2 oz])	7

Power Foods	PointsPlus® value
Muffin	
any type, 1 (130 g [4 1/4 oz])	11
Muffin, breakfast	
butter on English muffin, 1 (65 g [2 1/4 oz])	5
cheese and sausage on English muffin, 1 (125 g [4 oz])	11
egg, cheese, and Canadian bacon on English muffin, 1 (140 g [4 3/4 oz])	8
egg, cheese, and sausage on English muffin, 1 (165 g [5 3/4 oz])	13
Nachos	
cheese and jalapeño peppers, 6-8 nachos	17
cheese, beans, ground beef, and peppers, 6-8 nachos (275 g [9 oz])	16
cheese, 6-8 nachos (125 g [4 oz])	9
with cinnamon sugar, 6-8 nachos (110 g [3 3/4 oz])	17
Onion rings	
8-9 rings	8
Oysters	
battered or breaded and fried, 6 (150 g [5 oz])	10
Pancakes	
with butter and syrup, 2 (250 g [8 oz])	14
without butter and syrup, 1 serving (155 g [5 1/4 oz])	11
Pie, dessert	
fruit, 1 (8.5 cm [3 1/2"])	9
Pot pie	
any type, 1 (420 g [14 oz])	22
Potatoes, baked	
stuffed with bacon and cheese, 1 (285 g [9 2/3 oz])	13
stuffed with cheese, 1 (160 g [5 1/2 oz])	5
stuffed with sour cream and chives, 1 (160 g [5 1/2 oz])	5

▲ Power Foods	PointsPlus® value
stuffed with vegetables and cheese, 1 (400 g [13 1/3 oz])	12
with vegetables and cheese, 1 (390 g [13 oz])	11
Potatoes, hash brown	
125 ml (1/2 cup)	4
Poutine	
20 French fries with 60 g (2 oz) cheese and 125 ml (1/2 cup) sauce	19
Salad	
chef's, 1 (345 g [11 1/2 oz])	6
grilled chicken, without dressing, 1 (380 g [12 1/4 oz])	5
▲ side, without dressing, 1	0
taco, with chili con carne, 375 ml (1 1/2 cups)	7
taco, with shell, without dressing, 1	18
taco, without shell, without dressing, 1	10
vegetable, with cheese and egg, without dressing, 375 ml (1 1/2 cups)	3
vegetable, with chicken, without dressing, 375 ml (1 1/2 cups)	2
vegetable, with pasta and seafood, without dressing, 375 ml (1 1/2 cups)	10
vegetable, with shrimp, without dressing, 375 ml (1 1/2 cups)	3
vegetable, with turkey, ham and cheese, without dressing, 375 ml (1 1/2 cups)	7
Sandwich	
chicken fillet, plain, 1 (185 g [6 1/2 oz])	14
chicken fillet, with cheese, 1 (250 g [8 oz])	17
chicken, fried, 1 (205 g [7 1/4 oz])	12
egg and cheese, 1 (155 cm [5 1/4 oz])	9

▲ Power Foods	PointsPlus® value
fish and cheese, fried, 1 (185 g [6 1/2 oz])	14
fish with tartar sauce, 1 (160 g [5 1/2 oz])	12
grilled chicken, 1 (190 g [6 3/4 oz])	10
ham and cheese, 1 (155 cm [5 1/4 oz])	9
ham, egg, and cheese, 1 (150 g [5 oz])	9
lobster roll, 1 (130 g [4 1/4 oz])	6
lobster salad, 1 (135 g [4 1/2 oz])	8
Philly cheese steak, 1 (275 g [9 oz])	14
roast beef with cheese, 1 (170 g [6 oz])	12
roast beef, plain, 1 (150 g [5 oz])	9
steak, 1 (200 g [7 oz])	12
submarine with cold cuts, 1 (250 g [8 oz])	12
submarine with roast beef, 1 (215 g [7 1/2 oz])	11
submarine with tuna salad, 1 (275 g [9 oz])	16
Sauce	
donair, 30 ml (2 Tbsp)	2
Sausage biscuit	
1 (135 g [4 1/2 oz])	13
Scallops, fried	
breaded, 6 pieces (150 g [5 oz])	11
Shake	
milk, any flavour, 1 large (500 ml [16 fl oz])	16
milk, any flavour, 1 medium (375 ml [12 fl oz])	12
Shrimp	
breaded and fried, 6-8 shrimp (165 g [5 3/4 oz])	12
Taco	
hard, 1 (90 g [3 oz])	4
soft, 1 (100 g [3 1/2 oz])	4

ETHNIC & REGIONAL FAVOURITES

Canadian, Fast Food (cont'd)

▲ Power Foods	PointsPlus® value
Tostada	
beans and cheese, 1 (150 g [5 oz])	6
beans, beef, and cheese, 1 (250 g [8 oz])	9
beef and cheese, 1 (165 g [5 3/4 oz])	8
guacamole, 2 (280 g [9 1/4 oz])	10
Turnover	
fruit, any type, 1 (125 g [4 oz])	9

CANADIAN, ICE CREAM SHOP

	PointsPlus® value
Banana split	
3 scoops (375 ml [1 1/2 cups]) ice cream, 1 banana, 45 ml (3 Tbsp) syrup, and 125 ml (1/2 cup) whipped cream	21
Cream, whipped	
aerosol, 60 ml (1/4 cup)	1
Ice cream	
fat-free, sweetened with sugar, 1 scoop or 125 ml (1/2 cup)	2
light, sweetened with sugar, 1 scoop or 125 ml (1/2 cup)	3
premium, 1 scoop or 125 ml (1/2 cup)	8
regular, 1 scoop or 125 ml (1/2 cup)	4
vanilla, rich, 1 scoop or 125 ml (1/2 cup)	5
Ice cream cone only	
cake or wafer-type, 1 large (30 g [1 oz])	3
plain or sugar, 1 small (10 g [1/3 oz])	1
Ice cream soda	
375 ml (12 fl oz)	11
Ice cream, soft-serve	
French vanilla, 125 ml (1/2 cup)	5
Ice cream sundae	
any type, 1 large (185 g [6 1/2 oz])	13
any type, 1 scoop (125 ml [1/2 cup]) ice cream with syrup, nuts, and whipped topping (135 g [4 1/2 oz])	9

▲ Power Foods	PointsPlus® value
Ice cream sundae on a cone	
1 (100 g [3 1/2 oz])	9
Sherbet	
125 ml (1/2 cup)	3
Sprinkles	
any type, 15 ml (1 Tbsp)	0
Topping	
butterscotch, 30 ml (2 Tbsp)	3
caramel, regular or fat-free, 30 ml (2 Tbsp)	3
fruit, 15 ml (1 Tbsp)	2
fudge, regular, 15 ml (1 Tbsp)	2
nuts in syrup, 30 ml (2 Tbsp)	5
Topping, whipped	
dairy or nondairy, aerosol or frozen, 60 ml (1/4 cup)	1
dairy or nondairy, light or fat-free, aerosol or frozen, 30 ml (2 Tbsp)	0
dairy or nondairy, light or fat-free, aerosol or frozen, 75 ml (1/3 cup)	1
Yogourt, frozen	
fat-free, sweetened with sugar, 1 scoop or 125 ml (1/2 cup)	3
low-fat, 1 scoop or 125 ml (1/2 cup)	3

CANADIAN, SALAD BAR

	PointsPlus® value
Bacon bits	
imitation, 5 ml (1 tsp)	0
Beans	
▲ garbanzo (chick peas), cooked or canned, 125 ml (1/2 cup)	3
▲ garbanzo (chick peas), cooked or canned, 250 ml (1 cup)	7
▲ kidney, cooked, 125 ml (1/2 cup)	3
Beets	
▲ cooked, uncooked, or canned	0
pickled, 125 ml (1/2 cup)	2

▲ Power Foods	PointsPlus® value
Cheese, blue	
crumbled, 60 ml (1/4 cup) crumbled	3
Cheese, cottage	
regular (4%), plain, 250 ml (1 cup)	5
regular (4%), with fruit, 250 ml (1 cup)	6
Cheese, hard or semisoft	
regular, 2.5 cm (1") cube, 60 ml (1/4 cup) shredded, or 45 ml (3 Tbsp) grated or 30 g (1 oz)	3
Corn	
▲ baby ears, 250 ml (1 cup)	1
▲ kernels, cooked, 250 ml (1 cup)	4
Croutons	
plain, 250 ml (1 cup)	3
seasoned, 250 ml (1 cup)	5
Dressing, salad, creamy	
regular, 30 ml (2 Tbsp)	4
Dressing, salad, French	
regular, 15 ml (1 Tbsp)	2
Dressing, salad, Italian-type (other than creamy Italian)	
fat-free, 30 ml (2 Tbsp)	1
low-fat, 15 ml (1 Tbsp)	0
reduced-calorie, 30 ml (2 Tbsp)	1
regular, 30 ml (2 Tbsp)	2
Dressing, salad, mayonnaise-type	
regular, 15 ml (1 Tbsp)	2
Dressing, salad, Thousand Island	
15 ml (1 Tbsp)	1
Egg, whole	
▲ hard-boiled, 1 medium	2
Gelatin desserts	
prepared from dry mix, sweetened with sugar, 125 ml (1/2 cup)	2
Olives	
6 large or 10 small (30 g [1 oz])	1
Peas	
▲ chick (garbanzo beans), cooked or canned, 125 ml (1/2 cup)	3

▲ Power Foods	PointsPlus® value
▲ chick (garbanzo beans), cooked or canned, 250 ml (1 cup)	7
Pudding, rice	
250 ml (1 cup)	10
Salad	
carrot and raisin, 125 ml (1/2 cup)	8
▲ mixed greens	0
pasta, 125 ml (1/2 cup)	4
three-bean, 125 ml (1/2 cup)	5
Seeds	
caraway, flax, poppy, sesame, sunflower, 15 ml (1 Tbsp)	1
caraway, flax, poppy, sesame, sunflower, 5 ml (1 tsp)	0
Tomatoes	
▲ dried, not packed in oil, 1 medium	0
dried, packed in oil, drained, 1 medium	0

CANADIAN, SEAFOOD

	PointsPlus® value
Coconut shrimp	
4 jumbo (205 g [7 1/4 oz])	17
Crab cakes	
2 (65 g [2 1/4 oz] each or 7.5 cm [3"] round)	5
blue, 1 (60 g [2 oz])	2
Crab puffs	
6 (45 g [1 1/2"] rounds)	5
Fish	
▲ bass, striped, cooked, 1 fillet (170 g [6 oz])	5
▲ bluefish, cooked, 1 fillet (170 g [6 oz])	6
▲ cod, cooked, 1 fillet (90 g [3 oz])	2
▲ flounder, cooked, 1 fillet (170 g [6 oz])	4
▲ grouper, cooked, 1 fillet (170 g [6 oz])	4
▲ haddock, cooked, 1 fillet (170 g [6 oz])	4

ETHNIC & REGIONAL FAVOURITES

Canadian, Seafood, Fish (cont'd)

▲ Power Foods	PointsPlus® value
halibut, cooked, 1 fillet or steak (170 g [6 oz])	5
mackerel, 1 fillet (170 g [6 oz])	8
mahi mahi (dolphinfish), cooked, 1 fillet (170 g [6 oz])	4
orange roughy, cooked, 90 g (3 oz)	2
pollack, cooked, 1 fillet (170 g [6 oz])	4
pompano, cooked, 1 fillet (170 g [6 oz])	9
salmon, Atlantic wild, cooked, 1/2 fillet (160 g [5 1/2 oz])	7
salmon, farm-raised, cooked, 1 fillet (170 g [6 oz])	9
sea bass, cooked, 1 fillet (100 g [3 1/2 oz])	3
snapper, cooked, 1 fillet (170 g [6 oz])	5
sole, cooked, 1 fillet (170 g [6 oz])	4
swordfish, cooked, 1 fillet or steak (170 g [6 oz])	6
tilapia, cooked, 90 g (3 oz)	2
trout, cooked, 1 fillet (170 g [6 oz])	8
trout, rainbow, cooked, 1 fillet (170 g [6 oz])	6
tuna, cooked, 1 fillet or steak (170 g [6 oz])	5
whitefish, cooked, 1 fillet (160 g [5 1/2 oz])	6
Fish amandine	
1 fillet (250 g [8 oz])	13
Fish fillet	
fillet, grilled, with lemon pepper, 2 (9.5 cm [3 3/4 oz])	2
grilled, with garlic butter, 1 (110 g [3 3/4 oz])	3
Fish, stuffed	
baked, 190 g (6 3/4 oz)	9
Lobster Newburg	
250 ml (1 cup)	14
Lobster thermidor	
250 ml (1 cup)	14

▲ Power Foods	PointsPlus® value
Oysters	
fried, 10 (155 g [5 1/4 oz])	8
Oysters Rockefeller	
4 (60 g [2 oz])	3
Sauce	
tartar, 15 ml (1 Tbsp)	2
Scallops, fried	
20 small (100 g [3 1/2 oz])	6
Shellfish	
clams, cooked, 125 ml (1/2 cup) or 60 g (2 oz)	2
crabmeat, cooked, 125 ml (1/2 cup) or 60 g (2 oz)	1
crabmeat, lump, 90 g (3 oz)	2
crayfish, cooked, 16 or 125 ml (1/2 cup) or 60 g (2 oz)	1
lobster, cooked, 1/2 cup (75 g [2 1/2 oz])	2
lobster, cooked, 60 g (2 oz)	1
mussels, cooked, 125 ml (1/2 cup) or 60 g (2 oz)	2
oysters, cooked, 125 ml (1/2 cup)	2
oysters, cooked or uncooked, 6 medium (60 g [2 oz])	1
scallops, cooked, 4 large or 10 small (60 g [2 oz])	2
scallops, cooked, 90 g (3 oz)	2
shrimp, cooked, 60 g (2 oz)	1
squid, cooked, 90 g (3 oz)	2
Shrimp	
broiled, stuffed, 6 large (170 g [6 oz])	18
Shrimp, fried	
stuffed, 6 large (285 g [9 1/2 oz])	11
Shrimp puffs	
6 (45 g [1 1/2"] rounds)	5
Shrimp scampi	
9 medium (100 g [3 1/2 oz])	10
10 (150 g [5 oz])	9

Power Foods	PointsPlus® value
Soup	
lobster bisque, 250 ml (1 cup)	4
Squid, fried	
90 g (3 oz)	4

CANADIAN, STEAKHOUSE

Beef

Power Foods	PointsPlus® value
filet mignon, cooked, 1 small (125 g [4 oz])	10
filet mignon, cooked, 90 g (3 oz)	7
▲ filet mignon, trimmed, cooked, 1 small (125 g [4 oz])	5
▲ flank steak, trimmed, cooked, 1 slice (60 g [2 oz])	3
KC strip, cooked, 1 small (125 g [4 oz])	7
▲ KC strip, trimmed, cooked, 1 small (125 g [4 oz])	5
▲ KC strip, trimmed, cooked, 90 g (3 oz)	4
New York steak, cooked, 1 small (125 g [4 oz])	6
New York steak, trimmed, cooked, 90 g (3 oz)	4
porterhouse steak, cooked, 90 g (3 oz)	7
porterhouse steak, trimmed, cooked, 90 g (3 oz)	6
rib eye, trimmed, cooked, 90 g (3 oz)	5
round, steak or roast, cooked, 90 g (3 oz)	5
▲ round, steak or roast, trimmed, cooked, 90 g (3 oz)	3
▲ rump roast, trimmed, cooked, 1 slice (60 g [2 oz])	2
▲ rump roast, trimmed, cooked, 90 g (3 oz)	3

Power Foods	PointsPlus® value
sirloin, cooked, 90 g (3 oz)	5
sirloin, trimmed, cooked, 1 slice (60 g [2 oz])	3
sirloin, trimmed, cooked, 90 g (3 oz)	4
skirt steak, cooked, 90 g (3 oz)	5
▲ steak, lean, cooked (round or loin cuts other than those listed here with all visible fat trimmed), 1 small (125 g [4 oz])	5
steak, regular, cooked, 1 small (125 g [4 oz])	10
strip sirloin, cooked, 1 small (125 g [4 oz])	7
strip sirloin, cooked, 90 g (3 oz)	5
▲ strip sirloin, trimmed, cooked, 1 small (125 g [4 oz])	5
▲ strip sirloin, trimmed, cooked, 90 g (3 oz)	3
T-bone steak, cooked, 1 small (125 g [4 oz])	9
T-bone steak, cooked, 90 g (3 oz)	7
T-bone steak, trimmed, cooked, 1 small (125 g [4 oz])	7
T-bone steak, trimmed, cooked, 90 g (3 oz)	5
tenderloin, cooked, 1 slice (60 g [2 oz])	5
tenderloin, cooked, 90 g (3 oz)	7
▲ tenderloin, trimmed, cooked, 1 slice (60 g [2 oz])	2
▲ tenderloin, trimmed, cooked, 90 g (3 oz)	4
Bison (buffalo)	
▲ top sirloin, cooked, 125 g (4 oz)	5
Breadsticks	
any type other than soft, 1 long (18 cm x 1.25 cm [7 1/2" x 1/2"]) or 2 short (12.5 cm x 1.25 cm [5" x 1/2"])	1
soft, 1 (40 g [1 1/3 oz])	3

ETHNIC & REGIONAL FAVOURITES

Power Foods	PointsPlus® value
Cream, sour	
regular, 15 ml (1 Tbsp)	1
Onion, blooming	
1/4 of a 40 cm (16") diameter onion	6
Pepper steak	
170 g (6 oz)	14
Potatoes, baked	
▲ plain, 1 large (200 g [7 oz])	5
▲ plain, 1 medium (160 g [5 1/2 oz])	4
▲ plain, 1 small (90 g [3 oz])	2
Potatoes, mashed	
125 ml (1/2 cup)	3
garlic, 125 ml (1/2 cup)	5
Potatoes, scalloped	
125 ml (1/2 cup)	5
Rolls, dinner	
any type, 1 (60 g [2 oz])	5
Salad	
Caesar, 750 ml (3 cups)	7
cobb, without dressing, 750 ml (3 cups)	11
▲ tossed	0
Salisbury steak	
170 g (6 oz)	12
Sauce	
horseradish, 15 ml (1 Tbsp)	0
steak, 15 ml (1 Tbsp)	0
Steak au poivre	
170 g (6 oz) with 15 ml (1 Tbsp) sauce	13

CARIBBEAN

Power Foods	PointsPlus® value
Beans, black, with rice	
250 ml (1 cup)	6
Bistec de palomilla (Cuban fried steak)	
1 steak (170 g [6 oz])	11
Bread	
pan Cubano, 1 (16 cm x 7.5 cm [6 1/2" x 3"])	10
Cake	
Benny, 1 piece (5 cm x 7.5 cm [2" x 3"])	4
Chicken asopao	
250 ml (1 cup) with 1 piece chicken (290 g [10 oz])	9
Chuleta	
1 pork chop (170 g [6 oz])	12
Crab, deviled	
125 ml (1/2 cup)	4
Curry	
goat, 125 g (4 oz)	6
Fritters	
conch, 2 (50 g [1 3/4 oz])	3
Jamaican rice and peas	
250 ml (1 cup)	8
Jerk chicken breast	
without skin, 1 large breast (165 g [5 3/4 oz])	5
Johnny cake	
1 piece (6 cm [2 1/2"] square)	5
Lechon asado (roast pork)	
90 g (3 oz)	4
Macaroni and cheese	
Bahamian, 250 ml (1 cup)	9
Malanga	
▲ cooked, 1 large (200 g [7 oz])	5
▲ cooked, 175 ml (3/4 cup)	4
Peas, Bahamian style	
with rice, 250 ml (1 cup)	9
Plantain	
baked or boiled, 250 ml (1 cup)	5
fried, 250 ml (1 cup)	5
Plátanos maduros (fried sweet plantains)	
250 ml (1 cup)	5
Rice, Cuban	
250 ml (1 cup)	6
Ropa vieja	
250 ml (1 cup)	9

Power Foods	PointsPlus® value
Salad	
conch, 250 ml (1 cup)	3
Sandwich	
Cuban, 1/2 (16 m x 7.5 cm x 10 cm [6 1/2" x 3" x 4]")	12
Shellfish	
conch, cracked, 1 (15 cm [6"] long x 7.5 cm [3"])	10
Soup	
pigeon pea and dumpling, 375 ml (1 1/2 cups)	9
Souse, chicken	
1 leg and 1 thigh with skin (135 g [4 1/2 oz])	8
Stew	
carne guisado (Cuban beef stew), 250 ml (1 cup)	7

CHINESE

Power Foods	PointsPlus® value
Almond float	
250 ml (1 cup)	3
Beef and broccoli	
250 ml (1 cup)	4
Bubble tea (milk tea)	
250 ml (1 cup)	2
Char shiu bao (roast pork bun)	
1 (60 g [2 oz])	5
Chicken and broccoli	
250 ml (1 cup)	3
Chicken breast	
five spice, 1 (135 g [4 1/2 oz])	7
Chicken leg	
five spice with skin and bone, 1 thigh and drumstick (170 g [6 oz])	9
Chicken long rice	
250 ml (1 cup)	5
Chicken with cashews	
250 ml (1 cup)	11

Power Foods	PointsPlus® value
Chop suey	
beef, 250 ml (1 cup)	5
chicken, 250 ml (1 cup)	4
pork, 250 ml (1 cup)	5
vegetable, 250 ml (1 cup)	5
Chow fun	
beef, 250 ml (1 cup)	9
chicken, 250 ml (1 cup)	9
pork, 250 ml (1 cup)	9
shrimp, 250 ml (1 cup)	8
Chow mein	
beef, 250 ml (1 cup)	5
chicken, 250 ml (1 cup)	4
chicken subgum, 250 ml (1 cup)	4
pork, 250 ml (1 cup)	5
Cookies	
Chinese almond, 2 (30 g [1 oz])	4
fortune, 1 (5 g [1/4 oz])	1
Crab rangoon	
1 large (130 g [4 1/4 oz]) or 5 mini	5
Dim sum	
bean curd roll with shrimp and vegetables, 1 (12.5 cm [5"] long x 5 cm [2"] wide)	3
bean curd roll with vegetables, 1 (12.5 cm [5"] long x 3.5 cm [1 1/2"] wide)	2
sesame seed balls, 1 (7.5 cm x 7.5 cm [3" x 3"])	7
Duck, tea smoked	
60 g (2 oz)	3
Dumpling	
beef or pork, fried, 4 (185 g [6 1/2 oz])	7
beef or pork, steamed, 4 (165 g [5 3/4 oz])	7
chicken, fried, 4 (185 g [6 1/2 oz])	5
chicken, steamed, 4 (165 g [5 3/4 oz])	5
shrimp, fried, 4 (185 g [6 1/2 oz])	5
shrimp, steamed, 4 (165 g [5 3/4 oz])	5

ETHNIC & REGIONAL FAVOURITES

Power Foods	PointsPlus® value
vegetarian, fried, 4 (8.5 cm [3 1/2"] x 5 cm [2"] wide)	4
vegetarian, steamed, 4 (8.5 cm [3 1/2"] x 5 cm [2"] wide)	4
Egg foo yung	
beef, 1 (7.5 cm [3"] diameter)	4
chicken, 1 (7.5 cm [3"] diameter)	4
pork, 1 (7.5 cm [3"] diameter)	5
shrimp, 1 (7.5 cm [3"] diameter)	4
Egg roll	
beef, 1 (11 cm [4 1/2"] long)	6
chicken, 1 (11 cm [4 1/2"] long)	5
shrimp, 1 (11 cm [4 1/2"] long)	4
General Tso's chicken	
250 ml (1 cup)	17
Ginger fish	
250 ml (1 cup)	9
Hunan beef	
250 ml (1 cup)	10
Kung pao	
beef, 250 ml (1 cup)	12
chicken, 250 ml (1 cup)	9
pork, 250 ml (1 cup)	11
shrimp, 250 ml (1 cup)	10
Lettuce wrap	
beef, 2 (13.5 cm [5"] long x 7.5cm [3"] wide each)	5
chicken, 2 (13.5 cm [5"] long x 7.5 cm [3"] wide each)	4
Lo mein	
beef, 250 ml (1 cup)	10
chicken, 250 ml (1 cup)	9
pork, 250 ml (1 cup)	9
shrimp, 250 ml (1 cup)	9
vegetable, 250 ml (1 cup)	8
Lobster Cantonese	
250 ml (1 cup)	9
Mongolian beef	
250 ml (1 cup)	8

Power Foods	PointsPlus® value
Moo goo gai pan	
250 ml (1 cup)	7
Moo shoo	
chicken, 125 ml (1/2 cup) with 2 pancakes	8
pork, 125 ml (1/2 cup) with 2 pancakes	9
tofu, 125 ml (1/2 cup) with 2 pancakes	8
Noodles, cellophane	
cooked, 250 ml (1 cup)	5
Noodles, fried	
250 ml (1 cup)	8
Orange chicken	
250 ml (1 cup)	14
Pancakes, Chinese	
1 (30 g [1 oz])	2
Pancakes, scallion	
1 (12.5 cm [5"] diameter)	7
Peking duck	
60 g (2 oz) duck with 1 piece duck skin and 3 pancakes	11
Pepper steak	
Chinese, 250 ml (1 cup)	5
Pork and broccoli	
250 ml (1 cup)	4
Pork, Chinese roast	
250 ml (1 cup)	6
Pork with cashews	
250 ml (1 cup)	12
Rice, fried	
plain, 250 ml (1 cup)	10
with beef, 250 ml (1 cup)	10
with chicken, 250 ml (1 cup)	10
with pork, 250 ml (1 cup)	10
with shrimp, 250 ml (1 cup)	9
Sauce	
black bean, 5 ml (1 tsp)	0
brown, Chinese, 60 ml (1/4 cup)	1

ETHNIC & REGIONAL FAVOURITES

Power Foods	PointsPlus® value
duck, 15 ml (1 Tbsp)	1
hoisin, 5 ml (1 tsp)	0
kung pao, 30 ml (2 Tbsp)	2
oyster, 5 ml (1 tsp)	0
plum, 15 ml (1 Tbsp)	2
soy (shoyu), 15 ml (1 Tbsp)	0
soy (shoyu), low-sodium, 15 ml (1 Tbsp)	0
Sesame chicken	
250 ml (1 cup)	10
Sesame noodles	
250 ml (1 cup)	7
Shrimp and broccoli	
250 ml (1 cup)	3
Shrimp Cantonese	
250 ml (1 cup)	9
Shrimp toast	
1 piece (30 g [1 oz])	3
Shumai	
fried, 2 (5 cm [2"] diameter)	3
steamed, 2 (5 cm [2"] diameter)	3
Soup	
egg drop, 250 ml (1 cup)	1
hot and sour, 250 ml (1 cup)	3
shark fin, 250 ml (1 cup)	3
wonton, 250 ml (1 cup) with 4 wontons	5
Spareribs, barbecued	
Chinese, 2 (10 cm [4"] long)	4
Spring roll	
beef or pork, 1 (11 cm [4 1/2"] long)	6
chicken, 1 (11 cm [4 1/2"] long)	5
shrimp, 1 (11 cm [4 1/2"] long)	4
Stir-fry	
beef, with garlic or black bean sauce, 250 ml (1 cup)	8
broccoli, 250 ml (1 cup)	4
chicken, with garlic or black bean sauce, 250 ml (1 cup)	8

Power Foods	PointsPlus® value
mung beans, sprouted, 250 ml (1 cup)	2
pork, with garlic or black bean sauce, 250 ml (1 cup)	9
shrimp, with garlic or black bean sauce, 250 ml (1 cup)	7
vegetables with beef, 250 ml (1 cup)	4
vegetables with chicken, 250 ml (1 cup)	3
vegetables with pork, 250 ml (1 cup)	4
vegetables, with oil or sauce, 250 ml (1 cup)	4
vegetables, without sauce, 250 ml (1 cup)	1
Sweet and sour	
beef, 250 ml (1 cup)	13
chicken, 250 ml (1 cup)	11
pork, 250 ml (1 cup)	13
shrimp, 250 ml (1 cup)	11
Szechuan pork hotpot	
250 ml (1 cup)	6
Twice-cooked pork	
250 ml (1 cup)	10
Vegetables, Chinese	
with beef, 250 ml (1 cup)	7
with chicken, 250 ml (1 cup)	5
with peas, prepared with oil, 250 ml (1 cup)	5
with peas, prepared without oil, 250 ml (1 cup)	2
with pork, 250 ml (1 cup)	7
with shrimp, 250 ml (1 cup)	5
with tofu, 250 ml (1 cup)	4

EAST INDIAN

	PointsPlus® value
Aloo gobi	
250 ml (1 cup)	3
Aloo palak	
250 ml (1 cup)	4

ETHNIC & REGIONAL FAVOURITES

▲ Power Foods	PointsPlus® value
Beef masala	
250 ml (1 cup)	6
Bhuna gosht	
250 ml (1 cup)	9
Biryani	
chicken, 250 ml (1 cup)	11
lamb, 250 ml (1 cup)	15
Bread	
chapati, 1 piece (12.5 cm [5"] diameter)	3
naan, 1 piece (17 cm x 20 cm [7" x 8"] diameter)	5
Butter chicken	
250 ml (1 cup)	9
Cashew chicken	
90 g (3 oz) chicken with 75 ml (1/3 cup) sauce	7
Chana dal	
▲ 250 ml (1 cup)	5
Chana masala	
250 ml (1 cup)	9
Chicken jalfrezi	
250 ml (1 cup)	6
Chicken tikka	
125 g (4 oz)	5
Chili fish (macher jhol)	
1 fillet (170 g [6 oz])	13
Chutney	
tamarind, 30 ml (2 Tbsp)	2
30 ml (2 Tbsp)	1
Coconut rice	
Indian, 250 ml (1 cup)	6
Curry	
beef, 250 ml (1 cup)	11
Bengali, fish, 1 fillet (135 g [4 1/2 oz]) with 250 ml (1 cup) vegetables	11
chicken, 250 ml (1 cup)	10
egg, 250 ml (1 cup)	2
lamb, 250 ml (1 cup)	11

▲ Power Foods	PointsPlus® value
Dhansak	
250 ml (1 cup)	7
Fritters	
vegetable, 250 ml (1 cup)	12
Goat masala	
250 ml (1 cup)	6
Gosht shaha korma	
250 ml (1 cup)	15
Kashmiri (lamb meatballs)	
6 (100 g [3 1/2 oz])	11
Kheer	
125 ml (1/2 cup)	7
Kofta (vegetable balls without sauce)	
2 balls (90 g [3 oz])	6
Korma	
chicken, 250 ml (1 cup)	15
lamb, 250 ml (1 cup)	16
vegetable, 250 ml (1 cup)	12
Lamb masala	
250 ml (1 cup)	7
Mango lassi	
250 ml (1 cup)	3
Masala dosa	
with filling, 1 (15 cm [6"] diameter with 75 ml [1/3 cup] potato filling)	13
without filling, 1 (15 cm [6"] diameter)	12
Mung dal	
250 ml (1 cup)	6
Mutter paneer	
250 ml (1 cup)	13
Pakora, vegetable	
1 (5 cm x 7.5 cm [2" x 3"] or 50 g [1 3/4 oz])	4
Palak paneer	
250 ml (1 cup)	15
Palak vada (vegetable dumpling)	
fried, 1 (6 cm [2 1/2"] x 3.5 cm [1 1/2"])	5
steamed, 1 (6 cm [2 1/2"] x 3.5 cm [1 1/2"])	3

Power Foods	PointsPlus® value
Paneer, fried	
30 g (1 oz)	3
250 ml (1 cup)	6
Paratha	
10 cm (4") triangle	4
Puris	
1 (10 cm [4"] diameter)	3
Raita	
125 ml (1/2 cup)	2
Rajmah	
250 ml (1 cup)	8
Rogan josh	
250 ml (1 cup)	11
Saag gosht	
250 ml (1 cup)	7
Saag paneer	
250 ml (1 cup)	8
Samosa	
1 (6 cm [2 1/2"] x 6 cm [2 1/2"] x 7.5 cm [3"] triangle)	3
Soup	
mulligatawny, 250 ml (1 cup)	7
sambhar (Indian lentil), 250 ml (1 cup)	3
Stew	
bean and lentil (dal maharani), 250 ml (1 cup)	6
Tandoori chicken	
breast, without skin, 1 piece (135 g [4 1/2 oz])	4
thigh, without skin, 1 piece (90 g [3 oz])	4
Tandoori fish	
175 ml (3/4 cup)	5
Tandoori shrimp	
175 ml (3/4 cup)	3
Urad dal (split matpe beans without skin)	
250 ml (1 cup)	5
Vegetable pulao	
250 ml (1 cup)	4

Power Foods	PointsPlus® value
Vindaloo	
chicken, 250 ml (1 cup)	9
lamb, 250 ml (1 cup)	16
pork, 250 ml (1 cup)	10

EASTERN EUROPEAN

Power Foods	PointsPlus® value
Beef Stroganoff with noodles	
250 ml (1 cup) stroganoff with 250 ml (1 cup) noodles	17
Caviar (fish roe)	
any type, 30 g (1 oz)	2
Chicken Kiev	
1 piece (10 cm x 20 cm [4" x 8"])	18
Halvah	
1 piece (5 cm x 4.5 cm x 2.5 cm [2" x 1 3/4" x 1"])	6
Hungarian goulash	
250 ml (1 cup)	9
Kasha (buckwheat groats)	
▲ cooked, 250 ml (1 cup)	4
Kielbasa	
30 g (1 oz)	2
Kolache	
fruit-filled, 1 (7.5 cm [3"] diameter)	5
without filling, 1 (7.5 cm [3"] diameter)	4
Paprikash	
375 ml (1 1/2 cups) chicken mixture with 125 ml (1/2 cup) sauce	10
Pierogies	
cabbage, 2 (8.5 cm [3 1/2"] each)	8
cheese, 2 (8.5 cm [3 1/2"] each)	8
meat, 2 (8.5 cm [3 1/2"] each)	9
potato, 2 (8.5 cm [3 1/2"] each)	8
Sauerkraut	
▲ bottled or canned	0
Sausage	
Polish, 30 g (1 oz)	3
Soup	
cabbage, 250 ml (1 cup)	2

ETHNIC & REGIONAL FAVOURITES

FRENCH

Baba au rhum

1 (95 g [3 1/4 oz])	10

Beef Bourguignon

250 ml (1 cup)	15

Blanquette of veal

250 ml (1 cup)	6

Bouillabaisse

500 ml (2 cups)	9

Brioche

1 slice (30 g [1 oz])	3

Cassoulet

250 ml (1 cup)	12

Cheese, brie

30 g (1 oz)	3

Cheese, camembert

1 wedge (40 g [1 1/3 oz])	3

Cheese, goat

hard-type, 30 g (1 oz)	3
semisoft-type, 15 ml (1 Tbsp)	1
soft-type, 15 ml (1 Tbsp)	1

Chicken cordon bleu

1 (190 g [6 3/4 oz])	10

Chocolate mousse

250 ml (1 cup)	25

Coq au vin

500 ml (2 cups)	12

Coquilles St. Jacques

2 shells (405 g [13 1/2 oz])	9

Cream puff

1 (60 g [2 oz])	9

Crème brûlée

175 ml (3/4 cup)	12

Crème caramel

250 ml (1 cup)	8

Crème fraiche

30 ml (2 Tbsp)	3

Crêpes

chicken, 2 (290 g [10 oz])	12
plain, 1 (15 cm [6"] diameter)	2
seafood, 2 (330 g [11 oz])	12
Suzette, 2 (140 g [4 3/4 oz])	11

Croissant

apple, 1 medium (60 g [2 oz])	4
butter, 1 medium (60 g [2 oz])	6
cheese, 1 medium (60 g [2 oz])	6
chocolate-filled, 1 (12.5 cm [5"] long)	7
plain, 1 (12.5 cm [5"] long)	6

Croquettes

beef, 2 (75 g [2 1/2 oz] each)	10
chicken, 2 (75 g [2 1/2 oz] each)	9

Cruller

French, glazed, 1 (7.5 cm [3"] diameter)	5

Duck a l'orange

1/4 duck with 30 ml (2 Tbsp) sauce	15

Duck with fruit sauce

1/4 duck with skin and 125 ml (1/2 cup) sauce	16

Éclair

1 (155 cm [5 1/4 oz])	11

Escargots

6 snails with 30 ml (2 Tbsp) butter	6

Fish Veronique

1 fillet (170 g [6 oz])	12

Fondue, cheese

125 ml (1/2 cup) fondue with 60 g (2 oz) bread	12

Frog legs

fried, 2 (30 g [1 oz])	4

Fromage frais (soft cheese with fruit)

30 g (1 oz)	3

Mussels Mariniere

4 mussels with 45 ml (3 Tbsp) sauce	5

Napoleon

1 piece (11 cm x 5 cm x 3.5 cm [4 1/2" x 2" x 1 1/2"])	15

ETHNIC & REGIONAL FAVOURITES

▲ Power Foods	PointsPlus® value
Pâté	
liver, 1 slice (10.5 cm x 3.5 cm x 1.25 cm [4 1/4" x 1 1/2" x 1/2"])	3
Peach melba	
125 ml (1/2 cup) ice cream with 2 peach halves and raspberry sauce	9
Petit fours	
2 (4.5 cm x 3.5 cm x 2.5 cm [1 3/4" x 1 1/2" x 1"] each)	6
Petite marmite	
500 ml (2 cups)	8
Potatoes, au gratin	
250 ml (1 cup)	14
Profiterole	
1 small (30 g [1 oz])	3
Quenelles	
8 (6 cm x 3.5 cm x 2 cm [2 1/2" x 1 1/2" x 3/4"])	12
Quiche	
vegetable, 1/8 of a 22 cm (9") pie	9
Quiche Lorraine	
1/8 of a 22 cm (9") pie	11
Ratatouille	
250 ml (1 cup)	5
Salad	
Niçoise, with dressing, 1 L (4 cups)	20
Niçoise, without dressing, 1 L (4 cups)	9
Sandwich	
croque-monsieur, 1 (185 g [6 1/2 oz])	12
Sauce	
béarnaise, 60 ml (1/4 cup)	8
hollandaise, 60 ml (1/4 cup)	8
mornay, 60 ml (1/4 cup)	4
wine, 60 ml (1/4 cup)	3
Sausage in brioche	
1 slice (5 cm [2"] thick)	16
Sorbet, any flavour	
1 scoop or 125 ml (1/2 cup)	2

▲ Power Foods	PointsPlus® value
Soufflé	
cheese, 250 ml (1 cup)	5
fruit, 125 ml (1/2 cup)	4
Soup	
cherry, 250 ml (1 cup)	8
vichyssoise, 250 ml (1 cup)	3
Tarte aux fruits	
1/8 of 22 cm (9") tart	11
individual, 1 (10 cm [4"])	15

GERMAN

▲ Power Foods	PointsPlus® value
Apple kuchen	
215 g (7 1/2 oz)	12
Apple streusel	
125 ml (1/2 cup)	5
Dumpling	
potato, 6 (2.5 cm [1"] diameter)	3
Fritters	
apple, restaurant-type, 1 (125 g [4 oz])	12
Pepper, stuffed	
with beef and rice, 1 (225 g [7 3/4 oz])	9
Potato pancakes	
1 (95 g [3 1/4 oz]	2
Sachertorte	
1/16 of a 22 cm (9") cake	9
Salad	
potato, German, 125 ml (1/2 cup)	2
Sauerbraten	
90 g (3 oz) beef with 30 ml (2 Tbsp) gravy	6
Schaum torte	
with whipped cream, 1/10 of a 25 cm (10") pan	9
without whipped cream, 1/10 of a 25 cm (10") pan	4
Spaetzle	
125 ml (1/2 cup)	6

ETHNIC & REGIONAL FAVOURITES

▲ Power Foods	PointsPlus® value
Strudel, any type	
1 piece (13.5 cm x 5 cm [5 1/2" x 2"])	12
Wiener schnitzel	
1 slice (90 g [3 oz])	10

GREEK

▲ Power Foods	PointsPlus® value
Baklava	
1 piece (75 g [2 1/2 oz])	10
Cheese, feta	
crumbled, 5 ml (1 tsp)	0
crumbled, 15 ml (1 Tbsp)	1
crumbled, 60 ml (1/4 cup) or 40 g (1 1/3 oz)	3
crumbled, 250 ml (1 cup)	11
Dolma	
4 (95 g [3 1/4 oz])	5
Gyro	
1 (330 g [11 oz])	16
Kataifi	
1 piece (5 cm [2"] long)	7
Moussaka	
1 piece (7.5 cm x 10 cm [3" x 4"])	12
Pastitsio	
1 piece (8 cm x 7.5 cm [3 1/4" x 3"])	14
Saganaki	
1 piece (2.5 cm [1"] x 5 cm [2"] x 1.25 cm [1/2"] thick)	6
Salad	
Greek, with dressing, 750 ml (3 cups)	10
Greek, without dressing, 750 ml (3 cups)	3
yogourt and cucumber, 125 ml (1/2 cup)	1
tzatziki, 125 ml (1/2 cup)	2
Soup	
avgolemono, 250 ml (1 cup)	4
yogourt and cucumber, 250 ml (1 cup)	3

▲ Power Foods	PointsPlus® value
Souvlaki, chicken	
1 large or 2 small skewers (135 g [4 1/2 oz])	5
in pita bread, 1 (185 g [6 1/2 oz])	8
Souvlaki, lamb	
1 large or 2 small skewers (140 g [4 3/4 oz])	8
in pita bread, 1 (185 g [6 1/2 oz])	9
Spanakopita	
1 (7.5 cm [3"]) square or 250 ml (1 cup)	9

HAWAIIAN

▲ Power Foods	PointsPlus® value
Chicken hekka	
250 ml (1 cup)	7
Haupia (coconut pudding)	
5 cm (2") square	3
Huli huli chicken	
breast, with skin and bone, 1 (205 g [7 1/4 oz])	13
drumstick, with skin and bone, 1 (60 g [2 oz])	3
thigh, with skin and bone, 1 (90 g [3 oz])	5
Kahlua pig	
90 g (3 oz)	4
Lau lau (pork and fish in taro or spinach leaves)	
1 (215 g [7 1/2 oz])	8
Lomi lomi salmon	
125 ml (1/2 cup)	2
Manapua with char shiu filling	
1 (95 g [3 1/4 oz])	6
Mochi	
butter, 1 piece (5 cm [2"] square)	7
Mun doo	
fried, 4 (185 g [6 1/2 oz])	5
steamed, 4 (165 g [5 3/4 oz])	5

▲ Power Foods | *PointsPlus®* value

Musubi, spam

1 (8.5 cm x 5 cm x 2.5 cm [3 1/2" x 2" x 1"])	7

Poi

▲ 125 ml (1/2 cup) or 125 g (4 oz)	4

Saimin

250 ml (1 cup)	5

Salad

green papaya, with pork and shrimp, 250 ml (1 cup)	4
green papaya, without meat, 2 lettuce leaves filled with salad	2

Sauce

curry, Hawaiian-style, 60 ml (1/4 cup)	5

Soup

oxtail, Hawaiian-style, 250 ml (1 cup)	7

ITALIAN, PIZZERIA

Pizza, fast food, single serving

cheese, 1 (265 g [8 1/2 oz])	15

Pizza, thin crust, cheese, restaurant-type

1 small slice (1/8 of a 30 cm [12"] or 1/12 of a 40 cm [16"] pie)	5
1 large slice (1/8 of a 40-45 cm [16-18"] pie)	7

Pizza, thin crust, one-meat topping, restaurant-type

1 small slice (1/8 of a 30 cm [12"] or 1/12 of a 40 cm [16"] pie)	5
1 large slice (1/8 of a 40-45 cm [16-18"] pie)	8

Pizza, deep dish, one-meat topping, restaurant-type

1 small slice (1/8 of a 30 cm [12"] or 1/12 of a 40 cm [16"] pie)	8
1 large slice (1/8 of a 40-45 cm [16-18"] pie)	13

▲ Power Foods | *PointsPlus®* value

ITALIAN, RESTAURANT

Artichoke hearts

marinated, 125 ml (1/2 cup)	4

Artichokes

stuffed, 1 (225 g [7 3/4 oz])	15

Biscotti

chocolate, 1 regular, 2 small, or 8 mini (30 g [1 oz])	4
plain or fat-free, 1 regular, 2 small, or 8 mini (30 g [1 oz])	3

Bread, garlic

fresh, 1 slice (45 g [1 1/2 oz])	6

Bruschetta

1 slice (90 g [3 oz])	3

Calamari

fried, 125 ml (1/2 cup)	11
▲ grilled, 125 ml (1/2 cup)	1

Calzone

ham and cheese, 1 (13 cm x 15 cm [5 1/4" x 6"])	15

Cannelloni

cheese, with meat sauce, 2 shells with 125 ml (1/2 cup) sauce	22
cheese, with tomato sauce, 2 shells with 125 ml (1/2 cup) sauce	14
meat, with cream sauce, 2 shells with 125 ml (1/2 cup) sauce	19
meat, with tomato sauce, 2 shells with 125 ml (1/2 cup) sauce	15
spinach and cheese, with cream sauce, 2 shells with 125 ml (1/2 cup) sauce	17
spinach and cheese, with tomato sauce, 2 shells with 125 ml (1/2 cup) sauce	14

ETHNIC & REGIONAL FAVOURITES

▲ Power Foods	PointsPlus® value
Cannoli	
1 (8.5 cm [3 1/2"])	10
Caponata (eggplant appetizer)	
250 ml (1 cup)	5
Cappuccino	
▲ made with fat-free milk, 1 small (250 ml [8 fl oz])	1
▲ made with fat-free milk, 1 tall (375 ml [12 fl oz])	2
▲ made with fat-free milk, 1 grande (500 ml [16 fl oz])	2
made with low-fat milk, 1 small (250 ml [8 fl oz])	2
made with low-fat milk, 1 tall (375 ml [12 fl oz])	3
made with low-fat milk, 1 grande (500 ml [16 fl oz])	3
made with whole milk, 1 small (250 ml [8 fl oz])	2
made with whole milk, 1 tall (375 ml [12 fl oz])	3
made with whole milk, 1 grande (500 ml [16 fl oz])	4
ready-made from machine, any flavour, 250 ml (1 cup)	2
Cavatelli with sausage and broccoli	
250 ml (1 cup)	6
Cheese, gorgonzola	
30 g (1 oz)	3
Cheese, mozzarella	
fried, 2 slices (7 cm x 2.5 cm x 1.25 cm [2 3/4" x 1" x 1/2"] each)	10
Cheese, Parmesan	
grated, 30 ml (2 Tbsp)	1
shredded, 15 ml (1 Tbsp)	1
Cheese, provolone	
regular, 1 slice (30 g [1 oz])	3
Chicken cacciatore	
1/2 breast or 1 thigh and leg (185 g [6 1/2 oz])	11

▲ Power Foods	PointsPlus® value
Chicken marsala	
without bone, with sauce, 125 g (4 oz)	14
Chicken parmigiana	
with sauce, 150 g (5 oz) with 125 ml (1/2 cup) sauce	11
without sauce, 160 g (5 1/2 oz)	8
Chicken tetrazzini	
375 ml (1 1/2 cups)	15
Clams	
baked, 6 (75 g [2 1/2 oz])	7
breaded and fried, 20 (185 g [6 1/2 oz])	10
fried, 250 ml (1 cup)	11
Cookies	
amaretti, 1 (2.5 cm [1"] diameter)	3
sesame seed, 2 (5 cm [2"] long)	4
Dip	
artichoke, baked, 60 ml (1/4 cup)	6
Eggplant parmigiana	
with sauce, 1 piece (7.5 cm x 10 cm [3" x 4"]) with 125 ml (1/2 cup) Italian tomato sauce	14
without sauce, 1 piece (7.5 cm x 10 cm [3" x 4"])	11
Fettuccine Alfredo	
250 ml (1 cup)	17
Focaccia	
1/4 of a 25 cm (10") diameter	7
Gnocchi	
cheese, 250 ml (1 cup)	12
potato, 250 ml (1 cup)	5
spinach, 250 ml (1 cup)	13
Ices	
Italian, restaurant-type, 125 ml (1/2 cup)	2
Italian casserole (ground beef, pasta and cheese over rolls)	
1/8 of a 25 cm (10") round casserole	15

ETHNIC & REGIONAL FAVOURITES

▲ Power Foods	*PointsPlus®* value
Lasagna	
cheese, with tomato sauce, 1 piece (290 g [10 oz])	9
chicken, 250 ml (1 cup)	7
vegetable, 250 ml (1 cup)	8
vegetarian, with cheese, 1 piece (290 g [10 oz])	12
vegetarian, with cheese and spinach, 1 piece (300 g [10 1/2 oz])	10
with meat, 10 cm x 6 cm (4" x 2 1/2") or 250 ml (1 cup)	7
with meat sauce, 250 ml (1 cup)	7
Latte	
▲ made with fat-free milk, 1 small (250 ml [8 fl oz])	2
▲ made with fat-free milk, 1 tall (375 ml [12 fl oz])	3
▲ made with fat-free milk, 1 grande (500 ml [16 fl oz])	4
made with low-fat milk, 1 small (250 ml [8 fl oz])	3
made with low-fat milk, 1 tall (375 ml [12 fl oz])	4
made with low-fat milk, 1 grande (500 ml [16 fl oz])	5
made with whole milk, 1 small (250 ml [8 fl oz])	3
made with whole milk, 1 tall (375 ml [12 fl oz])	5
made with whole milk, 1 grande (500 ml [16 fl oz])	7
Linguine with red clam sauce	
250 ml (1 cup) linguine with 125 ml (1/2 cup) sauce	8
Linguine with white clam sauce	
250 ml (1 cup) linguine with 125 ml (1/2 cup) sauce	10
Macaroni	
regular, cooked, 250 ml (1 cup)	5
▲ whole-wheat, cooked, 250 ml (1 cup)	5

▲ Power Foods	*PointsPlus®* value
Manicotti	
with meat sauce, 2 pieces with 125 ml (1/2 cup) sauce	16
with tomato sauce, 2 pieces with 125 ml (1/2 cup) sauce	13
Meatballs	
with sauce, 2 meatballs and 125 ml (1/2 cup) Italian tomato sauce	13
without sauce, 2 (3 cm [1 1/4"] each)	10
Mushrooms, marinated	
125 ml (1/2 cup)	3
Mushrooms, stuffed	
4 (80 g [2 3/4 oz])	4
Osso bucco	
170 g (6 oz) veal with 60 ml (1/4 cup) sauce	12
Panettone	
1/12 of a 22 cm (9") tube or 45 g [1 1/2 oz])	7
Panini	
chicken, 1 (250 g [8 oz])	13
ham and cheese, 1 (215 g [7 1/2 oz])	13
turkey, restaurant-type, 1 (300 g [10 1/2 oz])	19
vegetable, 1 (390 g [13 oz])	12
Pasta	
regular, cooked, 250 ml (1 cup)	5
▲ whole-wheat, cooked, 250 ml (1 cup)	4
Pasta e fagioli	
250 ml (1 cup)	6
Pasta primavera	
with marinara sauce, 250 ml (1 cup) pasta with 175 ml (3/4 cup) sauce	7
with cream sauce, 250 ml (1 cup) pasta with 175 ml (3/4 cup) sauce	14
Pasta with garlic and oil	
250 ml (1 cup)	8

ETHNIC & REGIONAL FAVOURITES

Italian, Restaurant (cont'd)

▲ Power Foods	PointsPlus® value
Penne a la vodka	
250 ml (1 cup) pasta with 125 ml (1/2 cup) sauce	9
Polenta	
cooked, 125 ml (1/2 cup)	3
Ravioli	
cheese, with tomato sauce, 8 pieces or 250 ml (1 cup) with 125 ml (1/2 cup) sauce	19
cheese, without sauce, 8 pieces or 250 ml (1 cup)	16
meat, with tomato sauce, 8 pieces or 250 ml (1 cup) with 125 ml (1/2 cup) sauce	17
meat, without sauce, 8 pieces or 250 ml (1 cup)	14
Risotto	
125 ml (1/2 cup)	6
Salad	
tomato and mozzarella, without dressing, 2 large tomato slices with 60 g (2 oz) cheese	5
Sauce	
Alfredo, regular, 125 ml (1/2 cup)	10
Bolognese meat, 125 ml (1/2 cup)	6
clam, red, 125 ml (1/2 cup)	3
clam, white, 125 ml (1/2 cup)	5
marinara, 125 ml (1/2 cup)	3
meat, 125 ml (1/2 cup)	5
pesto, 30 ml (2 Tbsp)	4
puttanesca, 125 ml (1/2 cup)	12
tomato, Italian, 125 ml (1/2 cup)	3
Sausage	
Italian pork, cooked, 1 link (70 g [2 1/3 oz])	6
Soup	
Italian wedding, 250 ml (1 cup)	5
lentil, 250 ml (1 cup)	4
minestrone, 250 ml (1 cup)	5

▲ Power Foods	PointsPlus® value
Spaghetti	
regular, cooked, 250 ml (1 cup)	5
▲ whole-wheat, cooked, 250 ml (1 cup)	4
Spaghetti bolognese	
250 ml (1 cup) spaghetti with 125 ml (1/2 cup) sauce	12
Spaghetti carbonara	
250 ml (1 cup)	13
Spaghetti with marinara sauce	
250 ml (1 cup) spaghetti with 125 ml (1/2 cup) sauce	8
Spaghetti with meat sauce	
250 ml (1 cup) spaghetti with 125 ml (1/2 cup) sauce	11
Spaghetti with tomato sauce	
with meatballs, 250 ml (1 cup) spaghetti with 125 ml (1/2 cup) sauce and 2 meatballs	18
Spumoni	
125 ml (1/2 cup)	7
Stromboli	
1 slice (2.5 cm [1"] thick or 60 g [2 oz])	5
Tirami-su	
restaurant-type, 1 slice (140 g [4 3/4 oz])	12
Tortellini	
cheese, without sauce, 150 ml (2/3 cup)	4
meat, without sauce, 150 ml (2/3 cup)	4
Tortoni	
75 g (2 1/2 oz)	7
Turkey tetrazzini	
375 ml (1 1/2 cups)	15
Veal cutlet, breaded	
fried, 125 g (4 oz)	9
Veal marsala	
125 g (4 oz) veal with sauce	12

▲ Power Foods	PointsPlus® value
Veal parmigiana	
with sauce, 150 g (5 oz) veal with 125 ml (1/2 cup) tomato sauce	13
without sauce, 160 g (5 1/2 oz)	10
Veal piccata	
2 slices (125 g [4 oz])	10
Veal scaloppine	
2 pieces (135 g [4 1/2 oz])	9
Veal with peppers	
150 g (5 oz)	11
Vitello tonnato	
2 slices veal (125 g [4 oz]) with 125 ml (1/2 cup) sauce	16
Zabaglione	
125 ml (1/2 cup)	4
Zeppole	
1 (10 cm [4"] diameter)	7
Ziti, baked	
with meat, 250 ml (1 cup)	10
without meat, 250 ml (1 cup)	7
Zuppa di pesce	
500 ml (2 cups)	11
Zuppa Inglese	
1/16 of a 25 cm (10") cake	9

JAPANESE

▲ Power Foods	PointsPlus® value
Aburage (Japanese fried bean curd)	
1 piece (15 g [1/2 oz])	1
Curry	
Japanese, 250 ml (1 cup)	5
Dressing, salad, ginger	
30 ml (2 Tbsp)	2
Dressing, salad, sesame seed	
regular, 15 ml (1 Tbsp)	2
Edamame	
▲ in pods, 250 ml (1 cup)	3

▲ Power Foods	PointsPlus® value
Fish	
eel, cooked, 30 g (1 oz)	2
Gyoza	
3 (35 g [1 1/4 oz])	3
Katsu	
ahi, 2 slices (11 cm [4 1/2"] x 1.25 cm [1/2"] x 2 cm [3/4"] thick)	6
chicken, 2 slices (11 cm [4 1/2"] x 1.25 cm [1/2"] x 2 cm [3/4"] thick)	6
pork, 2 slices (11 cm [4 1/2"] x 1.25 cm [1/2"] x 2 cm [3/4"] thick)	7
Mochi	
1 piece (5 cm [2"] square)	2
Natto	
250 ml (1 cup)	10
Nebeyaki udon	
500 ml (2 cups)	7
Nikujaga	
250 ml (1 cup)	14
Noodles, Japanese, soba	
cooked, 250 ml (1 cup)	3
with sauce, 250 ml (1 cup)	12
Noodles, Japanese, somen	
cooked, 250 ml (1 cup)	6
Okonmiyaki, without sauce and mayonnaise (Japanese style pizza)	
1 (20 cm [8"] diameter)	9
Poke, ahi or tako	
125 ml (1/2 cup)	2
Rice, sushi	
cooked, 125 ml (1/2 cup)	3
Salad	
seaweed, 125 ml (1/2 cup)	1
Sashimi	
▲ any type except salmon or mackerel, 4 pieces (60 g [2 oz])	1
mackerel, 4 pieces (60 g [2 oz])	4
salmon, 4 pieces (60 g [2 oz])	2

ETHNIC & REGIONAL FAVOURITES

Power Foods	PointsPlus® value
Sauce	
shoyu (soy), 15 ml (1 Tbsp)	0
shoyu (soy), low-sodium, 15 ml (1 Tbsp)	0
tamari, 15 ml (1 Tbsp)	0
teriyaki, 15 ml (1 Tbsp)	0
Shabu shabu	
125 g (4 oz) beef, 60 g (2 oz) tofu, and 375 ml (1 1/2 cups) vegetables	10
Shoyu chicken	
1 thigh (90 g [3 oz])	6
Soup	
miso, 250 ml (1 cup)	2
suimono, 250 ml (1 cup)	2
Sukiyaki with sauce	
500 ml (2 cups) with 60 ml (1/4 cup) sauce	15
Sunomono	
125 ml (1/2 cup)	0
Sushi	
Alaskan roll, 2 pieces (2.5 cm [1"] high x 4.5 cm [1 3/4"] diameter)	3
California roll, 4 large pieces (2.5 cm [1"] high x 4.5 cm [1 3/4"] diameter) or 30 g (1 oz) each	4
cone, 1	3
inari, 1	3
kappa maki (cucumber roll), 4 medium pieces (3.5 cm [1 1/2"] diameter x 2 cm [3/4"] thick)	3
kappa maki (cucumber roll), 6 small pieces (2.5 cm [1"] diameter x 2.5 cm [1"] thick)	3
maki (vegetables and rice rolled with seaweed), 4 medium pieces (3.5 cm [1 1/2"] diameter x 2 cm [3/4"] thick)	3
maki (vegetables and rice rolled with seaweed), 6 small pieces (2.5 cm [1"] diameter x 2.5 cm [1"] thick)	3

Power Foods	PointsPlus® value
nigiri (sliced uncooked fish over rice), 4 medium pieces (3.5 cm [1 1/2"] diameter x 2 cm [3/4"] thick)	3
nigiri (sliced uncooked fish over rice), 6 small pieces (2.5 cm [1"] diameter x 2.5 cm [1"] thick)	3
nigiri uni (sea urchin), 4 medium pieces (5 cm [2"] long x 2 cm [3/4"] wide)	3
nigiri, albacore (white tuna), 4 medium pieces (5 cm [2"] long x 2 cm [3/4"] wide)	3
nigiri, amaebi (sweet shrimp), 4 medium pieces (5 cm [2"] long x 2 cm [3/4"] wide)	3
nigiri, conch, 4 medium pieces (5 cm [2"] long x 2 cm [3/4"] wide)	3
nigiri, ebi (cooked shrimp), 4 medium pieces (5 cm [2"] long x 2 cm [3/4"] wide)	3
nigiri, hamachi (yellow tail), 4 medium pieces (5 cm [2"] long x 2 cm [3/4"] wide)	3
nigiri, hirame (fluke), 4 medium pieces (5 cm [2"] long x 2 cm [3/4"] wide)	3
nigiri, hokigai (surf clam), 4 medium pieces (5 cm [2"] long x 2 cm [3/4"] wide)	3
nigiri, ika (squid), 4 medium pieces (5 cm [2"] long x 2 cm [3/4"] wide)	3
nigiri, ikura (salmon roe), 4 medium pieces (5 cm [2"] long x 2 cm [3/4"] wide)	3
nigiri, kani (crab), 4 medium pieces (5 cm [2"] long x 2 cm [3/4"] wide)	3
nigiri, maguro (tuna), 4 medium pieces (5 cm [2"] long x 2 cm [3/4"] wide)	3
nigiri, masago (smelt roe), 4 medium pieces (5 cm [2"] long x 2 cm [3/4"] wide)	3
nigiri, saba (mackerel), 4 medium pieces (5 cm [2"] long x 2 cm [3/4"] wide)	3

Power Foods	PointsPlus® value
nigiri, sake (fresh salmon), 4 medium pieces (5 cm [2"] long x 2 cm [3/4"] wide)	3
nigiri, smoked salmon, 4 medium pieces (5 cm [2"] long x 2 cm [3/4"] wide)	3
nigiri, suzuki (sea bass), 4 medium pieces (5 cm [2"] long x 2 cm [3/4"] wide)	3
nigiri, suzume, 4 medium pieces (5 cm [2"] long x 2 cm [3/4"] wide)	3
nigiri, tai (red snapper), 4 medium pieces (5 cm [2"] long x 2 cm [3/4"] wide)	3
nigiri, tairagai (scallops), 4 medium pieces (5 cm [2"] long x 2 cm [3/4"] wide)	3
nigiri, tako (octopus), 4 medium pieces (5 cm [2"] long x 2 cm [3/4"] wide)	3
nigiri, tobiko (flying fish roe), 4 medium pieces (5 cm [2"] long x 2 cm [3/4"] wide)	3
nigiri, unagi (fresh water eel), 4 medium pieces (5 cm [2"] long x 2 cm [3/4"] wide)	3
nori maki (uncooked fish and rice rolled with seaweed), 4 medium pieces (3.5 cm [1 1/2"] diameter x 2 cm [3/4"] thick)	3
nori maki (uncooked fish and rice rolled with seaweed), 6 small pieces (2.5 cm [1"] diameter x 2.5 cm [1"] thick)	3
Philadelphia roll, 2 large pieces (2.5 cm [1"] high x 4.5 cm [1 3/4"] diameter)	3
rainbow roll, 4 medium pieces (3.5 cm [1 1/2"] diameter x 2 cm [3/4"] thick)	3
rainbow roll, 6 small pieces (2.5 cm [1"] diameter x 2.5 cm [1"] thick)	3
spider roll, 6 pieces (5 cm [2"] diameter x 2.5 cm [1"] thick)	10

Power Foods	PointsPlus® value
tamago-yaki (omelette roll), 2 pieces (2 cm [3/4"] wide)	3
tempura roll, shrimp, 6 pieces (3.5 cm [1 1/2"] diameter x 2.5 cm [1"] thick)	10
tempura roll, vegetable, 6 pieces (3.5 cm [1 1/2"] diameter x 2.5 cm [1"] thick)	5
tuna roll, 4 medium pieces (3.5 cm [1 1/2"] diameter x 2 cm [3/4"] thick)	3
tuna roll, 6 small pieces (2.5 cm [1"] diameter x 2.5 cm [1"] thick)	3
tuna roll, spicy, 6 pieces (5 cm [2"] diameter x 2.5 cm [1"] thick)	7
unagi maki, 4 medium pieces (3.5 cm [1 1/2"] diameter x 2 cm [3/4"] thick)	3
unagi maki, 6 small pieces (2.5 cm [1"] diameter x 2.5 cm [1"] thick)	3
uni maki, 4 medium pieces (3.5 cm [1 1/2"] diameter x 2 cm [3/4"] thick)	3
uni maki, 6 small pieces (2.5 cm [1"] diameter x 2.5 cm [1"] thick)	3
yellow tail roll, 4 medium pieces (3.5 cm [1 1/2"] diameter x 2 cm [3/4"] thick)	3
yellow tail roll, 6 small pieces (2.5 cm [1"] diameter x 2.5 cm [1"] thick)	3
Tempura	
shrimp, 4 jumbo (110 g [3 3/4 oz])	13
vegetable, 250 ml (1 cup)	8
Teppan yaki (mixed grill of beef, chicken, shrimp and vegetables)	
375 ml (1 1/2 cups)	12

ETHNIC & REGIONAL FAVOURITES

▲ Power Foods	*PointsPlus®* value
Teriyaki	
beef, 2 slices (125 g [4 oz])	7
chicken, 2 slices (125 g [4 oz])	6
fish other than salmon, 125 g (4 oz)	6
salmon, 125 g (4 oz)	7
tofu, 250 ml (1 cup)	4
Tofu, fried	
1 piece (15 g [1/2 oz])	1
agadashi, 3.5 cm x 5 cm (1 1/2" x 2")	7
Tonkatsu	
beef, 175 ml (3/4 cup)	7
chicken, 175 ml (3/4 cup)	7
pork, 175 ml (3/4 cup)	9
Yaki-soba	
beef, 125 ml (1/2 cup) noodles with 125 ml (1/2 cup) beef and vegetables	5
chicken, 125 ml (1/2 cup) noodles with 125 ml (1/2 cup) chicken and vegetables	5
pork, 125 ml (1/2 cup) noodles with 125 ml (1/2 cup) pork and vegetables	5
Yakitori	
1 skewer (215 g [7 1/2 oz])	6
Yosenabe	
500 ml (2 cups)	5

JEWISH CUISINE

▲ Power Foods	*PointsPlus®* value
Bagel	
any type other than those listed here, 1 small (7.5 cm [3"] diameter) or 1/2 large (11 cm [4 1/2"] diameter) or 60 g (2 oz)	4
with cream cheese and lox, 1 large (185 g [6 1/2 oz])	14
Bialy	
1 (90 g [3 oz])	7
Blintz	
cheese, 1 (150 g [5 oz])	6
Borscht	
store-bought, 250 ml (1 cup)	2
Bread	
challah, 1 slice (12.5 cm x 7.5 cm x 2 cm [5" x 3" x 3/4"])	3
Cabbage, stuffed	
2 (5 cm x 6 cm [2" x 2 1/2"])	7
Chicken and meatball fricassee	
500 ml (2 cups)	10
Chicken in the pot	
without skin, 500 ml (2 cups)	12
Cholent	
250 ml (1 cup)	5
Cookies	
rugalach, 1 (6 cm [2 1/2"] x 3 cm [1 1/4"])	3
Fish	
lox, 30 g (1 oz)	1
sablefish, smoked, 30 g (1 oz)	2
▲ whitefish, smoked, 60 g (2 oz)	1
Flanken	
2 slices (125 g [4 oz])	8
Fruit compote	
125 ml (1/2 cup)	4
Gefilte fish	
1 piece (45 g [1 1/2 oz])	1
Hamantaschen	
1 piece (7.5 cm [3"] diameter)	3
Haroset	
60 ml (1/4 cup)	1
Herring	
chopped, 60 ml (1/4 cup)	4
pickled, 60 ml (1/4 cup)	2
Kasha varnishkes	
250 ml (1 cup)	7
Kishke	
1 small piece (20 g [3/4 oz])	2
Knish	
potato, 1 (8.5 cm [3 1/2"] square)	7

▲ Power Foods	*PointsPlus®* value
Kreplach	
boiled, 2 pieces (10 cm x 7.5 cm x 7.5 cm [4" x 3" x 3"] each)	6
fried, 2 pieces (10 cm x 7.5 cm x 7.5 cm [4" x 3" x 3"] each)	8
Kugel	
lukschen (noodle), with fruit, 1 piece (7.5 cm x 8 cm [3" x 3 1/4"])	9
lukschen (noodle), without fruit, 1 piece (7.5 cm x 8 cm [3" x 3 1/4"])	6
potato, 1 piece (7.5 cm x 8 cm [3" x 3 1/4"])	5
Liver	
chopped, 60 ml (1/4 cup)	5
Mandelbrot	
1 slice (7.5 cm x 5 cm x 1.25 cm [3" x 2" x 1/2"])	5
Matzo	
any variety, 1 board (30 g [1 oz])	3
Matzo brie	
1/4 of a 25 cm (10") round or 250 ml (1 cup)	5
Pastrami	
beef, extra lean, 1 slice (30 g [1 oz])	1
Potato latkes	
2 (8.5 cm [3 1/2"] diameter)	7
Schmaltz (chicken fat)	
15 ml (1 Tbsp)	3
Soup	
chicken, with matzo balls, 250 ml (1 cup) soup with 2 (3.5 cm [1 1/2"]) matzo balls	3
chicken, without matzo balls (broth only), 250 ml (1 cup)	0
mushroom barley, 250 ml (1 cup)	4
Tzimmes, vegetable	
175 ml (3/4 cup)	4

▲ Power Foods	*PointsPlus®* value
# KOREAN	
JapChae	
beef, 250 ml (1 cup)	8
chicken, 250 ml (1 cup)	9
pork, 250 ml (1 cup)	9
Kim chee	
▲ 125 ml (1/2 cup)	0
Korean barbecue beef	
125 g (4 oz)	7
Korean barbecue chicken thighs	
1 (150 g [5 oz])	12
Korean barbecue short ribs	
125 g (4 oz)	8
Pajun (Korean green onion and shrimp pancake)	
1 (15-20 cm [6-8"] diameter)	9
Soup	
oxtail, 250 ml (1 cup)	2
Stir-fry	
bulgogi (beef), 250 ml (1 cup)	5
# MEXICAN/TEX-MEX	
Arroz con pollo	
90 g (3 oz) chicken with 375 ml (1 1/2 cups) rice	15
Beans, refried	
125 ml (1/2 cup)	4
Burrito	
bean, 1 large (20 cm [8"])	10
bean, 1 small (170 g [6 oz])	7
beef and cheese, 1 large (20 cm [8"])	9
beef and cheese, 1 small (100 g [3 1/2 oz])	7
chicken and cheese, 1 large (20 cm [8"])	8
chicken and cheese, 1 small (170 g [6 oz])	6

ETHNIC & REGIONAL FAVOURITES

Power Foods	PointsPlus® value
vegetable, 1 (made with 15 cm [6"] tortilla)	6
Cake	
corn, sweet, 125 ml (1/2 cup)	10
Carne asada	
125 g (4 oz)	10
Carnitas	
250 ml (1 cup)	9
Chalupa (pork and bean dish)	
250 ml (1 cup)	7
Chicken adobo	
1 thigh (125 g [4 oz])	6
Chicken mole	
250 ml (1 cup)	9
Chili con carne	
canned, 250 ml (1 cup)	7
homemade, 250 ml (1 cup)	9
Chili rellenos	
beef and cheese, without sauce, 2 (215 g [7 1/2 oz])	19
beef, 1 (7.5 cm x 8.5 cm [3" x 3 1/2"])	12
chicken, 1 (7.5 cm x 8.5 cm [3" x 3 1/2"])	10
Coffee, Mexican	
175 ml (6 fl oz) with 30 ml (2 Tbsp) whipped cream	6
Cookies	
Mexican wedding, 2 (3.5 cm [1 1/2"] wide each)	2
Cornbread	
Mexican, 1/12 of a 25 cm (10") round or 95 g (3 1/3 oz)	8
Dip	
Mexican 7-layer, 125 ml (1/2 cup)	4
Empanadas	
2 (7.5 cm [3"] diameter)	6
Enchilada de camarones	
250 ml (1 cup)	5

Power Foods	PointsPlus® value
Enchiladas	
beef, 2 (300 g [10 1/2] oz)	13
cheese, 2 (26 g [8 1/2 oz])	12
chicken, 2 (300 g [10 1/2] oz)	11
pork, 2 (300 g [10 1/2] oz)	13
sour cream, 1 (160 g [5 1/2 oz])	9
Fajitas	
beef, 2 (275 g [9 oz])	13
chicken, 2 (26 g [8 1/2 oz])	10
pork, 2 (300 g [10 1/2 oz])	14
shrimp, 2 (275 g [9 oz])	10
vegetarian, 1 (160 g [5 1/2 oz])	6
Flauta	
beef, 1 (15 cm x 3 cm [6" x 1 1/4"])	12
chicken, 1 (15 cm x 3 cm [6" x 1 1/4"])	11
pork, 1 (15 cm x 3 cm [6" x 1 1/4"])	11
Gordita	
beef, 1 (7.5 cm [3"] diameter)	11
Guacamole	
60 ml (1/4 cup)	2
Huevos rancheros	
2 eggs on 2 tortillas	16
Ice cream, fried	
125 ml (1/2 cup)	12
Jalapeño poppers	
1 (45 g [1 1/2 oz])	4
King ranch chicken casserole	
250 ml (1 cup)	9
Mole poblano	
60 ml (1/4 cup)	5
Nachos	
beef, 4 (265 g [8 1/2 oz])	14
cheese, 4 (90 g [3 oz])	9
cheese and bean, 4 (185 g [6 1/2 oz])	10
chicken, 4 (265 g [8 1/2 oz])	13
with cheese sauce, 125 ml (1/2 cup) tortilla chips with 60 ml (1/4 cup) sauce	6

ETHNIC & REGIONAL FAVOURITES

▲ Power Foods	*PointsPlus*® value
Picadillo	
250 ml (1 cup)	11
Pico de gallo	
▲ fresh or canned, without added sugar or oil	0
Quesadilla	
beef, 1/2 of 170 g (6") diameter	7
cheese, 1/2 of 170 g (6") diameter	6
chicken, 1/2 of 170 g (6") diameter	7
vegetable, 1/2 of 170 g (6") diameter	7
Rice, with pigeon peas (arroz con gandules)	
250 ml (1 cup)	8
Salsa	
▲ black bean and corn, 125 ml (1/2 cup)	2
▲ fat-free	0
▲ peach, 125 ml (1/2 cup)	1
▲ peach, 30 ml (2 Tbsp)	0
pineapple, 125 ml (1/2 cup)	1
pineapple, 30 ml (2 Tbsp)	0
Sauce	
chili, green, 60 ml (1/4 cup)	0
chili, red, 15 ml (1 Tbsp)	0
chili, red, 60 ml (1/4 cup)	1
sofrito, 60 ml (1/4 cup)	4
taco, 15 ml (1 Tbsp)	0
Sopaipillas	
2 (10 cm x 7.5 cm [4" x 3"] each)	3
Soup	
chicken enchilada, 250 ml (1 cup)	6
chicken, with tortilla strips and shredded cheese, 250 ml (1 cup)	5
gazpacho, 250 ml (1 cup)	4
pozole (pork and hominy), 250 ml (1 cup)	5
tortilla, 250 ml (1 cup)	7
Stew	
menudo (beef tripe and hominy stew), 250 ml (1 cup)	7

▲ Power Foods	*PointsPlus*® value
Taco	
beef, 1 (100 g [3 1/2 oz])	6
breakfast, 1 (100 g [3 1/2 oz])	5
chicken, 1 (100 g [3 1/2 oz])	5
fish, 1 (130 g [4 1/4 oz])	5
pork, 1 (100 g [3 1/2 oz])	5
Tamale pie	
250 ml (1 cup)	12
Tamales	
2 (10 cm x 5 cm [4" x 2"])	10
Taquitos	
beef, 1 (13.5 cm [5 1/2"] x 3.5 cm [1 1/2"])	5
chicken, 1 (13.5 cm [5 1/2"] x 3.5 cm [1 1/2"])	3
Tortilla, corn	
1 medium (15 cm [6"] diameter or 30 g [1 oz])	2
1/2 large (290 g [10"] diameter) or 30 g (1 oz)	2
2 small (10 cm [4"] diameter) or 30 g (1 oz)	2
Tortilla, flour	
1 extra large (125 g [4 oz])	9
1 medium (15 cm [6"] diameter or 30 g [1 oz])	2
1/2 large (290 g [10"] diameter) or 30 g (1 oz)	2
2 small (10 cm [4"] diameter) or 30 g (1 oz)	2
Tortilla, wheat	
burrito-size, 1 large (25 cm [10"])	2
Tortilla, whole-wheat	
1 medium (17 cm [7"] diameter)	2
Tostada	
beef, 1 (255 g [8 1/4 oz])	11

ETHNIC & REGIONAL FAVOURITES

▲ Power Foods | *PointsPlus®* value   ▲ Power Foods | *PointsPlus®* value

MIDDLE EASTERN

Baba ganoush
60 ml (1/4 cup) — 3

Beef goulash
250 ml (1 cup) — 9

Chicken pilaf (kotta pilafi)
1 chicken breast with
250 ml (1 cup) pilaf — 8

Crackers
lavash, 1/4 of a 25 cm (10") cracker — 7

Doro wat
250 ml (1 cup) — 7

Falafel in pita
1 large pita with 4 falafel patties — 13

Falafel patties
4 (5 cm [2"] diameter each) — 8

Fattoush
500 ml (2 cups) — 7

Hummus
60 ml (1/4 cup) — 4

Kibbe
baked, 3 pieces
(3.5 cm [1 1/2"] squares) — 3

Rice pilaf
250 ml (1 cup) — 7

Sauce
tahini, 30 ml (2 Tbsp) — 5

Shawarma
chicken, 125 ml (1/2 cup) — 7
chicken, without skin and bone,
1 thigh (60 g [2 oz]) — 5

Tabouli
125 ml (1/2 cup) — 6

SCANDINAVIAN

Bread
lefse, 1 (20-25 cm [8-10"] diameter) — 6

Cheese, fontina
1 slice (30 g [1 oz]) — 3

Cookies
kringla, 2 (45 g [1 1/2 oz]) — 4
rosettes, 2 (7.5 cm x 7.5 cm
[3" x 3" each]) — 2

Dumpling
kroppkakor (potato), boiled,
1 (5 cm [2"] wide) — 3
kroppkakor (potato), fried,
1 (5 cm [2"] wide) — 4

Fish
salmon, smoked, 30 g (1 oz) — 1

Soup
knefla, 250 ml (1 cup) — 7

Swedish meatballs
6 (2.5 cm [1"] diameter) — 10

SOUTHEAST ASIA

Lumpia (Filipino spring rolls)
1 (11 cm x 2.5 cm x 3.5 cm
[4 1/2" x 1" x 1 1/2"]) — 6

Pancit canton (sautéed egg noodles)
250 ml (1 cup) — 6

SOUTHERN/SOUL

Apple brown Betty
250 ml (1 cup) — 6

Biscuits
homemade, 1 small
(5 cm [2"] diameter) or
1/2 large (45 g [1 1/2 oz]) — 3

▲ Power Foods	PointsPlus® value
Catfish, channel, breaded and fried	
1 fillet (90 g [3 oz])	5
Cereal, hot	
▲ grits, corn, cooked, 250 ml (1 cup)	5
Chicken and dumplings	
cooked, with skin, 90 g (3 oz) chicken with 2 dumplings	9
cooked, without skin, 90 g (3 oz) chicken with 2 dumplings	8
Chicken breast	
fried, with skin and bone, 1 (135 g [4 1/2 oz])	11
Chicken drumstick	
fried, with skin and bone, 1 (45 g [1 1/2 oz])	5
fried, without skin and bone, 1 (45 g [1 1/2 oz])	2
Chicken thigh	
fried, with skin and bone, 1 (90 g [3 oz])	8
Chitterlings	
cooked, 30 g (1 oz)	2
Corn	
cream-style, 250 ml (1 cup)	5
Cornbread	
1 piece (5 cm [2"] square)	3
Cornbread dressing	
250 ml (1 cup)	9
Fish	
▲ catfish, cooked, 1 fillet (170 g [6 oz])	6
Fish fillet	
fried, breaded with flour, 1 (170 g [6 oz])	13
fried, without flour, 1 (170 g [6 oz])	14
Fritters	
corn, 3 (6 cm x 5 cm [2 1/2" x 2]" each)	6

▲ Power Foods	PointsPlus® value
Gravy	
brown, 60 ml (1/4 cup)	3
cream, 60 ml (1/4 cup)	4
giblet, 60 ml (1/4 cup)	2
sausage, 60 ml (1/4 cup)	4
Greens	
cooked, seasoned with bacon or salt pork, 250 ml (1 cup)	4
Hush puppies	
2 (65 g [2 1/4 oz])	5
Macaroni and cheese	
250 ml (1 cup)	10
Okra	
fried, 250 ml (1 cup)	10
Sauce	
hot, any type, 5 ml (1 tsp)	0
pepper, 5 ml (1 tsp)	0
Soup	
split pea, 250 ml (1 cup)	4
Spoon bread	
125 ml (1/2 cup)	5
Steak, chicken-fried	
with cream gravy, 170 g (6 oz) with 60 ml (1/4 cup) cream gravy	18
without gravy, 170 g (6 oz)	14
Stew	
beef, 250 ml (1 cup)	7
Brunswick, 375 ml (1 1/2 cups)	7
Succotash	
▲ cooked, 250 ml (1 cup)	6
Sweet potato pie	
1/8 of a 22 cm (9") pie	11
Tomatoes, green, fried	
2 slices (3.5 cm [1 1/2"] thick)	5

ETHNIC & REGIONAL FAVOURITES

▲ Power Foods | *PointsPlus®* value

SPANISH

Ceviche

| 125 ml (1/2 cup) | 2 |

Flan

| 175 ml (3/4 cup) | 9 |

Paella

| 250 ml (1 cup) | 9 |

Red snapper Veracruz

| 170 g (6 oz) cooked fillet with 175 ml (3/4 cup) sauce | 12 |

Rice, Spanish

| 250 ml (1 cup) | 7 |

Sauce

| Spanish, 125 ml (1/2 cup) | 3 |

Soup

| black bean, 250 ml (1 cup) | 2 |

THAI

Chile beef (neua pad prik)

| 250 ml (1 cup) | 7 |

Coconut rice

| Thai, 250 ml (1 cup) | 10 |

Curry

green chicken (gaeng kheow wan gai), 250 ml (1 cup)	8
Massaman beef, 250 ml (1 cup)	21
panang, with beef, 250 ml (1 cup)	14
panang, with chicken, 250 ml (1 cup)	13
panang, with pork, 250 ml (1 cup)	15

Ginger chicken

| 250 ml (1 cup) | 8 |

Nam Prik

| 15 ml (1 Tbsp) | 1 |

Noodles, drunken

| 250 ml (1 cup) | 6 |

▲ Power Foods | *PointsPlus®* value

Noodles, rice

| cooked, 250 ml (1 cup) | 5 |

Pad Thai (rice noodles with chicken and shrimp)

| 250 ml (1 cup) | 10 |

Pudding, tapioca

| Thai, 125 ml (1/2 cup) | 4 |

Rice, fried

| kho-phat (Thai fried rice), 250 ml (1 cup) | 9 |

Salad

Thai beef, 250 ml (1 cup)	15
Thai chicken, 250 ml (1 cup)	12
Thai seafood, 500 ml (2 cups)	11

Satay

beef, with peanut sauce, 2 skewers with 60 ml (1/4 cup) sauce	12
beef, without peanut sauce, 2 skewers (90 g [3 oz])	5
chicken, with peanut sauce, 2 skewers with 60 ml (1/4 cup) sauce	12
chicken, without peanut sauce, 2 skewers (90 g [3 oz])	3

Sauce

chili, sriracha, 5 ml (1 tsp)	0
peanut satay, 15 ml (1 Tbsp)	1
peanut, spicy, 30 ml (2 Tbsp)	4

Seafood cakes (haw mok thalay)

| 175 ml (3/4 cup) | 9 |

Soup

| hot and spicy chicken, 250 ml (1 cup) | 4 |
| Thai chicken coconut, 250 ml (1 cup) | 10 |

Spring roll

| Thai, 1 (10 cm [4"] long) | 5 |

Sticky rice with mango

| 250 ml (1 cup) sliced mangoes with 125 ml (1/2 cup) sticky rice | 11 |

▲ Power Foods	*PointsPlus®* value
Stir-fry	
pad si-iew (beef with noodles), 250 ml (1 cup)	7
Thai chicken with basil	
without skin and bone, 1 breast (90 g [3 oz])	5
Thai coffee or tea	
250 ml (1 cup)	9
Thai crisp noodles	
250 ml (1 cup)	9
Thai grilled beef (nuea nam tok)	
125 ml (1/2 cup) on lettuce leaves	6
Tom yum kung	
250 ml (1 cup)	2

▲ Power Foods	*PointsPlus®* value
Spring roll	
Vietnamese, fresh, 1 (50 g [1 3/4 oz])	2
Vietnamese, fried, 1 (10 cm [4"] long)	5
Vietnamese beef balls (thit bo vien)	
6 (45 g [1 1/2 oz])	2

VIETNAMESE

	PointsPlus® value
Chao tom (shrimp mousse over sugar cane)	
4 pieces (100 g [3 1/2 oz])	2
Crêpes	
Vietnamese (banh xeo), 1 (20 cm x 17 cm [8" x 3"] or 200 g [7 oz])	17
Curry	
Vietnamese chicken, 250 ml (1 cup)	9
Imperial roll	
1 (11 cm [4 1/2"] long)	5
Lemon grass chicken	
250 ml (1 cup)	9
Nuoc cham	
15 ml (1 Tbsp)	0
Sauce	
Vietnamese spring roll dipping, 30 ml (2 Tbsp)	0
Soup	
asparagus crab, 250 ml (1 cup)	2
Vietnamese beef noodle, 250 ml (1 cup)	2

Restaurant Menus

A&W®

▲ Power Foods	*PointsPlus®* value

THE BURGER FAMILY®

Baby Burger®, 1	6
Cheddar Bacon Uncle Burger, 1	19
Grandpa Burger®, 1	20
Mama Burger®, 1	11
Papa Burger®, 1	15
Teen Burger®, 1	13
Uncle Burger™, 1	15
Add Cheese, 1	2

CHUBBY CHICKEN®

Chicken Grill® Deluxe, 1	8
Chubby Chicken® Burger, 1	13
Chubby Chicken® Pieces – Drumstick, 1 piece	4
Chubby Chicken® Pieces – Keel, 1 piece	8
Chubby Chicken® Pieces – Rib, 1 piece	9
Chubby Chicken® Pieces – Thigh, 1 piece	11
Chubby Chicken® Pieces – Wing, 1	5
Chubby Chicken® Strip Dipping Sauce – Barbecue, 1 serving	1
Chubby Chicken® Strip Dipping Sauce – Honey Mustard, 1 serving	3
Chubby Chicken® Strip Dipping Sauce – Sweet & Sour, 1 serving	1
Chubby Chicken® Strips, 3 pieces	8

HOT DOGS

Hot Dog, 1	10
Whistle Dog®, 1	12

▲ Power Foods	*PointsPlus®* value

OTHER FAVOURITES

Mozza Burger®, 1	16
Swiss Veggie Deluxe, 1	11

SALADS

Coleslaw, 1 individual portion	5
▲ Garden Greens, 1	1
Macaroni Salad, 1 individual portion	7
Hellman's Balsamic Dressing, 1 serving (28 ml)	4
Hellman's Light Italian Dressing, 1 serving (28 ml)	2
Hellman's Light Ranch Dressing, 1 serving (27 ml)	2

SIDES

Fresh Onion Rings, 1 serving	13
Fries, 1 small	7
Fries, 1 regular	11
Fries, 1 large	14

BREAKFAST

Bacon n' Egger®, 1	12
Classic Bacon & Eggs without Toast, 1	7
French Toast, with Syrup, 2 pieces	20
Hash Brown, 1	5
Homestyle Ham n' Egger®, 1	16
Homestyle Sausage n' Egger®, 1	15
Sausage n' Egger®, 1	15
White Toast, with Margarine, 2 slices	9
Whole Wheat Toast, with Margarine, 2 slices	9

▲ Power Foods	*PointsPlus®* value

DESSERTS

Apple Turnover, 1	8

FOUNTAIN BEVERAGES

A&W Root Beer®, 1 small	7
A&W Root Beer®, 1 regular	9
A&W Root Beer®, 1 large	15
Diet A&W Root Beer®, 1 small	0
Diet A&W Root Beer®, 1 regular	0
Diet A&W Root Beer®, 1 large	0

ARBY'S®

▲ Power Foods	PointsPlus® value
Baked Potato – Deluxe, 1 serving	17
Baked Potato – Mushroom & Swiss, 1 serving	20
Baked Potato – Sour Cream & Becel, 1 serving	12
Curly Fries, 1 small	7
Curly Fries, 1 medium	11
Curly Fries, 1 large	17
Homestyle Fries, 1 small	6
Homestyle Fries, 1 medium	9
Homestyle Fries, 1 large	16
Jalapeño Bites™, 1 regular (5 pieces)	8
Jalapeño Bites™, 1 large (10 pieces)	17
Loaded Potato Bites™, 5 pieces	9
Loaded Potato Bites™, 10 pieces	18
Mozzarella Sticks, 4 pieces	11
Mozzarella Sticks, 8 pieces	21

KIDS MEAL

2 Piece Chicken Tenders, 1 serving	7
Junior Roast Beef Sandwich, 1 serving	5

SHAKES & DESSERTS

Add icing, 1 serving (21 g)	2
Apple Turnover (no icing), 1	8
Blueberry Turnover (no icing), 1	8
Chocolate Chunk Cookies, 2 cookies	9
Chocolate Shake, 1	15
Jamocha Shake, 1	15
Strawberry Shake, 1	15
Vanilla Shake, 1	14

BOSTON PIZZA®

▲ Power Foods	*PointsPlus* value

STARTERS

Bandera Pizza Bread Sante Fe Ranch Dip, 1 starter serving	26
Boston's Breaded Barbecue Wings (starter size), 1 starter serving	15
Boston's Breaded Honey Garlic Wings (starter size), 1 starter serving	15
Boston's Breaded Hot Wings (starter size), 1 starter serving	14
Boston's Oven Roasted Mild Wings (starter size), 1 starter serving	12
Boston's Breaded Teriyaki Wings (starter size), 1 starter serving	15
Boston's Breaded Thai Wings (starter size), 1 starter serving	15
Boston's Oven Roasted Barbecue Wings (starter size), 1 starter serving	13
Boston's Oven Roasted Honey Garlic Wings (starter size), 1 starter serving	13
Boston's Oven Roasted Hot Wings (starter size), 1 starter serving	12
Boston's Oven Roasted Mild Wings (starter size), 1 starter serving	12
Boston's Oven Roasted Teriyaki Wings (starter size), 1 starter serving	13
Boston's Oven Roasted Thai Chili Wings (starter size), 1 starter serving	16
Boston's Pizza Bread, 1 starter serving	14
Cactus Cuts Potatoes & Dip, 1 starter serving	23
Calamari, 1 starter serving	12
Chicken Fingers, 1 starter serving	9
Chicken Fingers – Buffalo Style, 1 starter serving	9

▲ Power Foods	*PointsPlus* value
Cracked Pepper Dry Ribs, 1 starter serving	11
Garlic Pizza Fingers (with Donair Sauce), 1 starter serving	22
Garlic Twist Bread (single order), 1 starter serving	16
Nachos (with Sour Cream & Salsa), 1 starter serving	31
Oven Roasted Chicken Quesadilla (with sour cream & salsa), 1 starter serving	25
Southwest Potato Skins, 1 starter serving	17
Spicy Chicken Nachos (with Sour Cream & Salsa), 1 starter serving	33
Spinach & Artichoke Dip with Tortilla Chips, 1 starter serving	19
Sun-Dried Tomato Bruschetta, 1 starter serving	11
Taco Beef Nachos (with Sour Cream & Salsa), 1 starter serving	37
Thai Chicken Bites, 1 starter serving	14
Three Cheese Toast (single order), 1 starter serving	10

SOUPS & SALADS

Baked French Onion Soup, 1 serving	9
Baja Salad (chicken), 1 serving	15
Baja Salad (shrimp), 1 serving	14
Caesar Salad, 1 starter serving	7
Caesar Salad, 1 entree serving	14
Chipotle Chicken & Bacon Salad, 1 serving	17
Citrus Chicken Salad (grilled chicken), 1 serving	19
Crispy Chicken Pecan Salad (ranch dressing), 1 serving	32

Power Foods	PointsPlus® value
Garden Greens (with sun-dried tomato balsamic vinaigrette), 1 starter serving	4
Garden Greens (with sun-dried tomato balsamic vinaigrette), 1 entree serving	8
Greek Salad, 1 starter serving	9
Greek Salad, 1 entree serving	31
Spinach Salad, 1 starter serving	7
Spinach Salad, 1 entree serving	13

ENTREES

Baked Lemon Salmon Filet (with Tossed Garden Greens with Sundried Tomato Balsamic Vinaigrette), 1 serving	15
Cajun Rice Bowl, 1 serving	25
Certified Angus Beef Sirloin Steak, 1 serving	21
Chicken Parmesan (with Tossed Garden Greens with Sundried Tomato Balsamic Vinaigrette), 1 serving	20
Slow Roasted Pork Back Ribs, 1 serving	20
Steak Frites, 1 serving	35
Teriyaki Chicken Rice Bowl, 1 serving	35
The Ribber™, 1 serving	9

GOURMET PIZZA

Bacon Double Cheeseburger, 1 medium slice	6
Bacon Double Cheeseburger, Multigrain Crust, 1 medium slice	7
BBQ Chicken, 1 medium slice	5
BBQ Chicken, Multigrain Crust, 1 medium slice	5
BBQ Pulled Pork Pizza, 1 medium slice	5

Power Foods	PointsPlus® value
BBQ Pulled Pork Pizza, Multigrain Crust, 1 medium slice	5
Boston Royal, 1 medium slice	5
Boston Royal, Multigrain Crust, 1 medium slice	5
Bruschetta, 1 medium slice	7
Bruschetta, Multigrain Crust, 1 medium slice	7
Cajun Shrimp, 1 medium slice	8
Cajun Shrimp, Multigrain Crust, 1 medium slice	8
Deluxe, 1 medium slice	6
Deluxe, Multigrain Crust, 1 medium slice	6
Great White North, 1 medium slice	6
Great White North, Multigrain Crust, 1 medium slice	6
Hawaiian, 1 medium slice	6
Hawaiian, Multigrain Crust, 1 medium slice	6
La Quebecoise, 1 medium slice	5
La Quebecoise, Multigrain Crust, 1 medium slice	5
Meateor™, 1 medium slice	7
Meateor™, Multigrain Crust, 1 medium slice	5
Pepperoni, 1 medium slice	5
Pepperoni & Mushroom, 1 medium slice	5
Pepperoni & Mushroom, Multigrain Crust, 1 medium slice	5
Pepperoni, Multigrain Crust, 1 medium slice	5
Rustic Italian, 1 medium slice	7
Rustic Italian, Multigrain Crust, 1 medium slice	7
Spicy Perogy Pizza, 1 medium slice	7
Spicy Perogy Pizza, Multigrain Crust, 1 medium slice	7
Szechuan, 1 medium slice	5

BOSTON PIZZA®

▲ Power Foods	*PointsPlus®* value
Szechuan, Multigrain Crust, 1 medium slice	5
The Basic, 1 medium slice	4
The Basic, Multigrain Crust, 1 medium slice	4
The Pepper, 1 medium slice	6
The Pepper, Multigrain Crust, 1 medium slice	6
Tropical Chicken, 1 medium slice	7
Tropical Chicken, Multigrain Crust, 1 medium slice	7
Tuscan, 1 medium slice	6
Tuscan, Multigrain Crust, 1 medium slice	7
Vegetarian, 1 medium slice	5
Vegetarian, Multigrain Crust, 1 medium slice	5
Zorba the Greek, 1 medium slice	6
Zorba the Greek, Multigrain Crust, 1 medium slice	6

GOURMET PASTA

▲ Power Foods	*PointsPlus®* value
Baked Seven Cheese Ravioli (bolognese sauce), 1 full order	18
Baked Seven Cheese Ravioli (pomodoro sauce), 1 full order	20
Baked Shrimp and Feta Penne, 1 full order	30
Boston's Lasagna, 1 full order	17
Chicken and Mushroom Fettuccini, 1 full order	39
Chicken Cannelloni, 1 full order	13
Homestyle Lasagna, 1 full order	25
Jambalaya Fettuccini, 1 full order	40
Roasted Vegetable Lasagna, 1 full order	18
Scallop and Prawn Fettuccini, 1 full order	37

▲ Power Foods	*PointsPlus®* value
Smokey Mountain Spaghetti, 1 full order	47
Spicy Italian Penne, 1 full order	42
Tuscan Linguini, 1 full order	27

CREATE YOUR OWN PASTA

Power Foods	*PointsPlus®* value
Fettuccini with Alfredo, 1 full order	30
Fettuccini with Bolognese, 1 full order	21
Fettuccini with Creamy Tomato, 1 full order	26
Fettuccini with Pomodoro, 1 full order	23
Linguini with Alfredo (whole wheat), 1 full order	30
Linguini with Bolognese (whole wheat), 1 full order	20
Linguini with Creamy Tomato (whole wheat), 1 full order	27
Linguini with Pomodoro (whole wheat), 1 full order	23
Penne with Alfredo, 1 full order	27
Penne with Bolognese, 1 full order	17
Penne with Creamy Tomato, 1 full order	23
Penne with Pomodoro, 1 full order	20
Spaghetti with Alfredo, 1 full order	30
Spaghetti with Bolognese, 1 full order	21
Spaghetti with Creamy Tomato, 1 full order	27
Spaghetti with Pomodoro, 1 full order	23
Tortellini with Alfredo, 1 full order	25
Tortellini with Bolognese, 1 full order	15
Tortellini with Creamy Tomato, 1 full order	22
Tortellini with Pomodoro, 1 full order	18

▲ Power Foods	*PointsPlus®* value

DELICIOUS ALTERNATIVES

Chicken Stromboli, 1 serving	16
Lemon Baked Salmon Filet, 1 serving	7
Pollo Pomodoro Linguini, Whole Wheat, 1 serving	13
Spicy Garlic Chicken Pizza, Individual Size, 1 serving	17

SANDWICHES

BBQ Pulled Pork Sandwich, 1	23
Beef Dip Sandwich, 1	23
Boston Brute Sandwich, 1	28
Boston Cheesesteak Sandwich, 1	30
Boston Prime Rib Burger, 1	26
Boston's Prime Rib Burger with Bacon, 1	28
Boston's Prime Rib Burger with Cheese, 1	29
Boston's Prime Rib Burger with Cheese & Bacon, 1	31
Buffalo Chicken Sandwich, 1	25
Chicken Parmesan Sandwich, 1	22
Chicken Santa Fe Stromboli, 1	16
Chipotle Chicken Wrap, 1	14
Ciabatta Chicken Sandwich, 1	20
New York Steak Sandwich, 1	15
Panzerotti Roll, 1	22
Smoked Ham & Chicken Stromboli Sandwich, 1	20
Sundried Tomato, Cheese and Spinach Stromboli Sandwich, 1	19

SIDE DISHES

Caesar Salad, 1 side serving	5
Fries, 1 side serving	6
Garlic Mashed Potatoes, 1 side serving	8

▲ Power Foods	*PointsPlus®* value
Garlic Toast, 1 side serving	4
Peppercorn Sauce, 1 side serving	1
▲ **Prawns and Scallops,** 1 side serving	3
Rice, 1 side serving	5
Seasonal Vegetables, 1 side serving	3
Spaghetti with Bolognese, 1 side serving	10

KIDS MENU

▲ **Baked Salmon,** 1 serving	3
Bugs n' Cheese, 1 serving	16
Caesar Salad, 1 serving	4
Cheeseburger, 1 serving	13
Chicken Fingers with Honey Mustard Dipping Sauce, 1 serving	7
Fries, 1 serving	5
Garlic Mashed Potatoes, 1 serving	4
Gooey Grilled Cheese, 1 serving	10
Grilled Chicken Sandwich, no mayo, 1 serving	6
Grilled Chicken Sandwich, with mayonnaise, 1 serving	12
Lovely Linguini with Bolognese Sauce, 1 serving	10
Lovely Linguini with Pomodoro Sauce, 1 serving	11
Mighty Plump Perogies, 1 serving	13
Pint Sized Pizza, 1 serving	12
Pint Sized Pizza, Multigrain Dough, 1 serving	11
Rice, 1 serving	3
▲ **Steamed Vegetables,** 1 serving	0
Super Spaghetti with Pomodoro Sauce, 1 serving	11
Super Spaghetti, Bolognese Sauce, 1 serving	10
Tossed Salad with Raspberry Vinaigrette, 1 serving	2

BOSTON PIZZA®

PointsPlus®
value

KIDS DESSERTS

Bite Sized Brownie with Ice Cream, 1 serving	7
BP's Strawberry Dessert Pizza, 1 serving	15
▲ **Fruit Cup,** 1 serving	2
Jello, 1 serving	2
Mini Chocolate Pizza, 1 serving	2
Monster Cookie, 1 cookie	8
Pint Sized Sundae, 1 serving	8
Worms & Dirt, 1 serving	11

KIDS BEVERAGES

Grape Pop Rocks Beverage, 1 serving	2
Orange Iceberg Beverage, 1 serving	6
Shirley Temple, 1 serving	5

DESSERTS

Apple Crisp (served with ice cream), 1 serving	20
Chocolate Brownie Addiction (served with ice cream), 1 serving	16
Chocolate Explosion, 1 serving	24
Lava Cake (served with ice cream), 1 serving	14
Maple Blondie (with ice cream), 1 serving	26
New York Cheesecake, 1 serving	17
Tarte au Sucre, 1 serving	13

▲ Power Foods	*PointsPlus*® value

SALADS & DRESSINGS

Hawaiian Grilled Chicken Salad, 1 serving	8
Original Grilled Chicken Salad, 1 serving	7
Original Grilled Chicken Salad with Cranberry, Apple & Walnuts, 1 serving	8
Side Salad (without dressing), 1 side serving	3

SALAD DRESSINGS

Blue Cheese Dressing, 1 packet	9
House Dressing, 1 packet	6
Low Fat Balsamic Dressing, 1 packet	1
Thousand Island Dressing, 1 packet	7
Sesame Asian Dressing, 1 packet	3

CHARBROILED BURGERS

Big Hamburger, 1	12
Chili Cheeseburger, 1	22
Double Western Bacon Cheeseburger®, 1	26
Famous Star® with Cheese, 1	18
Jalapeno Burger ®, 1	20
Kid's Hamburger, 1	6
Super Star® with Cheese, 1	25
The Bacon Cheese Six Dollar Burger®, 1	29
The Guacamole Bacon Six Dollar Burger®, 1	28
The Jalapeno Six Dollar Burger®, 1	25
The Low Carb Six Dollar Burger®, 1	15
The Original Six Dollar Burger®, 1	24
The Western Bacon Six Dollar Burger®, 1	26
Western Bacon Cheeseburger®, 1	19

▲ Power Foods	*PointsPlus*® value

CHICKEN & OTHER CHOICES

Bacon Swiss Crispy Chicken Sandwich, 1	20
Carl's Catch Fish Sandwich®, 1	19
Charbroiled BBQ Chicken® Sandwich, 1	10
Charbroiled Chicken Club Sandwich®, 1	15
Charbroiled Santa Fe Chicken Sandwich®, 1	17
Kids Hand-Breaded Chicken Tenders (2 pieces), 2 pieces	6
Hand-Breaded Chicken Tenders (3 pieces), 3 pieces	9
Hand-Breaded Chicken Tenders (5 pieces), 5 pieces	15
Spicy Chicken Sandwich, 1	12

GREEN BURRITO SPECIALTIES

Taquitos – Chicken, 2	4
Taquitos – Chicken, 5	9

BREAKFAST

Bacon & Egg Burrito, 1	15
Breakfast Burger, 1	21
French Toast Dips®, without syrup, 5 pieces	12
Hash Brown Nuggets, 1 serving	9
Loaded Breakfast Burrito, 1	22
Sourdough Breakfast Sandwich (ham), 1	12
Steak & Egg Burrito, 1	17
Sunrise Croissant® Sandwich, 1	16

CARL'S JR.®

▲ Power Foods
PointsPlus® value

SIDES

Chicken Stars, 4 pieces	5
Chicken Stars, 6 pieces	7
Chicken Stars, 9 pieces	10
Chili Cheese Fries, 1 serving	22
CrissCut® Fries, 1 serving	11
Fish & Chips, 1 serving	19
Fried Zucchini, 1 serving	9
Natural Cut Fries, 1 kids serving	7
Natural Cut Fries, 1 small serving	8
Natural Cut Fries, 1 medium serving	12
Natural Cut Fries, 1 large serving	13
Onion Rings, 1 serving	12

HAND-SCOOPED ICE CREAM SHAKES & MALTS™

Chocolate Malt, 1 malt	21
Chocolate Shake, 1 shake	19
OREO® Cookie Malt, 1 malt	22
OREO® Cookie Shake, 1 shake	20
Strawberry Malt, 1 malt	21
Strawberry Shake, 1 shake	19
Vanilla Malt, 1 malt	21
Vanilla Shake, 1 shake	19

DESSERTS

Chocolate Cake, 1 serving	8
Chocolate Chip Cookie, 1	10
Strawberry Swirl Cheesecake, 1 serving	8

▲ Power Foods	*PointsPlus®* value
ENTRÉES	
Thai Tenderloin Salad **(28 g [1 oz] dressing)**, 1 serving	10
Cedar Planked Salmon **(plain baked potato, steamed** **vegetables)**, 1 serving	16
Filet Mignon (250 g [8 oz]) **(Quebec Only)**, 1 serving	15
Mango Mahi Mahi (plain baked **potato, steamed vegetables)**, 1 serving	12
Sirloin (250 g [8 oz]) (plain baked **potato, steamed vegetables)**, 1 serving	15

CHIPOTLE MEXICAN GRILL®

Power Foods	PointsPlus® value
APPETIZER	
Tortilla Chips, 1 serving (125 g [4 oz])	15
SALAD	
▲ **Romaine Lettuce,** 1 serving	0
TORTILLAS	
Flour Tortilla (burrito), 1	8
Flour Tortilla (taco), 1	2
FILLINGS	
Barbacoa, 1 portion (125 g [4 oz])	4
▲ **Black Beans,** 1 portion (125 g [4 oz])	3
Carnitas, 1 portion (125 g [4 oz])	5
Chicken, 1 portion (125 g [4 oz])	5
Cilantro-Lime Rice, 1 portion (90 g [3 oz])	3
▲ **Pinto Beans,** 1 portion (125 g [4 oz])	2
▲ **Steak,** 1 portion (125 g [4 oz])	5

Power Foods	PointsPlus® value
SALSA	
Corn Salsa, 1 taco portion (18 g [.67 oz])	0
▲ **Green Tomatillo Salsa,** 60 ml (2 fl oz)	0
▲ **Red Tomatillo Salsa,** 60 ml (2 fl oz)	0
▲ **Tomato Salsa,** 100 g (3 1/2 oz)	0
OTHER TOPPINGS & CONDIMENTS	
Cheese, 30 g (1 oz)	3
Guacamole, 100 g (3 1/2 oz)	4
▲ **Romaine Lettuce (tacos),** 30 g (1 oz)	0
Sour Cream, 60 g (2 oz)	3
Vinaigrette, 60 ml (2 fl oz)	8

COUNTRY STYLE BISTRO DELI

▲ Power Foods   *PointsPlus®* value

BREAKFAST BAGELS & BREAKFAST SANDWICHES

BLT Breakfast Sandwich, 1	7
Breakfast Bagel Deluxe, 1	13
Ham & Swiss Breakfast Bagel, Breakfast sandwich, 1	8
Plain Bagels, 1	5
Sausage & Egg Breakfast Bagels, Breakfast Sandwiches, 1	9
Sunriser Breakfast Bagels, Breakfast Sandwiches, 1	9
Western Breakfast Bagel, Breakfast Sandwich, 1	10

BISTRODELI

6" Assorted Club Bistrodeli, 1	12
6" Grilled Chicken Bistrodeli, 1	15
6" Meatball Deluxe Bistrodeli, 1	14
6" Original Steak & Cheese Bistrodeli, 1	14
6" Smokey Turkey Bistrodeli, 1	12
6" Traditional Egg Bistrodeli, 1	11
6" Traditional Tuna Bistrodeli, 1	10
6" Veggie & Cheese Bistrodeli, 1	9
Caesar Salad Bistrodeli, 1	4
Chicken Caesar Wrap Bistrodeli, 1	9
Garden Salad Bistrodeli, 1	3
Greek Salad Bistrodeli, 1	4
Greek Wrap Bistrodeli, 1	9
Spicy Buffalo Chicken Griller Bistrodeli, 1	9
The Clubhouse Griller Bistrodeli, 1	16
Tuscan Bacon Turkey Griller Bistrodeli, 1	14

SOUPS

Cheddar Cauliflower Soup, 1 serving	3
Chicken Gumbo Soup, 1 serving	2
Chicken Noodle Soup, 1 serving	3

▲ Power Foods   *PointsPlus®* value

Corn Chowder Soup, 1 serving	6
Cream of Asparagus Soup, 1 serving	4
Cream of Broccoli & Cheese Soup, 1 serving	5
Cream of Mushroom Soup, 1 serving	5
Cream of Potato Soup, 1 serving	5
Garden Vegetable Soup, 1 serving	2
Italian Wedding Soup, 1 serving	3
Minestrone Soup, 1 serving	2
Tomato Basil & Raviolini Soup, 1 serving	3
Turkey Vegetable & Rice Soup, 1 serving	3
Vegetable Beef Barley Soup, 1 serving	2

STEWS

Chicken Stew, 1 serving	5
Chili Stew, 1 serving	5
Chili with Cheddar Cheese Stew, 1 serving	6

BAGELS

Asiago Bagel, 1	6
Blueberry Bagel, 1	6
Cheddar Bagel, 1	6
Cranberry Walnut Flax Bagel, 1	6
Everything Bagel, 1	6

COUNTRY STYLE BISTRO DELI

Bagels (cont'd)

▲ Power Foods	*PointsPlus®* value
Honey Cinnamon Raisin Bagel, 1	5
Multigrain Bagel, 1	6
Poppy Seed Bagel, 1	6
Pumpernickel Bagel, 1	5
Sesame Bagel, 1	6
Sundried Tomato Bagel, 1	5
Whole Wheat Bagel, 1	5

COOKIES

Chocolate Chunk Cookie, 1	5
Oatmeal Cranberry Walnut Cookie, 1	5
Oatmeal Raisin Cookie, 1	4
Peanut Butter Cookie, 1	6
Triple Chocolate Cookie, 1	5
White Chocolate Macadamia Cookie, 1	5

CROISSANTS

Butter Cheese Croissant, 1	9
Butter Croissant, 1	7
Chocolatine Croissants, 1	8

DANISH

Apple Toffee Danish, 1	9
Cinnamon Bun (with Cream Cheese Icing) Danish, 1	9
Spinach & Cheese Danish, 1	8
Strawberry Cheese Danish, 1	8

DONUTS – CHOCOLATE CAKE

Chocolate Iced Donut, 1	7
Coconut Chocolate Cake Donut, 1	7
Glazed Donut, 1	6
Marble Iced Donut, 1	7
Sprinkled Chocolate Cake Donut, 1	7
Toasted Coconut Chocolate Cake Donut, 1	7
White Iced Donut, 1	7

▲ Power Foods	*PointsPlus®* value

DONUTS – COUNTRY BITS

Chocolate Cake Coconut Donut, 1	2
Chocolate Cake Glazed Donut, 1	2
Chocolate Cake Sprinkled Donut, 1	2
White Cake Coconut Donut, 1	2
White Cake Glazed Donut, 1	2
White Cake Sprinkled Donut, 1	2
Yeast Coconut Donut, 1	2
Yeast Filled Donut, 1	2
Yeast Glazed Donut, 1	2
Yeast Sprinkled Donut, 1	2

DONUTS – CRULLERS

Cherry Cruller, 1	9
Chocolate Cruller, 1	9
French Cruller, 1	5
Orange Cruller, 1	9
Plain Cruller, 1	7
Sour Cream Cruller, 1	8

DONUTS – WHITE CAKE

Chocolate Iced White Cake Donut, 1	7
Coconut Donut, 1	7
Glazed White Cake, 1	6
Marble Iced White Cake Donut, 1	7
Sprinkled White Cake Donut, 1	7
Toasted Coconut Donut, 1	7
White Iced White Cake Donut, 1	7

DONUTS – YEAST DONUTS

Apple & Spice Donut, 1	8
Banana Filled Donut, 1	8
Boston Creme, 1	8
Cherry Filled Donut, 1	8
Chocolate Raised Donut, 1	6
Dutchie, 1	23
Fritter, 1	8

COUNTRY STYLE BISTRO DELI

Power Foods	*PointsPlus®* value
Glazed Donut, 1	6
Lemon Filled Donut, 1	8
Maple Raised Donut, 1	6
Sprinkled Donut, 1	7
Strawberry Filled Donut, 1	8
Vanilla Raised Donut, 1	6

"GOOD 4 U" MUFFINS

Banana Mango Muffin, 1	11
Fruit & Flax Fibre Muffin, 1	8
Pomegranate Bran Muffin, 1	9
Twelve Grain Muffins, 1	10
Whole Wheat Blueberry Muffin, 1	10

MUFFINS

Apple Cinnamon Muffin, 1	11
Apple Oatmeal Muffin, 1	12
Banana Nut Muffin, 1	12
Blueberry Muffin, 1	11
Carrot Muffin, 1	11
Chocolate Chip Muffin, 1	13
Corn Muffin, 1	13
Golden Raisin Bran Muffin, 1	10
Lemon Cranberry Muffin, 1	11
Low Fat Blueberry Bran Muffin, 1	8
Morning Glory Muffin, 1	11
Raspberry Yogurt Muffin, 1	13
Reduced Fat Apple Oatmeal Muffin, 1	10
Reduced Fat Fruit & Fibre Muffin, 1	8
Strawberry Banana Yogurt Muffin, 1	12
Whole Grain Banana Muffin, 1	12

TARTS

Pecan Butter Tart, 1	10
Raisin Butter Tart, 1	10

Power Foods	*PointsPlus®* value

TEA BISCUIT

Blueberry Tea Biscuit, 1	4
Cheese Tea Biscuit, 1	5
Plain Tea Biscuit, 1	4
Raisin Tea Biscuit, 1	5

COLD BEVERAGES

Chocolate Milk, 250 ml (8 fl oz)	5
Fountain Pop, 300 ml (10 fl oz)	3
Iced Cappuccino, 300 ml (10 fl oz)	4
Iced Mocha Cappuccino, 300 ml (10 fl oz)	10
Iced Vanilla Cappuccino, 300 ml (10 fl oz)	8
Milk, 250 ml (8 fl oz)	3
Pomegranate Blueberry Freeze, 300 ml (10 fl oz)	4
Tropical Drinks, 300 ml (10 fl oz)	3

HOT BEVERAGES

Coffee, Single Cream, Single Sugar, 300 ml (10 fl oz)	1
Decaf Coffee, Single Cream, Single Sugar, 300 ml (10 fl oz)	1
French Vanilla Frothy Coffee, 300 ml (10 fl oz)	3
Hot Chocolate, 300 ml (10 fl oz)	3
Tea, Single Milk, Single Sugar, 300 ml (10 fl oz)	1

SPECIALITY DRINKS

Belgian Hot Chocolate, 300 ml (10 fl oz)	2
Cappuccino, 300 ml (10 fl oz)	2
Caramel Latte, 300 ml (10 fl oz)	5
Espresso, 40 ml (1 1/2 fl oz)	0
Green Tea Latte, 300 ml (10 fl oz)	5
Latte, 300 ml (10 fl oz)	2
Mocha Latte, 300 ml (10 fl oz)	2
Vanilla Latte, 300 ml (10 fl oz)	2

DAIRY QUEEN®

▲ Power Foods	*PointsPlus®* value
BLIZZARD TREATS®	
Banana Cream Pie Blizzard, 1 mini	11
Banana Cream Pie Blizzard, 1 small	16
Banana Cream Pie Blizzard, 1 medium	21
Banana Cream Pie Blizzard, 1 large	30
Banana Split Blizzard, 1 mini	8
Banana Split Blizzard, 1 small	12
Banana Split Blizzard, 1 medium	16
Banana Split Blizzard, 1 large	22
Chocolate Xtreme Blizzard, 1 mini	11
Chocolate Xtreme Blizzard, 1 small	18
Chocolate Xtreme Blizzard, 1 medium	26
Chocolate Xtreme Blizzard, 1 large	38
Cookie Dough Blizzard, 1 mini	12
Cookie Dough Blizzard, 1 small	20
Cookie Dough Blizzard, 1 medium	29
Cookie Dough Blizzard, 1 large	36
Crispy Crunch® Blizzard, 1 mini	10
Crispy Crunch Blizzard, 1 small	14
Crispy Crunch Blizzard, 1 medium	22
Crispy Crunch Blizzard, 1 large	29
Double Fudge Cookie Dough Blizzard, 1 mini	12
Double Fudge Cookie Dough Blizzard, 1 small	21
Double Fudge Cookie Dough Blizzard, 1 medium	28
Double Fudge Cookie Dough Blizzard, 1 large	35
French Silk Pie Blizzard, 1 mini	12
French Silk Pie Blizzard, 1 small	19
French Silk Pie Blizzard, 1 medium	25
French Silk Pie Blizzard, 1 large	37
Georgia Mud Fudge® Blizzard, 1 mini	12

▲ Power Foods	*PointsPlus®* value
Georgia Mud Fudge Blizzard, 1 small	18
Georgia Mud Fudge Blizzard, 1 medium	27
Georgia Mud Fudge Blizzard, 1 large	39
Hawaiian Blizzard, 1 mini	8
Hawaiian Blizzard, 1 small	12
Hawaiian Blizzard, 1 medium	16
Hawaiian Blizzard, 1 large	22
Midnight Truffle Blizzard, 1 mini	12
Midnight Truffle Blizzard, 1 small	22
Midnight Truffle Blizzard, 1 medium	29
Midnight Truffle Blizzard, 1 large	37
Mint OREO® Blizzard, 1 mini	11
Mint OREO Blizzard, 1 small	15
Mint OREO Blizzard, 1 medium	19
Mint OREO Blizzard, 1 large	27
OREO® Cookies Blizzard, 1 mini	11
OREO Cookies Blizzard, 1 small	15
OREO Cookies Blizzard, 1 medium	19
OREO Cookies Blizzard, 1 large	29
Reese® Peanut Butter Cups® Blizzard, 1 mini	10
Reese Peanut Butter Cups Blizzard, 1 small	17
Reese Peanut Butter Cups Blizzard, 1 medium	23
Reese Peanut Butter Cups Blizzard, 1 large	30
Rolo® Blizzard, 1 mini	10
Rolo Blizzard, 1 small	17
Rolo Blizzard, 1 medium	27
Rolo Blizzard, 1 large	36
Skor® Blizzard, 1 mini	11
Skor Blizzard, 1 small	16
Skor Blizzard, 1 medium	23
Skor Blizzard, 1 large	32

▲ Power Foods	*PointsPlus*® value
Smarties® Chocolate Candy Blizzard, 1 mini	10
Smarties Chocolate Candy Blizzard, 1 small	18
Smarties Chocolate Candy Blizzard, 1 medium	22
Smarties Chocolate Candy Blizzard, 1 large	30
Strawberry CheeseQuake® Blizzard, 1 mini	9
Strawberry CheeseQuake Blizzard, 1 small	14
Strawberry CheeseQuake Blizzard, 1 medium	19
Strawberry CheeseQuake Blizzard, 1 large	25
Turtle Pecan Cluster Blizzard, 1 mini	11
Turtle Pecan Cluster Blizzard, 1 small	19
Turtle Pecan Cluster Blizzard, 1 medium	30
Turtle Pecan Cluster Blizzard, 1 large	44

WAFFLE TREATS

Chocolate Coated Waffle Cone with Soft Serve, 1	15
Chocolate Covered Strawberry Waffle Bowl Sundae, 1	22
Fab Fudge Waffle Bowl Sundae, 1	20
Fudge Brownie Temptation Waffle Bowl Sundae, 1	26
Plain Waffle Cone with Soft Serve, 1	12
Turtle Waffle Bowl Sundae, 1	22

▲ Power Foods	*PointsPlus*® value

DQ® CONES

Chocolate Cone, 1 kids	5
Chocolate Cone, 1 small	7
Chocolate Cone, 1 medium	10
Chocolate Cone, 1 large	14
Dipped Cone, Chocolate, 1 kids	6
Dipped Cone, Chocolate, 1 small	9
Dipped Cone, Chocolate, 1 medium	13
Dipped Cone, Chocolate, 1 large	18
Vanilla Cone, 1 kids	5
Vanilla Cone, 1 small	6
Vanilla Cone, 1 medium	9
Vanilla Cone, 1 large	13

DQ® SUNDAES

Sundae, Caramel, 1 small	8
Sundae, Caramel, 1 medium	12
Sundae, Caramel, 1 large	16
Sundae, Cherry, 1 small	7
Sundae, Cherry, 1 medium	10
Sundae, Cherry, 1 large	14
Sundae, Chocolate, 1 small	8
Sundae, Chocolate, 1 medium	11
Sundae, Chocolate, 1 large	15
Sundae, Hot Fudge, 1 small	8
Sundae, Hot Fudge, 1 medium	12
Sundae, Hot Fudge, 1 large	17
Sundae, Marshmallow, 1 small	8
Sundae, Marshmallow, 1 medium	11
Sundae, Marshmallow, 1 large	16
Sundae, Pineapple, 1 small	6
Sundae, Pineapple, 1 medium	9
Sundae, Pineapple, 1 large	13
Sundae, Raspberry, 1 small	7
Sundae, Raspberry, 1 medium	10

DAIRY QUEEN®

▲ Power Foods	PointsPlus® value
Sundae, Raspberry, 1 large	15
Sundae, Strawberry, 1 small	7
Sundae, Strawberry, 1 medium	10
Sundae, Strawberry, 1 large	13

SHAKES

	PointsPlus® value
Shake, Caramel, 1 small	16
Shake, Caramel, 1 medium	21
Shake, Caramel, 1 large	28
Shake, Cherry, 1 small	14
Shake, Cherry, 1 medium	18
Shake, Cherry, 1 large	23
Shake, Chocolate, 1 small	15
Shake, Chocolate, 1 medium	20
Shake, Chocolate, 1 large	26
Shake, Coffee, 1 small	14
Shake, Coffee, 1 medium	18
Shake, Coffee, 1 large	22
Shake, Hot Fudge, 1 small	16
Shake, Hot Fudge, 1 medium	21
Shake, Hot Fudge, 1 large	28
Shake, Raspberry, 1 small	15
Shake, Raspberry, 1 medium	20
Shake, Raspberry, 1 large	25
Shake, Strawberry, 1 small	14
Shake, Strawberry, 1 medium	18
Shake, Strawberry, 1 large	23
Shake, Vanilla, 1 small	15
Shake, Vanilla, 1 medium	19
Shake, Vanilla, 1 large	24

MOOLATTÉ® FROZEN BLENDED COFFEE

Cappuccino MooLatté, 1 small	13
Cappuccino MooLatté, 1 medium	16
Cappuccino MooLatté, 1 large	20
Caramel MooLatté, 1 small	15
Caramel MooLatté, 1 medium	18

▲ Power Foods	PointsPlus® value
Caramel MooLatté, 1 large	24
French Vanilla MooLatté, 1 small	14
French Vanilla MooLatté, 1 medium	17
French Vanilla MooLatté, 1 large	22
Mocha MooLatté, 1 small	14
Mocha MooLatté, 1 medium	19
Mocha MooLatté, 1 large	24

ARCTIC RUSH® FROZEN BEVERAGES

Arctic Rush, All Flavours, 1 small	7
Arctic Rush, All Flavours, 1 medium	8
Arctic Rush, All Flavours, 1 large	11

MORE TREATS

Peanut Buster®, 1	20
Parfait Banana Split, 1	15
OREO Brownie EarthQuake® Treat, 1	21
Pecan Mudslide® Treat, 1	18
Arctic Rush® Float, All Flavours, 1 small	9
Arctic Rush Float, All Flavours, 1 medium	11
Arctic Rush Float, All Flavours, 1 large	15
Arctic Rush Freeze, All Flavours, 1 small	10
Arctic Rush Freeze, All Flavours, 1 medium	13
Arctic Rush Freeze, All Flavours, 1 large	17

NOVELTIES

Chocolate Dilly® Bar, 1	6
Buster Bar® Treat, 1	13
DQ Sandwich, 1	5
Fudge Bar, 1	2
Vanilla Orange Bar, 1	2
DQ Litre, 1 L	5

▲ Power Foods	PointsPlus® value
BURGERS (WEIGHTS ARE BASED ON PRECOOKED MEASUREMENTS)	
1/4 lb. Bacon Cheese GrillBurger®, 1	17
1/4 lb. GrillBurger with Cheese, 1	14
1/2 lb. FlameThrower® GrillBurger, 1	27
1/4 lb. Mushroom Swiss GrillBurger, 1	16
1/2 lb. GrillBurger with Cheese, 1	21
DQ Ultimate® Burger, 1	20
Original Double Cheeseburger, 1	17
Original Cheeseburger, 1	11

BASKETS (DOES NOT INCLUDE A DRINK)	
Chicken Strip Basket™ – with Gravy, 4 pieces	21
Chicken Strip Basket – with Gravy, 6 pieces	27
Chicken Quesadilla Basket Veggie Quesadilla Basket, 1 serving	32
Veggie Quesadilla Basket, 1 serving	30

HOT DOGS	
All-Beef Chili Cheese Dog, 1	9
All-Beef Hot Dog, 1	7

IRON GRILLED	
Iron Grilled Turkey Sandwich, 1	13
Iron Grilled Supreme BLT Sandwich, 1	15

SANDWICHES, SALADS & WRAPS	
Crispy Chicken Sandwich, 1	14
Grilled Chicken Sandwich, 1	10
Crispy FlameThrower Chicken Sandwich, 1	22
Crispy Chicken Salad, 1	10

▲ Power Foods	PointsPlus® value
Grilled Chicken Salad, 1	7
Side Salad, 1	1
Crispy Chicken Wrap, 1	7
Grilled Chicken Wrap, 1	5
Crispy FlameThrower Chicken Wrap, 1	8

SIDE ITEMS	
French Fries, 1 kids serving	7
French Fries, 1 regular serving	8
French Fries, 1 large serving	13
Onion Rings, 1	7
Poutine, 1 (260 g [5 oz])	17
Poutine, 1 (520 g [11 oz])	33

CONDIMENTS	
Ketchup Packet, 1 packet	0
Mayonnaise, 1 packet	3
Mustard Packet, 1 packet	0

KIDS' MEALS (DOES NOT INCLUDE A DRINK OR A TREAT)	
All-Beef Hot Dog Kid's Meal with Fries, 1	12
All-Beef Hot Dog Kids' Meal with Applesauce, 1	9
All-Beef Hot Dog Kids' Meal with Banana, 1	10
Cheeseburger Kids' Meal with Fries, 1	15
Cheeseburger Kids' Meal with Applesauce, 1	13
Cheeseburger Kids' Meal with Banana, 1	14
Chicken Strip Kids' Meal with Fries, 1	12
Chicken Strip Kids' Meal with Applesauce, 1	8

DAIRY QUEEN®

Power Foods	*PointsPlus*® value
Chicken Strip Kids' Meal with Banana, 1	10
Hamburger Kids' Meal with Fries, 1	15
Hamburger Kids' Meal with Applesauce, 1	11
Hamburger Kids' Meal with Banana, 1	12
Grilled Cheese Kids' Meal with Fries, 1	13
Grilled Cheese Kids' Meal with Applesauce, 1	10
Grilled Cheese Kids' Meal with Banana, 1	11

CHILLERS

Lemonade Chiller, Classic, 1 small	8
Lemonade Chiller, Classic, 1 medium	12
Lemonade Chiller, Classic, 1 large	19
Lemonade Chiller, Raspberry, 1 small	10
Lemonade Chiller, Raspberry, 1 medium	14
Lemonade Chiller, Raspberry, 1 large	23
Lemonade Chiller, Strawberry, 1 small	9
Lemonade Chiller, Strawberry, 1 medium	13
Lemonade Chiller, Strawberry, 1 large	21

DRINKS

Pepsi®, 1 small	5
Pepsi®, 1 medium	6
Pepsi®, 1 large	9
Diet Pepsi, 1 small	0

Power Foods	*PointsPlus*® value
Diet Pepsi, 1 medium	0
Diet Pepsi, 1 large	0
7-Up®, 1 small	5
7-Up®, 1 medium	6
7-Up®, 1 large	9
Lipton Brisk Iced Tea®, 1 small	3
Lipton Brisk Iced Tea®, 1 medium	4
Lipton Brisk Iced Tea®, 1 large	6
Minute Maid®, 1 small	6
Minute Maid®, 1 medium	7
Minute Maid®, 1 large	11
Coca Cola®, 1 small	5
Coca Cola®, 1 medium	6
Coca Cola®, 1 large	9
Diet Coca Cola®, 1 small	0
Diet Coca Cola®, 1 medium	0
Diet Coca Cola®, 1 large	0
Barq's®, 1 small	5
Barq's®, 1 medium	7
Barq's®, 1 large	10
Sprite®, 1 small	5
Sprite®, 1 medium	6
Sprite®, 1 large	9
Nestea®, 1 small	3
Nestea®, 1 medium	4
Nestea®, 1 large	6
Bottled Water, 1	0
Coffee, 1 (375 ml [12 fl oz])	0
Milk, whole, 1 (250 ml [8 fl oz])	4

XTRA STUFF

Banana Slices, 28 g (1 oz)	1
Caramel Topping, 28 g (1 oz)	2
Cheesecake Pieces, 28 g (1 oz)	3
Cherry Topping, 28 g (1 oz)	1

Power Foods	*PointsPlus®* value
Brownie Pieces, 28 g (1 oz)	3
Choco Chunks, 28 g (1 oz)	4
Chocolate Chip Cookie Dough Pieces, 28 g (1 oz)	4
Chocolate Topping, 28 g (1 oz)	2
Cocoa Fudge, 28 g (1 oz)	4
Coconut Flakes, 14 g (1/2 oz)	2
Crispy Crunch Pieces, 28 g (1 oz)	4
Hot Fudge Topping, 28 g (1 oz)	3
OREO Cookie Pieces, 28 g (1 oz)	4
Peanuts, 28 g (1 oz)	5
Pecan Pieces, 14 g (1/2 oz)	3
Pineapple Topping, 28 g (1 oz)	1
Rainbow Sprinkles, 4 g (1/8 oz)	1
Raspberry Topping, 28 g (1 oz)	2
Reese Peanut Butter Cups Pieces, 28 g (1 oz)	4
Skor Pieces, 28 g (1 oz)	4
Smarties Chocolate Candies, 28 g (1 oz)	3
Strawberry Topping, 28 g (1 oz)	1
Whipped Topping, 28 g (1 oz)	3

DQ® CAKES

Cake, decorations not included, 1 slice (1/8 of 20 cm [8"] cake)	12
Cake, decorations not included, 1 slice (1/12 of 25 cm [10"] cake)	12
Heart Cake, decorations not included, 1 slice (1/10 of cake)	6
Log Cake, decorations not included, 1 slice (1/8 of 20 cm [8"] cake)	7
Sheet Cake, decorations not included, 1 slice (1/24 of cake)	7
Chocolate Xtreme Blizzard Cake, 1 slice (1/8 of 20 cm [8"] cake)	16

Power Foods	*PointsPlus®* value
Chocolate Xtreme Blizzard Cake, 1 slice (1/12 of 25 cm [10"] cake)	18
OREO Blizzard Cake, 1 slice (1/8 of 20 cm [8"] cake)	17
OREO Blizzard Cake, 1 slice (1/12 of 25 cm [10"] cake)	15
Reese Peanut Butter Cups Blizzard Cake, 1 slice (1/8 of 20 cm [8"] cake)	16
Reese Peanut Butter Cups Blizzard Cake, 1 slice (1/12 of 25 cm [10"] cake)	16
Treatzza Pizza®, Peanut Butter Fudge, 1 slice (1/8 of pizza)	6
Treatzza Pizza, Skor®, 1 slice (1/8 of pizza)	5
Treatzza Pizza, Smarties®, 1 slice (1/8 of pizza)	5
Treatzza Pizza, Strawberry Banana, 1 slice (1/8 of pizza)	5
Raspberry Torte, 1 slice (1/8 of pizza)	12
Mocha Torte, 1 slice (1/8 of pizza)	13
Turtle Torte, 1 slice (1/8 of pizza)	13

DENNY'S®

SLAMS

All-American Slam®, 1 serving	22
Belgian Waffle Slam®, 1 serving	23
Fit Slam®, 1 serving	10
French Toast Slam®, 1 serving	21
Lumberjack Slam®, 1 serving	25
The Grand Slamwich® with Hash Browns, 1 serving	41

BUILD YOUR OWN GRAND SLAM®

Bacon Strips, 2 slices	2
Buttermilk Biscuit, 1 biscuit	5
Chicken Sausage Patty, 1 patty	3
Eggs, 2 eggs	7
Eggs, Whites, 2 egg whites	1
English Muffin, no Margarine, 1 muffin	3
Grilled Ham Slice, 1 slice	3
Grits with Margarine, 1 serving	6
Hash Browns, 1	6
Oatmeal with milk, 290 g (10 oz)	5
Pancakes, Buttermilk, 2 pancakes	9
Pancakes, Hearty Wheat, 2 pancakes	8
Sausage Links, 2 links	5
Seasonal Fruit, 125 g (4 oz)	2
Slices of Toast with Margarine, 2 slices	7
Turkey Bacon Strips, 2 slices	2
Yogurt, Low Fat, 170 g (6 oz)	4

SKILLETS

Bananas Foster French Toast Skillet, 1 serving	23
Prime Rib Skillet, 1 serving	22
Santa Fe Skillet, 1 serving	19
Ultimate Skillet, 1 serving	20

FAVOURITES

Bacon Avocado Burrito with Hash Browns, 1 serving	27
Banana Pecan Pancake Breakfast, 1 serving	20
Country-Fried Steak & Eggs, 1 serving	18
Harvest Oatmeal Breakfast, 1 serving	14
Moons over my Hammy®, 1 serving	20
Southwestern Steak Burrito with Hash Browns, 1 serving	30
T-Bone Steak & Eggs, 1 serving	20

OMELETTES

Fit Fare® Omelette, 1 serving	10
Moons over my Hammy Omelette™ with hash browns, 1 serving	21
Ultimate Omelette, 1 serving	16
Veggie-Cheese Omelette, 1 serving	12
Western Omelette with Hash Browns, 1 serving	19

SCRAMBLES

Heartland Scramble®, 1 serving	31
Meat Lover's Scramble, 1 serving	30

▲ Power Foods | *PointsPlus®* value
▲ Power Foods | *PointsPlus®* value

BREAKFAST SIDES

Bacon Strips, 4 slices	4
Bagel & Cream Cheese, 1 serving	9
Bowl of Harvest Oatmeal with Milk, 1 serving	10
Cheddar Cheese Hash Browns, 1 serving	8
Chicken Sausage Patty, 2 patties	6
Everything Hash Browns with Onions Cheese & Country Gravy, 1 serving	10
Grits with Margarine, 1 serving	3
Pancake Puppies®, 1 serving	10

APPETIZERS

Basket of Puppies without Syrup, 1 serving	14
Cheese Burger Flatbread, 1 serving	23
Chicken Strips with Buffalo Sauce, 1 serving	19
Chicken Strips with Sweet & Tangy BBQ Sauce, 1 serving	22
Chicken Wings with Buffalo Sauce, 250 g (1/2 lb)	8
Chicken Wings with Sweet & Tangy BBQ Sauce, 250 g (1/2 lb)	12
Half Size Sampler™, 1 serving	24
Half Size Zesty Nachos, 1 serving	18
Mozzarella Cheese Sticks, 1 serving	15
Sampler™, 1 serving	38
Smothered Cheese Fries, 1 serving	23
Three-Dip & Chips, 1 serving	15
Zesty Nachos, 1 serving	36

SOUPS, SALADS & SIDES

Broccoli & Cheddar Soup, 1 serving	10
Chicken Deluxe Salad – Chicken Strips, 1 serving	16
Chicken Deluxe Salad – Grilled Chicken, 1 serving	9
Chicken Noodle Soup, 1 serving	6
Clam Chowder, 1 serving	7
Cranberry Apple Chicken Salad with Balsamic Vinaigrette, no bread, 1 serving	10
Dippable Veggies with Ranch Dressing, 1 side serving	6
French Fries, salted, 1 serving	12
Garden Salad with Dressing, 1 serving	3
Half Size Cranberry Apple Chicken Salad with Balsamic Vinaigrette, no bread, 1 serving	8
Loaded Baked Potato Soup, 1 serving	12
Onion Rings, 1 serving	15
Seasoned Fries, 1 serving	18
Vegetable Beef Soup, 1 serving	4

DINNER CLASSICS

Chicken Strips with bread (add choices), 1 serving	20
Country-Fried Steak with gravy (add choices), 1 serving	32
Fish & Chips (add dinner bread choice), 1 serving	42
Fit Fare® Sweet & Tangy BBQ Chicken with Broccoli & Corn, 1 serving	16
Fit Fare® Tilapia Ranchero, 1 serving	14

DENNY'S®

Dinner Classics (cont'd)

▲ Power Foods	*PointsPlus®* value
Lemon Pepper Grilled Tilapia with bread (add choices), 1 serving	20
Mushroom Swiss Chopped Steak with Bread (add choices), 1 serving	28
Prime Rib & Chicken Sizzlin' Skillet, 1 serving	24
Sweet & Tangy BBQ Chicken with bread & Veggies, 1 serving	26
T-Bone Steak & Breaded Shrimp with Bread (add choices), 1 serving	24
T-Bone Steak & Shrimp Skewer with Bread (add choices), 1 serving	27
T-Bone Steak with Bread, 1 serving	22
Tilapia Ranchero with Bread, 1 serving	18

55+ MENU

Senior Belgian Waffle Slam®, 1 serving	14
Senior Club Sandwich, 1 serving	14
Senior Country-Fried Steak with bread, 1 serving	19
Senior Fit Fare® Grilled Chicken, 1 serving	14
Senior Fit Fare® Omelette, 1 serving	13
Senior French Toast Slam® with egg, 1 serving	15
Senior Grilled Cheese Deluxe Sandwich, 1 serving	14
Senior Grilled Chicken with Bread, 1 serving	10
Senior Grilled Shrimp Skewer with Bread, 1 serving	12
Senior Lemon Pepper Grilled Tilapia with Bread, 1 serving	16
Senior Omelette, 1 serving	12
Senior Scrambled Eggs & Cheddar Breakfast, 1 serving	26

▲ Power Foods	*PointsPlus®* value
Senior Soup & Salad, 1 serving	12
Senior Starter™, 1 serving	6

BURGERS

Bacon Cheddar Burger, 1	22
Bacon Slamburger™, 1	26
Classic Cheeseburger, 1	20
Double Cheeseburger, 1	35
Mushroom Swiss Burger, 1	22
Patty Melt, 1	27
Veggie Burger with Balsamic Vinaigrette & Fit Fare® Fresh Veggies, 1	14
Western Burger, 1	26

SANDWICHES

Bacon, Lettuce & Tomato, 1	14
Chicken Avocado Sandwich, 1	13
Chicken Ranch Melt with Dressing, 1	25
Club Sandwich, 1	17
Hickory Grilled Chicken Sandwich, 1	24
Prime Rib Philly Melt, 1	18
Spicy Buffalo Chicken Melt, 1	23
The Super Bird®, 1	16

DINNER SIDES

Broccoli, 1 side serving	1
Coleslaw, 1 side serving	7
Corn, 1 side serving	2
Dippable Veggies (no dressing), 1 side serving	0
Fiesta Corn, 1 side serving	4
French Fries (salted), 1 side serving	11

DENNY'S®

Power Foods	PointsPlus® value
Garlic Dinner Bread, 2 pieces	5
Golden-Fried Shrimp, 6 pieces	5
Green Beans, 1 side serving	1
Grilled Shrimp Skewer, 1 skewer	2
Hash Browns, 1	6
Mashed Potatoes, 1 side serving	7
Red-Skinned Potatoes, 1 side serving	5
Sautéed Spinach, 1 side serving	2
Sautéed Spinach with Pico De Gallo & Bacon, 1 side serving	3
Smoked Cheddar Mashed Potatoes, 1 side serving	7
Tomato Slices, 3 slices	0
Vegetable Rice Pilaf, 1 side serving	5

CONDIMENTS

Balsamic Vinaigrette, Low Fat, 30 oz (1 oz)	1
BBQ Sweet & Spicy, 45 g (1.5 oz)	3
Bleu Cheese Dressing, 30 oz (1 oz)	3
Caesar Dressing, 30 oz (1 oz)	3
Croutons, 5 g (1/4 oz)	3
Fat Free Italian Dressing, 30 oz (1 oz)	0
Fat Free Ranch Dressing, 30 oz (1 oz)	0
French Dressing, 30 oz (1 oz)	2
Honey Mustard Dressing, 30 oz (1 oz)	4
Maple-Flavoured Syrup, 45 ml (3 Tbsp)	4
Marinara Sauce, 60 g (2 oz)	1
Pico de Gallo, 90 g (3 oz)	1
Ranch Dressing, 30 oz (1 oz)	4
Sour Cream, 45 g (1.5 oz)	3
Sugar-Free Maple-Flavoured Syrup, 45 ml (3 Tbsp)	1
Thousand Island Dressing, 30 oz (1 oz)	3
Whipped Margarine, 30 oz (1 oz)	2

KIDS' MEAL ENTRÉES

Cheesy @ the Plate, 1 serving	10
Chocolate Chip-In Pancakes, 1 serving	12
Finish Line Fries, 1 serving	11
Game-On Grapes, 1 serving	3
Home Plate Mashed Potatoes with Brown Gravy, 1 serving	7
Jr. Grand Slam®, 1 serving	10
Pit Stop Pizza, 1 serving	16
Slam® Dribblers, 1 serving	12
Slap Shot Slider, 1 slider	8
Softball Pancake with meat, 1 serving	7
Spaghetti, Set, Go!, 1 serving	6
Track & Cheese, 1 serving	8
Triple Play Nuggets with BBQ Sauce, 1 serving	9

KIDS' MEAL SIDES

Apple Dunkers with Caramel Sauce, 1 serving	3
Fishing Goldfish Crackers, 1 side serving	7
High Diving Veggies with Ranch Dressing, 1 side serving	6
Tumbling Vanilla Yogurt with Strawberry Topping, 1 serving	5

KIDS' MEAL DESSERTS

Kids' OREO® Blender Blaster, 1 (375 ml [12 fl oz])	18
Soccer Shake, 1 (330 ml [11 fl oz])	13
Sundae Sundae Sundae!, 1 serving	8

DENNY'S®

DESSERTS

Apple Pie, 1 serving	13
Banana Split, 1 serving	22
Caramel Apple Crisp, 1 serving	20
Caramel Topping, 45 g (1.5 oz)	5
Cherry Topping, 60 g (2 oz)	2
Chocolate French Silk Pie, 1 serving	21
Chocolate Peanut Butter Silk Pie, 1 serving	19
Chocolate Topping, 45 g (1.5 oz)	1
Chopped Nuts, 30 g (1 oz)	6
Coconut Cream Pie, 1 serving	18
Cookies & Cream Pie, 1 serving	18
Floats (Root Beer or Coca-Cola®), 1 (500 ml [16 fl oz])	12
Fudge Topping, 45 g (1.5 oz)	4
Glazed Pecans, 35 g (1.25 oz)	6
Hershey®'s Chocolate Cake, 1 serving	16
Hot Fudge Brownie a la Mode, 1 serving	23
Ice Cream, 1 scoop	8
Key Lime Pie, 1 serving	15
Lemon Meringue Layer Pie, 1 serving	14
Milk Shakes, 1 (375 ml [12 fl oz])	16
New York Style Cheesecake, 1 serving	14
Oreo® Blender Blaster™, 1 (400 ml [14 fl oz])	25
Oreo® Cookie Pieces, 25 g (0.8 oz)	3
Pecan Pie, 1 serving	20
Pumpkin Pie, 1 serving	13
Strawberry Topping, 45 g (1.5 oz)	1
Turtle Cheesecake, 1 serving	21

SMOOTHIES

Groovy Mango, 1 (500 ml [16 fl oz])	8
Strawberry Banana Bliss, 1 (500 ml [16 fl oz])	7
Sweet Georgia Peach, 1 (500 ml [16 fl oz])	7

BEVERAGES

Cherry Cherry Limade™, 1 (450 ml [15 fl oz])	5
Chocolate Milk, 1 small	4
Chocolate Milk, 1 large	7
Coffee, 1 (250 ml [8 fl oz])	0
Family Size Juice Carafe, 1 carafe	21
Flavoured Cappuccino, 1 (250 ml [8 fl oz])	4
Hot Chocolate, 1 (250 ml [8 fl oz])	4
Hot Tea, 1 (250 ml [8 fl oz])	0
Iced Tea, 1 (450 ml [15 fl oz])	0
Island Splash, 1 (450 ml [15 fl oz])	7
Juice, 1 small	5
Juice, 1 large	8
Lemonade, 1 (450 ml [15 fl oz])	4
Milk, 1 small	6
Milk, 1 large	3
OJ Strawberry Mango, 1 (450 ml [15 fl oz])	7
Pacific Chiller, 1 (450 ml [15 fl oz])	6
Pineapple Dream™, 1 (450 ml [15 fl oz])	5
Raspberry Nestea®, 1 (450 ml [15 fl oz])	2
Soft Drinks, 1 (375 ml [12 fl oz])	2
Strawberry Lemonade, 1 (450 ml [15 fl oz])	5
Strawberry Mango Pucker™, 1 (450 ml [15 fl oz])	6

▲ Power Foods	PointsPlus® value

DIPPIN' DOTS CHILLZ™

Chocolate Frozen Dairy Dessert, 125 ml (1/2 cup)	2
Sour Blue Razz Flavored Ice, 125 ml (1/2 cup)	2
Wango Rainbo™ Flavored Ice, 125 ml (1/2 cup)	1

DOTS 'N CREAM (10% BUTTERFAT)

Berry Crème Ice Cream, 125 ml (1/2 cup)	5
Caramel Cappuccino™ Ice Cream, 125 ml (1/2 cup)	5
Mint Chocolate Ice Cream, 125 ml (1/2 cup)	6

▲ Power Foods	PointsPlus® value

DOTS 'N CREAM (14% BUTTERFAT)

Banana Split Ice Cream, 125 ml (1/2 cup)	6
Caramel Cappuccino™ Ice Cream, 125 ml (1/2 cup)	5
Mint Chocolate Ice Cream, 125 ml (1/2 cup)	7
Orange Crème de la Crème™ Ice Cream, 125 ml (1/2 cup)	5
Vanilla Bean Ice Cream, 125 ml (1/2 cup)	6
Vanilla Over the Rainbow™ Ice Cream, 125 ml (1/2 cup)	6
Wild About Chocolate™ Ice Cream, 125 ml (1/2 cup)	7

DOMINO'S PIZZA®

Power Foods	PointsPlus® value
Banana Peppers, 1 serving	0
Beef, 1 serving	1
Black Olives, 1 serving	0
Brooklyn Style Pepperoni, 1 serving	1
Cheddar Cheese, 1 serving	1
Chicken, 1 serving	1
Extra Cheese, 1 serving	1
Garlic, 1 serving	0
Green Olives, 1 serving	1
Green Pepper, 1 serving	0
Ham, 1 serving	0
Jalapenos, 1 serving	0
Mushroom, 1 serving	0
Pepperoni, 1 serving	1
Philly Meat, 1 serving	0
Pineapple, 1 serving	0
Provolone, 1 serving	2
Sausage, 1 serving	2
Tomatoes, 1 serving	0

SPECIALTY PIZZA

Pepperoni, 1 slice, medium	6
Pepperoni, 1 slice, large	8
Pepperoni & Bacon, 1 slice, medium	9
Pepperoni & Bacon, 1 slice, large	16
Pepperoni & Sausage, 1 slice, medium	6
Pepperoni & Mushroom, 1 slice, large	8
Pepperoni & Sausage, 1 slice, large	9
Pepperoni Feast®, 1 slice, medium	4
Pepperoni Feast®, 1 slice, large	5
Philly Cheese Steak, 1 slice, medium	3
Philly Cheese Steak, 1 slice, large	3
Sausage, 1 slice, medium	6
Sausage, 1 slice, large	8

Power Foods	PointsPlus® value

OVEN BAKED SANDWICHES

Chicken Bacon Ranch, 1	24
Chicken Parmesan, 1	20
Italian, 1	23
Philly Cheese Steak, 1	18
Extra Cheese (sandwich topping), 1 serving	2
Extra Chicken (sandwich topping), 1 serving	2
Extra Meat (Italian sandwich topping), 1 serving	3
Extra Meat (Philly sandwich topping), 1 serving	1
Extra Veggies (Italian sandwich topping), 1 serving	0
Extra Veggies (Philly sandwich topping), 1 serving	0

BREAD SIDES

Breadsticks, 1 piece	3
Cheesy Bread, 1 piece	3
Cinna Stix®, 1 slice	3
Garlic Dipping Sauce, 1 container	7
Italian Dipping Sauce, 1 container	1
Marinara Dipping Sauce, 1 container	1
Sweet Icing, 1 container	7

CHICKEN SIDES

Barbecue Buffalo Wings, 2 pieces	6
Buffalo Chicken Kickers®, 2 pieces	3
Hot Buffalo Wings, 2 pieces	5
Blue Cheese Dipping Sauce, 1 container	6
Hot Dipping Sauce, 1 container	1
Ranch Dipping Sauce, 1 container	6

EAST SIDE MARIO'S

Power Foods	PointsPlus® value
STARTERS	
Baked Garlic Shrimp, 1 serving	10
Bruschetta for one, 1 order	9
Bruschetta for two, 1 order (whole)	16
Budda Boomers, 1 serving	23
Calamari Fritti (no dips), 1 serving	13
Cheddar Cheese Sticks, 1 serving	12
Chicken Wings – (no sauce, no carrots / celery or blue cheese), 1 serving	30
Garlic Parmesan Wings (no carrots / celery or blue cheese), 1 serving	24
Blue Cheese Dip, 1 serving (46 g)	5
Hot Sauce, 1 serving (43 g)	3
Medium Sauce, 1 serving (43 g)	3
Mild Sauce, 1 serving (54 g)	4
Mussels Marinara (Atlantic only), 1 serving	15

SOUPS & SALADS	
Chicken Garden Salad, 1 serving	10
Entrée Caesar, 1 serving	16
Entrée Garden, 1 serving	8
Garden Salad for 2 or more (large red bowl), 1 order (whole)	10
Caesar Salad for 2 or more (large red bowl), 1 order (whole)	22
ESM House Vinaigrette, 1 serving (29 g)	5
Grilled Chicken Caesar Salad, 1 serving	18
Italian Minestrone Soup, 1 serving	2
Italian Wedding Soup, 1 serving	2
Salmon Salad (Quebec only) without dressing, 1 serving	14

Power Foods	PointsPlus® value
Side Caesar Salad/ Single Serving of Unlimited (small red bowl), 1 side serving	11
Side Garden Salad/ Single Serving of Unlimited (small red bowl), 1 side serving	5
Tuscan Chicken Salad, 1 serving	13

EVERYDAY VALUES	
Cheese Pizza, 1 slice	5
Fettuccine Alfredo, 1 serving	15
Penne Arrabbiata, 1 serving	15
Penne Napolitana, 1 serving	15
Pepperoni Pizza, 1 slice	5
Spaghettini Bolognese, 1 serving	13

CLASSICS	
Baked Penne Bolognese, 1 serving	20
Cheese Cappelletti, 1 serving	24
Linguine Chicken Amatriciana, 1 serving	29
Linguine Chicken Tettrazini, 1 serving	28
Mario's Classic Chicken Parmigiana – no side choice, 1 serving	12
Mario's Classic Lasagna, 1 serving	13
Sausage and Pepper Penne, 1 serving	26
Seafood Linguine, 1 serving	18
Spaghettini and Meatballs, 1 serving	24
Spaghettini Primavera, 1 serving	21
Veal Parmigiana – no side choice, 1 serving	14

EAST SIDE MARIO'S

Power Foods	PointsPlus® value

TASTES OF LITTLE ITALY

Chicken Marsala – (no side vegetables or side choice), 1 serving	9
Chicken Picatta – (no side vegetables or side choice), 1 serving	10
Firecracker Shrimp Penne, 1 serving	24
Hell's Kitchen Chicken – (no side vegetables or side choice), 1 serving	12
Orecchiette Genovese Alfredo, 1 serving	28
Scallop Carbonara, 1 serving	36
Side Crustini, 1 side serving	1
Spaghettini with Mushrooms, 1 serving	35
Spinach & Ricotta Milanese, 1 serving	19
Vernazza Peppercorn Alfredo (no crustini), 1 serving	29

FROM THE NEIGHBOURHOOD

1/2 Rotisserie Chicken – (no side choice or dipping sauce), 1 serving	26
1/4 Rotisserie Chicken – Dark – (no side choice or dipping sauce), 1 serving	14
1/4 Rotisserie Chicken – White – (no side choice or dipping sauce), 1 serving	11
Chicken Strips – no side choice or plum sauce, 1 serving	14
Fish & Chips – no side choice or tartar sauce, 1 serving	14
Half Rack Back Ribs – (no side choice), 1 serving	30
Full Rack Back Ribs – (no side choice), 1 serving	59

Power Foods	PointsPlus® value

Grilled Atlantic Salmon (with sauce, no vegetables or side choice), 1 serving	14
New York Striploin – (no vegetables or side choice), 1 serving	8
Plum Sauce for dipping, 1 serving (53 g)	3
Rotisserie Chicken Dipping Sauce, 44 ml (1 1/2 fl oz)	0
Side Tartar Sauce, 1 serving (55 g)	9

SIDE SERVINGS

French Fries, 1 side serving	10
Mario's Potatoes, 1 side serving	11
Roasted Vegetables (zucchini, carrots, peppers, grape tomatoes), 1 side serving	2
Side Arabiatta Sauce, 1 side serving	1
Side Garlic Aioli, 1 side serving	8
Side Homeloaf (no margarine), 1 side serving	8
Side Napolitana Sauce, 1 side serving	2

LUNCH PASTAS

Cheese Cappelletti, 1 serving	12
Linguine Chicken Amatriciana, 1 serving	17
Linguine Chicken Tettrazini, 1 serving	16
Orecchiette Genovese Alfredo, 1 serving	17
Sausage and Pepper Penne, 1 serving	15
Seafood Linguine, 1 serving	13
Spaghettini and Meatballs, 1 serving	17
Spaghettini Primavera, 1 serving	12

EAST SIDE MARIO'S

▲ Power Foods   *PointsPlus*®
value

PIADINI

Chicken Caesar Piadini, 1	22
Grilled Portobello Mushroom & Spinach Piadini, 1	22
Tuscan Chicken Piadini, 1	14

SANDWICHES (NOT INCLUDING SIDE SERVING)

Chicken Parmigiana Sandwich, 1	13
Mariboli Wrap, 1	16
New York Steak Sandwich (West only), 1	16
Philly Cheesesteak (Ontario, Quebec and East), 1	23
Portobello Panini, 1	28
Roasted Chicken & Provolone Panini, 1	25
Traditional Burger, 1	18
Tuscan Turkey Club, 1	19

PIZZA (NOT INCLUDING QUEBEC)

Build Your Own Pizza (cheese & sauce only), 1 slice	5
Four Meat Pizza, 1 slice	7
Goat Cheese & Grilled Chicken Pizza, 1 slice	5
Hawaiian Pizza, 1 slice	6
Margherita Pizza, 1 slice	5
New Yorker Pizza, 1 slice	5
Roasted Chicken & Bacon Pizza, 1 slice	6
Sausage & Hot Pepper Pizza, 1 slice	6
Vegetarian Pizza, 1 slice	5

EXTREME PITA®

Power Foods	PointsPlus® value

FRESH SALADS

Grilled Chicken Caesar, 1 serving	9
Mandarin Chicken Salad, 1 serving	12
Maple-Dijon Chicken Salad, 1 serving	5
Traditional Greek, 1 serving	8

CHEF INSPIRED PITAS

Bourbon Chipotle Chicken, 1 small	9
Buffalo Chicken, 1 small	9
Chicken Caesar, 1 small	8
Chicken Shawarma, 1 regular	12
Chicken Souvlaki, 1 small	9
Chicken Souvlaki, 1 regular	16
Fiesta Mexicana, 1 small	8
Mandarin Chicken, 1 small	9
Maple Dijon Chicken, 1 small	6
Thai Beef, 1 small	8
Thai Chicken, 1 small	7

CLASSIC PITAS

Big Country (chicken & steak), 1 regular	11
Grilled Steak, 1 small	6
Meatball, 1 small	13

FLATBAKED PITAS

Bourbon Chipotle Chicken, 1 serving	12
Buffalo Chicken, 1 serving	11
Extreme Classic, 1 serving	12
Hawaiian Luau, 1 serving	13
Mediterranean Chicken, 1 serving	11
Pepperoni Extreme, 1 serving	11
Rustic Italian, 1 serving	11
Thai Beef, 1 serving	12
Thai Chicken, 1 serving	11

FREESTYLE PITAS

Chipotle Steak, 1 regular	14
Club, 1 small	7
Club, 1 regular	10
Falafel, 1 small	7
Falafel, 1 regular	12
Grilled Chicken, 1 small	5
Grilled Chicken, 1 regular	9
Gyro, 1 small	9
Gyro, 1 regular	13
Philly Steak, 1 small	7
Philly Steak, 1 regular	12
Rustic Italian, 1 small	9
Tuna, 1 small	5
Veggie, 1 small	4
Veggie, 1 regular	4

TOPPINGS

Cheddar Cheese, 30 g (1 oz)	3
Feta Cheese, 30 g (1 oz)	2
Mozzarella Cheese, 15 g (1/2 oz)	1
Mozzarella Cheese, 30 g (1 oz)	3
Standard Vegetable Mix, 1 small serving	0
Standard Vegetable Mix, 1 regular serving	1

SIDES & APPETIZERS

Bruschetta Pita, 1 serving	6
Cheesy Garlic Pita with Hummus, 1 serving	9
Hummus dip, 1 serving	4
Pita Chips, 1 serving	4
Tzatziki Dip, 1 serving	2

EXTREME PITA®

PointsPlus®
value

DRESSINGS & SAUCES

BBQ Regular, 1 small	1
Bourbon Chipotle, 1 small	1
Chipotle Mayo, 1 small	1
Dijonaisse, 1 small	1
Greek Feta & Oregano, 1 small	2
Honey Mustard, 1 small	1
Hot Cajun BBQ, 1 small	1
Hot Cajun BBQ, 1 regular	2
Hot Sauce, 1 small	0
Hot Sauce, 1 regular	0
Hummus dip, 1 small	1
Hummus dip, 1 regular	2
Light Caesar, 1 small	1
Light Mayonnaise, 1 small	1
Maple Dijon Vinaigrette, 1 small	1
Pepita Mole Sauce, 1 small	1
Sour Cream, 1 small	1
Spicy Asian Sesame, 1 small	2
Sweet Chili Thai, 1 small	1
Tzatziki Dip, 1 small	0
Tzatziki Dip, 1 regular	1

KIDS MENU

BBQ4U Pita, 1 serving	5
Beefosaurus Rex Pita, 1 serving	6
Cheese Flatbaked Pita, 1 serving	6
Fee-Fi-Fo-Hummus Pita, 1 serving	6
Ham & Cheese Pita, 1 serving	7
Pepperoni Flat Baked Pita, 1 serving	7
Sweet Chicken Little Pita, 1 serving	5

GOLDEN SPOON® FROZEN YOGURT

▲ Power Foods	*PointsPlus*® value
REGULAR CONE	
Cone, 1	0
Heath Bar® Low-Fat Frozen Yogurt, any flavour, 1 regular cone	6
Non-Fat Frozen Yogurt, any flavour, 1 regular	4
WAFFLE CONE	
Heath Bar® Low-Fat Frozen Yogurt, any flavour, 1 waffle cone	8
Non-Fat Frozen Yogurt, any flavour, 1 waffle cone	6

HARVEY'S®

Power Foods	*PointsPlus®* value
Crispy Chicken Bun, 1	5
Grilled Chicken Sandwich, 1 serving	7
Grilled Chicken, 1 serving	3
Grilled Chicken Bun, 1 serving	4
Warm Grilled Chicken BLT Salad, 1 serving	5
Warm Grilled Chicken Salad, 1 serving	4
Chicken Strips – 2 pieces, 1 serving	6
Chicken Strips – 3 pieces, 1 serving	8
Hot Dog with Bun, 1	8
Hot Dog, 1	4
Hot Dog Bun, 1	4
Bacon Cheddar Dog, 1	11

SIDE ORDERS

Fries – Kids, 1 kids serving	13
Fries – Regular, 1 regular serving	9
Fries – Large, 1 large serving	11
Frings, 1 serving	14
Onion Rings – Regular, 1 regular serving	8
Onion Rings – Large, 1 large serving	15
Poutine, 1 serving	22
▲ **Side Garden Salad,** 1 side serving	0

SALAD DRESSINGS

Asian Sesame Dressing, 1 serving	2
Balsamic Vinaigrette Dressing, 1 serving	2
Creamy Caesar Dressing, 1 serving	3
Creamy Garlic Peppercorn Ranch Dressing, 1 serving	3

Power Foods	*PointsPlus®* value

MAIN MENU ITEMS

Original Hamburger, 1	10
Original Cheeseburger, 1	12
Original Bacon Cheeseburger, 1	13
Original Burger Patty, 1	5
Original Bun, 1	5
L'il Original, 1	5
L'il Original with Cheese, 1	7
L'il Original with Bacon and Cheese, 1	7
Harvey's Great Canadian Burger, 1	15
Harvey's Great Canadian Burger with Cheese, 1	17
Harvey's Great Canadian Burger with Bacon and Cheese, 1	18
Harvey's Great Canadian Burger Patty, 1	9
Harvey's Great Canadian Bistro Bun, 1	6
Veggie Burger, 1	7
Veggie Burger Whole Wheat Bun, 1	4
Crispy Chicken Sandwich, 1	12
Crispy Chicken, 1	8

▲ Power Foods	*PointsPlus®* value

BREAKFAST ITEMS

Breakfast Club, 1 serving	11
Breakfast Club Deluxe, 1 serving	14
Extra Egg, 1 serving	3
Homefries, 1 serving	8
Toast (white), 2 slices	5
Toast (whole wheat), 2 slices	4

GARNISHES

Bacon, 3 strips	1
Barbecue Sauce, 1 serving	1
Frank's RedHot Sauce, 1 serving	0
Hot Peppers, 1 serving	0
Ketchup, 1 serving	0
Lettuce, 1 serving	0
Light Mayonnaise, 1 serving	1
Mustard, 1 serving	0
▲ **Onions,** 1 serving	1
Pickle, 2 slices	0
Real Canadian Cheddar Cheese Slice, 1 serving	2
Relish, 1 serving	0
▲ **Tomato,** 2 slices	0

DIPPING SAUCES

Barbecue Sauce, 1 serving	2
Honey Mustard, 1 serving	5
Plum Sauce, 1 serving	2
Sweet N' Sour Sauce, 1 serving	2

KIDS COMBOS

Hamburger Meal, 1 serving	22
Cheeseburger Meal, 1 serving	24
Chicken Strip Meal, 3 pieces	20
Hot Dog Meal, 1 serving	20

▲ Power Foods	*PointsPlus®* value

DESSERTS

Apple Pie, 1	6

BEVERAGES

2% Partially Skimmed Milk, 1 serving (250 mL [8 fl oz])	3
2% Partially Skimmed Chocolate Milk, 1 serving (250 mL [8 fl oz])	4
Chocolate Milkshake, 1 serving (397 mL [14 fl oz])	20
Mug Rootbeer, 1 regular (473 mL [15 fl oz])	6

JOHNNY ROCKETS®

▲ Power Foods

	PointsPlus® value

STARTERS

American Fries, 1 serving	13
Cheese Fries, 1 serving	20
Chili Bowl, 1 serving	16
Chili Cheese Fries, 1 serving	24
Half Rings and Half Fries, 1 serving	22
Onion Rings, 1 serving	23
Rocket Wings – Hot Rocket Fuel, 1 serving	17
Rocket Wings – Plain, 1 serving	16
Rocket Wings – Sweet Barbeque, 1 serving	18
Rocket Wings – Traditional, 1 serving	18
Salad, Side, 1 side serving	2

SALADS

Chicken Club Salad with Breaded Chicken, 1 serving	17
Garden Salad, 1 serving	7

HAMBURGERS

#12 Burger, 1	26
Bacon Cheddar Double Burger, 1	29
Bacon Cheddar Single Burger, 1	30
Chili Cheese Hamburger, 1	24
Mini Chili Cheese Dogs, 1	32
Patty Melt Burger, 1	23
Rocket Double Burger, 1	37
Rocket Single Burger, 1	25
Route 66 Burger, 1	26
Smoke House Double Burger, 1	45
Smoke House Single Burger, 1	30
Streamliner Burger, 1	11
The Houston Burger, 1	28
The Original Burger, 1	23

▲ Power Foods

	PointsPlus® value

CHICKEN

Chicken Club Sandwich, 1	19
Chicken Tenders, 1 serving	23
Grilled Chicken Breast Sandwich, 1	17

OTHER FAVOURITES

BLT Sandwich on Rye Bread, 1	16
BLT Sandwich on Sourdough Bread, 1	14
BLT Sandwich on Wheat Bread, 1	16
BLT Sandwich on White Bread, 1	15
Caesar Salad, 1	12
Chicken Caesar Salad, 1	15
Chicken Club Salad with Grilled Chicken, 1	13
Chili Dog, 1	22
Grilled American Cheese Sandwich on Rye Bread, 1	14
Grilled American Cheese Sandwich on Sourdough Bread, 1	12
Grilled American Cheese Sandwich on Wheat Bread, 1	14
Grilled American Cheese Sandwich on White Bread, 1	13
Grilled Cheddar Cheese Sandwich on Rye Bread, 1	15
Grilled Cheddar Cheese Sandwich on Sourdough Bread, 1	14
Grilled Cheddar Cheese Sandwich on Wheat Bread, 1	15
Grilled Cheddar Cheese Sandwich on White Bread, 1	14
Grilled Swiss Cheese Sandwich on Rye Bread, 1	17
Grilled Swiss Cheese Sandwich on Sourdough Bread, 1	15
Grilled Swiss Cheese Sandwich on Wheat Bread, 1	17

JOHNNY ROCKETS®

Power Foods	PointsPlus® value
Grilled Swiss Cheese Sandwich on White Bread, 1	16
Hot Dog, 1	11
Philly Cheese Steak Sandwich with Pepperjack Cheese, 1	20
Philly Cheese Steak with American Cheese Sandwich, 1	20
Philly Cheesestake Sandwich with Swiss Cheese, 1	21
Philly Cheesestake with Cheddar Cheese, 1	20
The Houston Burger, 1	23
Tuna Melt on Rye Bread, 1	23
Tuna Melt on Sourdough Bread, 1	21
Tuna Melt on Wheat Bread, 1	22
Tuna Melt on White Bread, 1	12
Tuna Melt Sandwich on Rye Bread, 1	23
Tuna Melt Sandwich on Sourdough Bread, 1	21
Tuna Melt Sandwich on Wheat Bread, 1	22
Tuna Melt Sandwich on White Bread, 1	22
Tuna Salad Sandwich on White Bread, 1	20

EXTRA EXTRAS

American Cheese, 1 serving	2
Cheddar Cheese, 1 serving	2
Chili, 1 serving	3
Hamburger Patty, 1 serving	10
Pepperjack Cheese, 1 serving	2
Swiss Cheese, 1 serving	2

Power Foods	PointsPlus® value

DELUXE SHAKES

Black Forest, 1	25
Chocolate Peanut Butter, 1	29
Chocolate Vanilla Twist, 1	25
Mocha Fudge, 1	31
Orange Dreamsicle, 1	21
Strawberry Banana, 1	25

KERNELS®

PointsPlus®
value

POPCORN

Air Caramel, 50 g	6
Jalapeno Jack, 50 g	6
Low Fat Caramel, 50 g	5
Original Buttersalt, 50 g	7

▲ Power Foods	*PointsPlus®* value

ORIGINAL RECIPE® CHICKEN

Boneless Chicken Filet, 1	5
Drumstick, 1	3
Keel, 1	8
Keel (skin removed), 1	5
Rib, 1	6
Rib (skin removed), 1	4
Thigh, 1	8
Thigh (skin removed), 1	4
Wing, 1	4

SANDWICHES

Big Crunch® Sandwich, 1	16
Big Fresh Sandwich, 1	12
Boxmaster Sandwich, 1	22
Classic Sandwich, 1	12
Classic Sandwich (no mayonnaise), 1	9
Crispy Chicken Strips BBQ Bacon Ranch Twister™, 1	16
Crispy Chicken Strips Original Twister™, 1	13
Crispy Chicken Strips Roasted Garlic Caesar Twister™, 1	17
Double Down Sandwich, 1	14
Grilled Chicken BBQ Bacon Ranch Twister, 1	13
Grilled Chicken Roasted Garlic Caesar Twister™, 1	11
Grilled Chicken Sandwich, 1	10
Grilled Chicken Strips Original Twister™, 1	11
Homestyle Snacker Sandwich, 1	4
Sandwich Snackwich®, 1	10
Spicy Big Crunch® Sandwich, 1	17

▲ Power Foods	*PointsPlus®* value

SALADS/DRESSINGS/DIPPING SAUCES

Coleslaw, 1 individual serving	3
Macaroni Salad, 1 individual serving	5
Potato Salad, 1 individual serving	5
Tangy Caesar Salad with Grilled Chicken, 1 serving	5
Caesar Salad (no dressing), 1 serving	2
Caesar Light Dressing, 1 serving	4
Mighty Caesar Dressing, 1 serving	8
Croutons, 1 pack	2
Honey Mustard Dipping Sauce, 1 serving	2
Plum Dipping Sauce, 1 serving	1
Sweet BBQ Dipping Sauce, 1 serving	1

SNACKABLES/SIDES

Chicken Fries®, 5 pieces	4
▲ **Corn,** 1 individual serving	2
Crispy Strips®, 3 pieces	7
French Fries, 1 individual serving	9
Gravy, 1 individual serving	1
Hot Wings®, 5 pieces	11
Popcorn Chicken, 1 kids serving	10

OTHER MENU ITEMS

Chicken Nuggets – Kids, 4 nuggets	5
Popcorn Chicken, 1 small serving	13
Poutine, 1 serving	26

DESSERTS

Apple Turnover, 1	6
Chocolate Delite Cake (McCain), 1	6
Lemon Meringue Pie Slice, 1/5 of pie	8
Mini Brownies, 2 brownies	5

LA POPESSA

SALADS

	PointsPlus® value
Caesar Salad, 100 g (3 1/2 oz)	7
Caesar Salad with Chicken, 100 g (3 1/2 oz)	6
Chef Salad, 100 g (3 1/2 oz)	4
Chef Salad with Chicken, 100 g (3 1/2 oz)	4

PASTA

Garlic, 100 g (3 1/2 oz)	6
Mixed Herbs, 100 g (3 1/2 oz)	6
Regular, 100 g (3 1/2 oz)	6
Spinach, 100 g (3 1/2 oz)	6
Three-Flavour, 100 g (3 1/2 oz)	9
Whole Wheat, 100 g (3 1/2 oz)	6

SAUCES

Sauce à l'Ail, 100 g (3 1/2 oz)	12
Sauce Alfredo, 100 g (3 1/2 oz)	6
Sauce Arabiata, 100 g (3 1/2 oz)	3
Sauce Atlantique, 100 g (3 1/2 oz)	4
Sauce aux Fines Herbes, 100 g (3 1/2 oz)	14

	PointsPlus® value
Sauce Bavaroise, 100 g (3 1/2 oz)	4
Sauce Bayonne, 100 g (3 1/2 oz)	3
Sauce Bolognèse, 100 g (3 1/2 oz)	4
Sauce Cacciatore, 100 g (3 1/2 oz)	3
Sauce Calabrèse, 100 g (3 1/2 oz)	12
Sauce Californienne, 100 g (3 1/2 oz)	3
Sauce Carbonara, 100 g (3 1/2 oz)	6
Sauce Cardinal, 100 g (3 1/2 oz)	3
Sauce Créole, 100 g (3 1/2 oz)	3
Sauce Florentine, 100 g (3 1/2 oz)	4
Sauce Gorgonzola, 100 g (3 1/2 oz)	5
Sauce Grenoble, 100 g (3 1/2 oz)	5
Sauce Manhattan, 100 g (3 1/2 oz)	2
Sauce Méditéranéenne, 100 g (3 1/2 oz)	3
Sauce Mexicaine, 100 g (3 1/2 oz)	8
Sauce Montagnaise, 100 g (3 1/2 oz)	5
Sauce Moule Rosa, 100 g (3 1/2 oz)	4
Sauce Napolitain, 100 g (3 1/2 oz)	3
Sauce Orientale, 100 g (3 1/2 oz)	5
Sauce Orléans, 100 g (3 1/2 oz)	3
Sauce Pesto, 100 g (3 1/2 oz)	15
Sauce Printanière, 100 g (3 1/2 oz)	3
Sauce Putanesca, 100 g (3 1/2 oz)	3
Sauce Ratatouille, 100 g (3 1/2 oz)	3
Sauce Romanoff, 100 g (3 1/2 oz)	4
Sauce Rosée, 100 g (3 1/2 oz)	5
Sauce Royale, 100 g (3 1/2 oz)	4
Sauce St-Jacques, 100 g (3 1/2 oz)	4
Sauce Stroganoff, 100 g (3 1/2 oz)	3
Sauce Tériyaki, 100 g (3 1/2 oz)	4
Sauce Trois Fromage, 100 g (3 1/2 oz)	5
Sauce Végétarienne, 100 g (3 1/2 oz)	2
Sauce Vongole, 100 g (3 1/2 oz)	3
Sauce Zuricoise, 100 g (3 1/2 oz)	3

 Power Foods	*PointsPlus®* value
PANINIS	
Chicken, 100 g (3 1/2 oz)	7
Chicken & Goat Cheese, 100 g (3 1/2 oz)	8
Ham & Cheese, 100 g (3 1/2 oz)	7
Smoked Salmon, 100 g (3 1/2 oz)	7
Vegetarian, 100 g (3 1/2 oz)	7

 Power Foods	*PointsPlus®* value

WAIT LESS PLATTERS (SERVED WITH SIDE SALAD, FRESH FRUIT SALAD & COTTAGE CHEESE)

Chick'n' Lick'n® Wait Less Platter, 1 serving	9
Gobbler® Wait Less Platter, 1 serving	11
Homeburger® Wait Less Platter, 1 serving	14
Nature Burger® Wait Less Platter, 1 serving	12

CHILI

Beef Chili, 1 serving	7
Nature Chili® – soy based vegetarian chili, 1 serving	6

SANDWICHES (NO TOPPINGS)

Lick's Triple Cheese Blend – Mozzarella, Monterey Jack and Medium Cheddar, 1	3
Chick'n' Lick'n® on Whole Wheat Enriched Bun, 1	6
Chick'n' Lick'n® – chicken breast – no bun, 1	2
Cottage Cheese – 4%, 1	2
Gobbler® – turkey patty – no bun, 1	4
Gobbler® on Whole Wheat Enriched Bun, 1	8
Homeburger® – beef patty – no bun, 1	7
Homeburger® on Whole Wheat Enriched Bun, 1	11
Nature Burger® – soy based vegetarian patty – no bun, 1	5
Nature Burger® on Whole Wheat Enriched Bun, 1	8
White Bun, 1	7
Whole Wheat Enriched Bun, 1	4

MCDONALD'S®

▲ Power Foods   *PointsPlus*® value   ▲ Power Foods   *PointsPlus*® value

SANDWICHES

Big Mac®, 1 serving	14
Big Xtra®, 1 serving	14
Double Quarter Pounder® without Cheese, 1 serving	17
Hamburger, 1 serving	6
McDouble™, 1 serving	10
Bacon Cheeseburger, 1 serving	9
Cheeseburger, 1 serving	8
Double Cheeseburger, 1 serving	11
Quarter Pounder® with Cheese, 1 serving	14
Angus Bacon & Cheese, 1 serving	21
Angus Deluxe, 1 serving	21
Angus Mushroom and Swiss Burger, 1 serving	20
Crispy Chicken Classic Sandwich, 1 serving	12
Grilled Chicken Classic Sandwich, 1 serving	10
Junior Chicken Sandwich, 1 serving	10
McChicken® Sandwich, 1 serving	13
Southwest Crispy Chicken Sandwich, 1 serving	16
Southwest Grilled Chicken Sandwich, 1 serving	13
Grilled Chicken Snack Wrap®, 1 serving	6
Mac Snack Wrap, 1 serving	9
Spicy Buffalo Chicken Snack Wrap®, 1 serving	7
Spicy Buffalo Chicken Snack Wrap® with Grilled Chicken, 1 serving	6
BLT Sandwich, 1 serving	12
Chicken Fajita, 1 serving	5
Filet-O-Fish® Sandwich, 1 serving	11
Grilled Cheese Sandwich, 1 serving	7

FRENCH FRIES

French Fries – Small, 1 serving	6
French Fries – Medium, 1 serving	10
French Fries – Large, 1 serving	15

CHICKEN McNUGGETS®

White Meat Chicken McNuggets® (4), 1 serving	6
White Meat Chicken McNuggets® (6), 1 serving	9
White Meat Chicken McNuggets® (10), 1 serving	15
White Meat Chicken McNuggets® (20), 1 serving	30
Barbeque Sauce, 1 serving	1
Honey Sauce, 1 serving	2
Sweet & Sour Sauce, 1 serving	1

SALADS

Mighty Caesar Entrée Salad, 1 serving	6
Mighty Caesar Entrée with Warm Crispy Chicken, 1 serving	11
Mighty Caesar Entrée with Warm Grilled Chicken, 1 serving	9
Side Caesar Salad, 1 serving	3
Side Garden Fresh Salad, 1 serving	1
Spicy Thai Chicken Salad with Warm Grilled Chicken, 1 serving	5
Spicy Thai Chicken with Warm Crispy Chicken, 1 serving	7
Spicy Thai Salad, 1 serving	2

SALAD DRESSINGS

Renée's® Asian Sesame Dressing, 1 packet	4
Renée's® Balsamic Vinaigrette, 1 packet	3

MCDONALD'S®

▲ Power Foods	*PointsPlus®* value
Renée's® Mighty Caesar Dressing, 1 packet	8
Renée's® Mighty Caesar Light Dressing, 1 packet	4
Renée's® Ravin' Raspberry Vinaigrette, 1 packet	2

BREAKFAST

Bacon & Egg Bagel, 1 serving	14
Bacon 'n Egg McMuffin® Sandwich, 1 serving	8
Bacon, Egg & Cheese McGriddles® Sandwich, 1 serving	11
Breakfast BLT Bagel, 1 serving	13
Breakfast Burrito, 1 serving	8
Egg McMuffin® Sandwich, 1 serving	8
English Muffin with Trans Fat Free Liquid Margarine, 1 serving	5
Hash Browns, 1 serving	4
Hotcakes with Syrup and Becel® Margarine, 1 serving	15
Sausage McGriddles® Sandwich, 1 serving	11
Sausage McMuffin® with Egg Sandwich, 1 serving	12
Sausage, Egg & Cheese McGriddles® Sandwich, 1 serving	15

MUFFINS

Muffin – Blueberry, 1 serving	11
Muffin – Carrot, 1 serving	12
Muffin – Cranberry Orange, 1 serving	10
Muffin – Double Chocolate with Oreo® Crumble, 1 serving	12
Muffin – Fruit & Fibre, 1 serving	10
Muffin – Golden Bran & Raisin, 1 serving	10

▲ Power Foods	*PointsPlus®* value

CONDIMENTS

Becel Margarine Portions, 1 portion	2
Big Mac® Sauce Packet, 1 packet	2
Granulated Nuts Packet, 1 packet	1
Ketchup Packet, 1 packet	0
Peanut Butter Packet, 1 packet	3
Salsa Sauce Packet, 1 packet	0
Vinegar Packet, 1 packet	0

DESSERTS

Apple Slices with Caramel Dip, 1 serving	3
Baked Apple Pie, 1 serving	8
Cinnamon Melts®, 1 serving	13
Cone – Vanilla, 1 serving	6
Fruit 'n Yogurt Parfait, 1 serving	5
McFlurry® Dessert – Oreo®, Small, 1 serving	14
McFlurry® Dessert – Oreo®, Large, 1 serving	19
McFlurry® Dessert – Rolo®, Small, 1 serving	15
McFlurry® Dessert – Rolo®, Large, 1 serving	19
McFlurry® Dessert – Smarties®, Small, 1 serving	14
McFlurry® Dessert – Smarties®, Large, 1 serving	19
'Original Recipe' McDonaldland® Cookies, 1 serving	5
'Original Recipe' McDonaldland® Cookies – Fun Size, 1 serving	1
Sundae – Hot Caramel, 1 serving	10
Sundae – Hot Fudge, 1 serving	9
Sundae – Strawberry, 1 serving	8

▲ Power Foods	PointsPlus® value

TRIPLE THICK MILKSHAKE®/ McFLURRY® DESSERTS

Triple Thick Milkshake® – Chocolate, Small, 1 serving	15
Triple Thick Milkshake® – Chocolate, Medium, 1 serving	21
Triple Thick Milkshake® – Chocolate, Large, 1 serving	32
Triple Thick Milkshake® – Strawberry, Small, 1 serving	15
Triple Thick Milkshake® – Strawberry, Medium, 1 serving	20
Triple Thick Milkshake® – Strawberry, Large, 1 serving	30
Triple Thick Milkshake® – Vanilla, Small, 1 serving	15
Triple Thick Milkshake® – Vanilla, Medium, 1 serving	20
Triple Thick Milkshake® – Vanilla, Large, 1 serving	30

BEVERAGES

1% Partly Skimmed Milk, 1 serving (200 ml [6 1/2 fl oz])	2
1% Partly Skimmed Milk, 1 serving (250 ml [8 fl oz])	3
1% Party Skimmed Chocolate Milk, 1 serving (200 ml [6 1/2 fl oz])	4
1% Partly Skimmed Chocolate Milk, 1 serving (250 ml [8 fl oz])	5
Apple Juice, 1 serving	2
Barq's® Root Beer – Small, 1 serving	4
Barq's® Root Beer – Medium, 1 serving	6
Barq's® Root Beer – Large, 1 serving	9
Barq's® Root Beer – Child, 1 serving	3
Caramel Iced Coffee – Small, 1 serving	3

▲ Power Foods	PointsPlus® value
Caramel Iced Coffee – Large, 1 serving	6
Carnation Hot Chocolate – Small, 1 serving	5
Coca-Cola® – Small, 1 serving	4
Coca-Cola® – Medium, 1 serving	6
Coca-Cola® – Large, 1 serving	9
Coca-Cola® – Child, 1 serving	3
Coca-Cola Zero® – Small, 1 serving	0
Coca-Cola Zero® – Medium, 1 serving	0
Coca-Cola Zero® – Large, 1 serving	0
Coca-Cola Zero® – Child, 1 serving	0
Diet Coke® – Small, 1 serving	0
Diet Coke® – Medium, 1 serving	0
Diet Coke® – Large, 1 serving	0
Diet Coke® – Child, 1 serving	0
Fruitopia® Strawberry Passion Awareness® – Small, 1 serving	5
Fruitopia® Strawberry Passion Awareness® – Medium, 1 serving	7
Fruitopia® Strawberry Passion Awareness® – Large, 1 serving	10
Fruitopia® Strawberry Passion Awareness® – Child, 1 serving	3
Hot Chocolate – Small, 1 serving	5
Iced Coffee – Small, 1 serving	3
Iced Coffee – Large, 1 serving	6
Nescafé Frothy – French Vanilla (Small), 1 serving	5
Nescafé Frothy – Mackintosh Toffee (Small), 1 serving	5
Nestea® Iced Tea – Small, 1 serving	3
Nestea® Iced Tea – Medium, 1 serving	4
Nestea® Iced Tea – Large, 1 serving	6
Nestea® Iced Tea – Child, 1 serving	2
Orange Juice – Small, 1 serving	4
Orange Juice – Medium, 1 serving	5

MCDONALD'S®

▲ Power Foods	PointsPlus® value
Orange Juice – Large, 1 serving	6
Sprite® – Small, 1 serving	4
Sprite® – Medium, 1 serving	6
Sprite® – Large, 1 serving	8
Sprite® – Child, 1 serving	3
Vanilla Iced Coffee – Small, 1 serving	3
Vanilla Iced Coffee – Large, 1 serving	6

The menu items listed above are available at participating McDonald's® restaurants in Canada. Some menu items may not be available at all restaurants. Menu items are subject to change without notice. For the most current nutritional information, visit www.mcdonalds.ca.

▲ Power Foods	PointsPlus® value

ANTIPASTI

Bite-sized sausages starter, 1 serving	8
Fried Calamari, 1 serving	8
Fries, 1 small serving	14
Fries, 1 large serving	26
Garlic Bread Au Gratin, 1 serving	9
Italian Poutine, 1 serving	25
Mixed Platter, 1 serving	34
Pizza bread, 1 serving	16
Poutine, 1 serving	24
Sausage & Meatball Duetto, 1 serving	18
Spicy Fries, 1 small serving	14
Spicy Fries, 1 large serving	24
Sunshine Dip, 1 serving	22
Tomatoes and Bocconcini*, 1 serving	14

SOUP

Beef and Barley, 1 serving	2
Chicken Noodle, 1 serving	3
Cream of Broccoli, 1 serving	5
Cream of Carrot, 1 serving	4
Cream of Mushroom, 1 serving	5
Cream of Potato and Leek, 1 serving	6
Minestrone, 1 serving	3
Turkey and Wild Rice, 1 serving	2

INSALATA

Caesar, 1 small serving	5
Caesar, 1 entrée serving	10
Chicken and Pasta, 1 serving	24
Chicken Caesar, 1 serving	13
Fruits de Mer*, 1 serving	25
House, 1 small serving	10

▲ Power Foods	PointsPlus® value
House, 1 entrée serving	19
Salmon Salad, 1 serving	22

PASTA

Campagnola Pennine with Bite-Sized Sausages, 1 serving	25
Campagnola Pennine with Bite-Sized Sausages, 1/2 portion	12
Campagnola Pennine with Chicken, 1 serving	22
Campagnola Pennine with Chicken, 1/2 portion	11
Chicken & Broccoli Pennine, 1 serving	23
Fettucine Alfredo, 1 serving	19
Fettucine Carbonara, 1 serving	27
Fettucine Carbonara, 1/2 portion	13
Lasagna Classica, 1 serving	25
Lasagna Classica, 1/2 portion	13
Lasagne di Mikes*, 1 serving	46
Linguine al Diavolo*, 1 serving	20
Linguine al Salmone, 1 serving	27
Linguine al Salmone, 1/2 portion	15
Linguine di Mare*, 1 serving	29
Linguine di Mare*, 1/2 portion	15
Manicotti Parmigiana, 1 serving	22
Pennine Arrabbiata, 1 serving	14

MIKES RESTAURANTS

▲ Power Foods	PointsPlus® value
Pennine Arrabbiata, 1/2 portion	7
Seafood Linguine, 1 serving	22
Seafood Linguine, 1/2 portion	12
Spaghetti with Meat Sauce, 1 serving	21
Spaghetti with Meat Sauce, 1/2 portion	10
Spaghetti with Meatballs, 1 serving	26
Tortellini with Rosée Sauce, 1 serving	32

PASTA COMBINATIONS*

Pasta (spaghetti, pennine, fettucine, linguine), 1 serving	1
Alfredo Sauce, 1 serving	1
Arrabbiata Sauce, 1 serving	0
Meat Sauce, 1 serving	1
Neapolitan Sauce, 1 serving	0
Rosée Sauce, 1 serving	1
Bite-Sized Meatballs, 5 meatballs	6
Bite-Sized Sausages, 5 sausages	4
Campagnola Shrimp, 5 shrimp	2
Chicken Breast Strips, 1 serving	2
House Vegetables, 1 serving	2

GONDOLAS (NO SIDE)

Asparagus & Capicollo, 1 serving	13
Chicken, Bacon and Cheddar, 1 serving	20
Four-Cheese, 1 serving	17
Philly Steak and Pepper Sauce, 1 serving	18
Shrimp, 1 serving	16
Vegetable and Goat Cheese, 1 serving	15

▲ Power Foods	PointsPlus® value

SUNSHINE® PIZZAS

BBQ Chicken, 1 serving	30
Field of Dreams, 1 serving	26

CLASSIC PIZZAS

All-Dressed (regular crust), 1 serving (15 cm [6"] pizza)	15
All-Dressed (regular crust), 1 serving (22 cm [9"] pizza)	32
All-Dressed (regular crust), 1 serving (30 cm [12"] pizza)	49
All-Dressed (thin crust), 1 serving (15 cm [6"] pizza)	11
All-Dressed (thin crust), 1 serving (22 cm [9"] pizza)	25
All-Dressed (thin crust), 1 serving (30 cm [12"] pizza)	42
Calabrese (regular crust), 1 serving (15 cm [6"] pizza)	16
Calabrese (regular crust), 1 serving (22 cm [9"] pizza)	32
Calabrese (regular crust), 1 serving (30 cm [12"] pizza)	48
Calabrese (thin crust), 1 serving (15 cm [6"] pizza)	12
Calabrese (thin crust), 1 serving (22 cm [9"] pizza)	25
Calabrese (thin crust), 1 serving (30 cm [12"] pizza)	40
Carbonara (regular crust), 1 serving (15 cm [6"] pizza)	14
Carbonara (regular crust), 1 serving (22 cm [9"] pizza)	31
Carbonara (regular crust), 1 serving (30 cm [12"] pizza)	46
Carbonara (thin crust), 1 serving (15 cm [6"] pizza)	11
Carbonara (thin crust), 1 serving (22 cm [9"] pizza)	24

MIKES RESTAURANTS

Power Foods	PointsPlus® value
Carbonara (thin crust), 1 serving (30 cm [12"] pizza)	38
Carnivore (regular crust), 1 serving (15 cm [6"] pizza)	17
Carnivore (regular crust), 1 serving (22 cm [9"] pizza)	35
Carnivore (regular crust), 1 serving (30 cm [12"] pizza)	59
Carnivore (thin crust), 1 serving (15 cm [6"] pizza)	13
Carnivore (thin crust), 1 serving (22 cm [9"] pizza)	27
Carnivore (thin crust), 1 serving (30 cm [12"] pizza)	51
Chicken Alfredo (regular crust), 1 serving (15 cm [6"] pizza)	12
Chicken Alfredo (regular crust), 1 serving (22 cm [9"] pizza)	23
Chicken Alfredo (regular crust), 1 serving (30 cm [12"] pizza)	36
Chicken Alfredo (thin crust), 1 serving (15 cm [6"] pizza)	8
Chicken Alfredo (thin crust), 1 serving (22 cm [9"] pizza)	16
Chicken Alfredo (thin crust), 1 serving (30 cm [12"] pizza)	29
Hawaiian (regular crust), 1 serving (15 cm [6"] pizza)	14
Hawaiian (regular crust), 1 serving (22 cm [9"] pizza)	28
Hawaiian (regular crust), 1 serving (30 cm [12"] pizza)	41
Hawaiian (thin crust), 1 serving (15 cm [6"] pizza)	10
Hawaiian (thin crust), 1 serving (22 cm [9"] pizza)	20
Hawaiian (thin crust), 1 serving (30 cm [12"] pizza)	34
International (regular crust), 1 serving (15 cm [6"] pizza)	17
International (regular crust), 1 serving (22 cm [9"] pizza)	39

Power Foods	PointsPlus® value
International (regular crust), 1 serving (30 cm [12"] pizza)	59
International (thin crust), 1 serving (15 cm [6"] pizza)	13
International (thin crust), 1 serving (22 cm [9"] pizza)	32
International (thin crust), 1 serving (30 cm [12"] pizza)	51
Margherita (regular crust), 1 serving (22 cm [9"] pizza)	28
Margherita (regular crust), 1 serving (30 cm [12"] pizza)	44
Margherita (thin crust), 1 serving (22 cm [9"] pizza)	20
Margherita (thin crust), 1 serving (30 cm [12"] pizza)	37
Neapolitan (regular crust), 1 serving (15 cm [6"] pizza)	13
Neapolitan (regular crust), 1 serving (22 cm [9"] pizza)	28
Neapolitan (regular crust), 1 serving (30 cm [12"] pizza)	42
Neapolitan (thin crust), 1 serving (15 cm [6"] pizza)	10
Neapolitan (thin crust), 1 serving (22 cm [9"] pizza)	20
Neapolitan (thin crust), 1 serving (30 cm [12"] pizza)	34
Pepperoni (regular crust), 1 serving (15 cm [6"] pizza)	14
Pepperoni (regular crust), 1 serving (22 cm [9"] pizza)	32
Pepperoni (regular crust), 1 serving (30 cm [12"] pizza)	48
Pepperoni (thin crust), 1 serving (15 cm [6"] pizza)	11
Pepperoni (thin crust), 1 serving (22 cm [9"] pizza)	24
Pepperoni (thin crust), 1 serving (30 cm [12"] pizza)	41
Polpette (regular crust), 1 serving (22 cm [9"] pizza)	30

MIKES RESTAURANTS

Classic Pizzas (cont'd)

▲ Power Foods	*PointsPlus®* value
Polpette (regular crust), 1 serving (30 cm [12"] pizza)	45
Polpette (thin crust), 1 serving (22 cm [9"] pizza)	23
Polpette (thin crust), 1 serving (30 cm [12"] pizza)	37
Seafood (regular crust), 1 serving (15 cm [6"] pizza)	15
Seafood (regular crust), 1 serving (22 cm [9"] pizza)	33
Seafood (regular crust), 1 serving (30 cm [12"] pizza)	51
Seafood (thin crust), 1 serving (15 cm [6"] pizza)	12
Seafood (thin crust), 1 serving (22 cm [9"] pizza)	26
Seafood (thin crust), 1 serving (30 cm [12"] pizza)	43
Three-Cheese (regular crust), 1 serving (15 cm [6"] pizza)	13
Three-Cheese (regular crust), 1 serving (22 cm [9"] pizza)	28
Three-Cheese (regular crust), 1 serving (30 cm [12"] pizza)	40
Three-Cheese (thin crust), 1 serving (15 cm [6"] pizza)	9
Three-Cheese (thin crust), 1 serving (22 cm [9"] pizza)	20
Three-Cheese (thin crust), 1 serving (30 cm [12"] pizza)	32
Vegetarian (regular crust), 1 serving (15 cm [6"] pizza)	13
Vegetarian (regular crust), 1 serving (22 cm [9"] pizza)	27
Vegetarian (regular crust), 1 serving (30 cm [12"] pizza)	41
Vegetarian (thin crust), 1 serving (15 cm [6"] pizza)	9
Vegetarian (thin crust), 1 serving (22 cm [9"] pizza)	20
Vegetarian (thin crust), 1 serving (30 cm [12"] pizza)	33

▲ Power Foods	*PointsPlus®* value
HOT ITALIAN SUBS (NO SIDES)	
Chicken, 1 (17 cm [7"])	12
Chicken, 1 (25 cm [10"])	17
Co-Star®, 1 (17 cm [7"])	14
Co-Star®, 1 (25 cm [10"])	21
Delirio di Mikes, 1 (17 cm [7"])	13
Delirio di Mikes, 1 (25 cm [10"])	19
Encore, 1 (17 cm [7"])	11
Encore, 1 (25 cm [10"])	16
Hot Luke®, 1 (17 cm [7"])	17
Hot Luke®, 1 (25 cm [10"])	25
Parrain® au Gratin, 1 (17 cm [7"])	15
Parrain® au Gratin, 1 (25 cm [10"])	21
Pompei di Mikes, 1 (17 cm [7"])	20
Pompei di Mikes, 1 (25 cm [10"])	27
Primavera di Mikes, 1 (17 cm [7"])	14
Primavera di Mikes, 1 (25 cm [10"])	20
Superstar®, 1 (17 cm [7"])	14
Superstar®, 1 (25 cm [10"])	20
FOCACCIAS (NO SIDE)	
Chicken and Bacon, 1 serving	19
Chicken and Marinated Vegetables, 1 serving	16
Soprano di Mikes, 1 serving	22
The Classic Hamburger, 1 serving	16
The Classic Hamburger with Bacon, 1 serving	19
The Classic Hamburger with Cheese, 1 serving	19
The Classic Hamburger with Cheese and Bacon, 1 serving	22
The Siciliano Hamburger, 1 serving	22

MIKES RESTAURANTS

▲ Power Foods

PointsPlus® value

SPECIALITÀ TRATTORIA (INCLUDES HOUSE VEGETABLES, BUT NOT A CHOICE OF SIDE)

Chicken Campagnola, 1 serving	14
Chicken Campagnola, 1/2 portion	11
Chicken Parmigiana, 1 serving	11
Osso Bucco*, 1 portion	15
Osso Bucco*, 2 portions	26
Roasted Salmon, 1 serving	9
Scaloppine di Vitello al Limone*, 1 serving	16
Tilapia Fillet Campagnola, 1 serving	7
Tilapia Fillet*, 1 serving	17
Veal Campagnola, 1 serving	14
Veal Parmigiana, 1 serving	12

DUETTOS

All-Dressed Pizza (regular) and Caesar Salad, 1 serving	23
All-Dressed Pizza (thin) and Caesar Salad, 1 serving	19
All-Dressed Pizza and Spaghetti with Meat sauce, 1 serving	28
Carbonara Pizza and Fettuccine Carbonara, 1 serving	35
Cheese and Tomato Bruschetta Rolls and Fettuccine Bruschetta, 1 serving	31
Cheese and Tomato Bruschetta Rolls and Fettuccine Carbonara, 1 serving	31
Goat Cheese and Vegetable Pizza and Linguine Alfredo with Mushrooms, 1 serving	29
International Pizza (regular) and Pennine with Meat Sauce, 1 serving	28
International Pizza (thin) and Pennine with Meat Sauce, 1 serving	24

▲ Power Foods

PointsPlus® value

Margherita Pizza and Pennine with Neapolitan Sauce Napolitaine, 1 serving	22
Philly Steak Sub and Pennine with Meat Sauce, 1 serving	21
Seafood Pizza (regular) and Fettucine Alfredo, 1 serving	28
Seafood Pizza (thin) and Fettucine Alfredo, 1 serving	24
Spaghetti with Meat sauce and Caesar Salad, 1 serving	19
Vegetarian Pizza and Pennine with Rosée Sauce, 1 serving	24

SIDES

Fries, 1 serving	14
Garlic Bread, 1 serving	6
House Vegetables, 1 serving	2
Linguine with Campagnola Sauce, 1 serving	7
Linguine with Neapolitan Sauce, 1 serving	7
Pennine with Neapolitan Sauce, 1 serving	4
Spicy Fries, 1 serving	14
Three-Herb Potatoes, 1 serving	9

BEVERAGES

2% Milk, 1 small serving	3
2% Milk, 1 large serving	5
Apple Juice, 1 small serving	3
Apple Juice, 1 large serving	4
Orange Juice, 1 small serving	3
Orange Juice, 1 large serving	4
Soda (Diet Pepsi), 1 serving	0
Soda (Pepsi), 1 serving	6
Tomato Juice, 1 small serving	1
Tomato Juice, 1 large serving	1

MIKES RESTAURANTS

▲ Power Foods

	PointsPlus® value
Vegetable Cocktail, 1 small serving	1
Vegetable Cocktail, 1 large serving	2

DESSERTS

Apple Crisp, 1 serving	23
Apple Indulgence, 1 serving	13
Brownie Eruption, 1 serving	33
Double Chocolate Indulgence, 1 serving	14
Dulce de Leche Cheesecake, 1 serving	17
Espresso Chocolate Cake, 1 serving	20
Piccolo Vesuvio, 1 serving	21
Pizzelato with Berry Syrup, 1 serving	8
Pizzelato with Brown Sugar Sauce, 1 serving	11
Pizzelato with Caramel Sauce, 1 serving	11
Pizzelato with Chocolate Sauce, 1 serving	9
Pizzelato with Strawberry Syrup, 1 serving	9
Praline Indulgence, 1 serving	19
Profiterole Trio, 1 serving	18
Sugar Pie, 1 serving	15
Sugar Pie with Ice Cream, 1 serving	18
The Alps, 1 serving	24
Tiramisu, 1 serving	12

*Offered in Trattoria di Mikes Restaurants.

▲ Power Foods | *PointsPlus®* value

APPETIZERS
(SERVING SIZE BASED ON 1/4 OF APPETIZER)

Chicken Souvlaki Stick, 1 stick	4
Garlic Bun, 1	8
Hummus, 28 g (1 oz)	1
Mediterranean Spinach Dip, 57 g (2 oz)	5
MR. GREEK® Fried Kalamari, 85 g (3 oz)	5
MR. GREEK® Grilled Kalamari, 85 g (3 oz)	4
Pork Souvlaki Stick, 1 stick	5
Saganaki, 28 g (1 oz)	5
Spanakopita, 28 g (1 oz)	2
Tzatziki, 28 g (1 oz)	1
Vienna Bread Slice, 1 slice	4
Whole Wheat Pita Bread, 1	4

SALADS

Caesar Salad (with dressing), 1 side serving	9
Caesar Salad (with dressing), 1 regular serving	14
Caesar Salad (with dressing), 1 entrée serving	14
Chicken Caesar (with dressing), 1 medium serving	16
Chicken Village (with dressing), 1 regular serving	15
Greek Salad (without dressing), 1 side serving	3
Greek Salad (without dressing), 1 regular serving	5
Greek Salad (without dressing), 1 entrée serving	5
Chicken Greek (without dressing), 1 medium serving	7
MR. GREEK® Dressing, 57 ml (2 fl oz)	9

▲ Power Foods | *PointsPlus®* value

SPANIKOPITA & GREEK SALAD

Spanikopita & Greek Salad, 1 serving	10

PERFECT PITAS®
(INCLUDES SANDWICH TOPPINGS)

Chicken Filet Pita, 1	7
Chicken Souvlaki Pita, 1	9
Falafel Pita, 1	11
Pork Souvlaki Pita, 1	11
Traditional Gyro Pita, 1	16
Veggie Pita, 1	8
Add Feta, 28 g (1 oz)	2

WRAPS (INCLUDES SANDWICH TOPPINGS)

Chicken Caesar Wrap, 1	17
Chicken Greek Wrap, 1	18

ORIGINAL SOUVLAKI
(WITHOUT SIDE OPTIONS)

Original Chicken, 2 pieces	8
Original Pork, 2 pieces	11
Original Pork, 3 pieces	16

MR. GREEK® EXPRESS

PointsPlus® value

PointsPlus® value

CLASSIC SOUVLAKI
(WITHOUT SIDE OPTIONS)

Classic Chicken, 1 serving	7
Classic Lamb, 1 serving	11
Classic Pork, 1 serving	14

GYROS (WITHOUT SIDE OPTIONS)

Classic Gyro, 1 serving	22
Original Gyro, 1 serving	16

BURGERS

Chicken Filet, 1	3
Hercules Burger, 1	23
Prime Rib Burger, 1	19
Swiss Cheese, 1 slice	2
Cheddar Cheese, 1 slice	2

MEAL SIDES

French Fries (fried in trans fat free oil, from frozen), 1 serving (with meal)	13
MR. GREEK® Rice, 1 serving (with meal)	11
MR. GREEK® Potatoes, 1 serving (with meal)	5
Roasted Seasonal Vegetables, 1 serving (with meal)	2
Sauteed Green Beans, 1 serving (with meal)	4

SIDES

French Fries (Fried in trans fat free oil, from frozen), 1 serving	8
MR. GREEK® Fries, 1 serving	21
MR. GREEK® Potatoes, 1 serving	7
MR. GREEK® Rice, 1 serving	20
Roasted Seasonal Vegetables, 1 serving	3
Sauteed Green Beans, 1 serving	7

KID'S MENU

Cyclops Souvlaki with Pita (chicken), 1 serving	4
Cyclops Souvlaki with Pita (pork), 1 serving	8
Herc's Chicken Strips, 1 serving	4
Super Hero Gyro, 1 serving	8

DESSERT

Classic Baklava, 1 piece	4

MR. GREEK® MEDITERRANEAN GRILL

▲ Power Foods

PointsPlus® value

APPETIZERS
(SERVING SIZE BASED ON 1/4 OF APPETIZER)

Chicken Souvlaki Stick, 1	4
Garlic Shrimp Paros, 28 g (1 oz)	4
Grilled Octopus, 57 g (2 oz)	1
Gyro, 57 g (2 oz)	4
Keftedes, 1	5
Maria's Dolmades, 1 (57 g [2 oz])	6
MR. GREEK® Fried Kalamari, 85 g (3 oz)	5
MR. GREEK® Grilled Kalamari, 85 g (3 oz)	4
Pork Souvlaki Stick, 1	5
Saganaki, 28 g (1 oz)	5
Sautéed Mushrooms, 85 g (3 oz)	2
Shrimp Santorini, 28 g (1 oz)	5
Spanakopita, 28 g (1 oz)	2

SALADS

Caesar Salad, 1 entrée serving	14
Greek Salad, 1 entrée serving	5
Greek Salad with Chicken, 1 entrée serving	7
Greek Salad Dressing, 57 ml (2 fl oz)	9
Village Salad, 1 regular serving	13
Village Salad with Chicken, 1 entrée serving	15
Fire-Grilled Chicken Breast, 142 g (5 oz)	2
Grilled Kalamari, 142 g (5 oz)	8
Grilled Salmon Filet, 227 g (8 oz)	12
Grilled Shrimp, 5 shrimp	4

BREADS & HOT DIPS
(SERVING SIZE BASED ON 1/4 OF APPETIZER)

Feta Bruschetta, 1/4 plate	6
Hummus, 28 g (1 oz)	2
Mediterranean Spinach Dip, 57 g (2 oz)	5

▲ Power Foods

PointsPlus® value

Taramosalata, 28 g (1 oz)	3
Tirokafteri, 28 ml (1 fl oz)	2
Tzatziki, 28 g (1 oz)	1
Whole Wheat Pita Bread, 1	4

SOUP OF THE DAY

Avgolemono, 250 ml (8 fl oz)	3
Fasolada, 250 ml (8 fl oz)	3
Lentil Soup, 250 ml (8 fl oz)	3

GRILLED & GREEK SPECIALTIES
(WITHOUT SIDE OPTIONS)

Fresh Taverna Chicken, 1/2 chicken	16
Grilled Chicken & Garlic Shrimp Paros, 1 serving	11
Grilled Chicken & Shrimp Santorini, 1 serving	13
Grilled Lamb Chops, 4 chops (113 g [4 oz] each)	19
Grilled Lamb Chops & Chicken Filet, 1 serving	13
Kotopoulo (Chicken filet), 2 pieces	4
Lamb "Anaki" Fournou, 284 g (10 oz)	23
Yiayia's Moussaka, 1 serving	23

MR. GREEK® MEDITERRANEAN GRILL

▲ Power Foods   *PointsPlus®* value   ▲ Power Foods   *PointsPlus®* value

PASTA & SEAFOODS
(WITHOUT SIDE OPTIONS)

Garlic Shrimp Paros, 1 serving	15
Keftedes and Spaghetti, 1 serving	42
MR. GREEK® Fried Kalamari, 1 serving	19
MR. GREEK® Grilled Kalamari, 1 serving	25
Roasted Vegetable Penne, 1 serving	31
Salmon Filet, 1 serving	22
Shrimp Linguine, 1 serving	29
Shrimp Santorini, 1 serving	19
Taverna Chicken Penne, 1 serving	45

HOT OFF THE GRILL®

Full Rack Ribs, 510 g (18 oz)	50
Ribeye, 340 g (12 oz)	13
Striploin, 284 g (10 oz)	14

WORLD FAMOUS SOUVLAKI & GYROS
(WITHOUT SIDE OPTIONS)

Classic Chicken Gyro, 1 serving	15
Classic Gyro, 1 serving	22
Original Chicken Gyro, 1 serving	12
Original Gyro, 1 serving	16
Classic Chicken Souvlaki, 1 serving	7
Classic Lamb Souvlaki, 1 serving	11
Classic Pork Souvlaki, 1 serving	14
Original Chicken Souvlaki, 2 (85 g [3 oz] each)	8
Original Pork Souvlaki, 2 (85 g [3 oz] each)	16
Vegetable Souvlaki, 1 skewer	5

TRADITIONAL FARE
(INCLUDES SANDWICH TOPPINGS)

Chicken Greek Wrap, 1 serving	14
Chicken Souvlaki Pita, 1 serving	9
Greek salad, 1 side serving	3
Gyro Pita, 1 serving	16
Island Fish & Chips, 1 serving	19
Pork Souvlaki Pita, 1 serving	11
Taverna Chicken, 1/4 chicken	8

MEAL SIDES

French Fries (Fried in trans fat free oil, from frozen), 1 serving (with meal)	8
French Fries (Fried in trans fat free oil, from frozen), 1 serving (with meal)	13
MR. GREEK® Potatoes, 1 serving (with meal)	5
MR. GREEK® Rice, 1 serving (with meal)	11
Roasted Seasonal Vegetables, 1 serving (with meal)	2
Sautéed Green Beans, 1 serving (with meal)	4

SIDES & EXTRAS

MR. GREEK® Potatoes, 1 serving	7
MR. GREEK® Rice, 1 serving	20
Roasted Seasonal Vegetables, 1 serving	3
Sautéed Green Beans, 1 serving	7
Extra Feta, 28 g (1 oz)	2

MR. GREEK® MEDITERRANEAN GRILL

▲ Power Foods

PointsPlus® value

KID'S MENU

Chicken Licken Penne, 1 serving	21
Cyclops Souvlaki with Pita (Chicken), 1 serving	8
Cyclops Souvlaki with Pita (Pork), 1 serving	8
Herc's Chicken Strips, 1 serving	4
Poseidon's Plate, 1 serving	6
Spanakopita, 1 serving	7
Super Hero Gyro, 1 serving	8

DESSERTS

Berry Burst, 1 serving	6
Choc-a-Lot, 1 serving	17
Classic Baklava, 1 serving	4
Cookies and Cream, 1 serving	17
French Vanilla Ice Cream, 1 serving	5
Key Lime Cheesecake, 1 serving	12
Mango Madness, 1 serving	12
Oh Fudge Caramel Caked, 1 serving	15
Tiramisu Cheesecake Wonder, 1 serving	12

OPA! SOUVLAKI OF GREECE

▲ Power Foods — PointsPlus® value

SALAD

Caesar Salad, 1 small serving	6
Caesar Salad, 1 large serving	9
Caesar Salad with Bacon Bits, 1 small serving	8
Caesar Salad with Bacon Bits, 1 large serving	11
Greek Salad, 1 small serving	5
Greek Salad, 1 large serving	8

SALAD & CALAMARI

Calamari with Caesar Salad, 1 serving	13
Calamari with Greek Salad, 1 serving	12

SALAD & SOUVLAKI

Chicken Souvlaki and Caesar Salad, 1 serving	15
Chicken Souvlaki and Greek Salad, 1 serving	15
Lamb Souvlaki and Caesar Salad, 1 serving	18
Lamb Souvlaki and Greek Salad, 1 serving	18

▲ Power Foods — PointsPlus® value

Pork Souvlaki and Caesar Salad, 1 serving	18
Pork Souvlaki and Greek Salad, 1 serving	18
Shrimp Souvlaki and Caesar Salad, 1 serving	14
Shrimp Souvlaki and Greek Salad, 1 serving	14

SOUVLAKI PLATTER

Chicken Souvlaki Platter with Caesar Salad, 1 serving	26
Chicken Souvlaki Platter with Greek Salad, 1 serving	26
Lamb Souvlaki Platter with Caesar Salad, 1 serving	29
Lamb Souvlaki Platter with Greek Salad, 1 serving	29
Pork Souvlaki Platter with Caesar Salad, 1 serving	29
Pork Souvlaki Platter with Greek Salad, 1 serving	29
Shrimp Souvlaki Platter with Caesar Salad, 1 serving	25

SPANIKOPITA PLATTER

Spanikopita Platter with Caesar Salad, 1 serving	14
Spanikopita Platter with Greek Salad, 1 serving	14
Spanikopita Platter with Rice and Potato, 1 serving	24

SOUVLAKI WRAP COMBOS

Chicken Pita Wrap Meal with Caesar Salad, 1 serving	15
Chicken Pita Wrap Meal with Fries, 1 serving	24

▲ Power Foods	*PointsPlus®* value
Chicken Pita Wrap Meal with Greek Salad, 1 serving	14
Lamb Pita Wrap Meal with Caesar Salad, 1 serving	18
Lamb Pita Wrap Meal with Fries, 1 serving	27
Lamb Pita Wrap Meal with Greek Salad, 1 serving	18
Pork Pita Wrap Meal with Caesar Salad, 1 serving	17
Pork Pita Wrap Meal with Fries, 1 serving	27
Pork Pita Wrap Meal with Greek Salad, 1 serving	17

PITA WRAP

	PointsPlus® value
Chicken Pita Wrap, 1 serving	10
Lamb Pita Wrap, 1 serving	13
Pork Pita Wrap, 1 serving	13
Veggie Pita with Jalapenos & Lettuce, 1 serving	9
Veggie Pita without Jalapenos & Lettuce, 1 serving	9
Add Feta Cheese to Pita Wrap, 1 serving	1

SIDES

	PointsPlus® value
Chicken Souvlaki, 1 serving	4
Lamb Souvlaki, 1 serving	7
OPA! Fries, 1 serving	14
OPA! Tzatziki, 1 serving (57 g [2 oz])	2
OPA! Tzatziki, 1 serving (113 g [4 oz])	4
OPA! Tzatziki, 1 serving (227 g [8 oz])	8
Pork Souvlaki, 1 serving	6
Shrimp Souvlaki, 1 serving	2
Side Calamari, 1 serving	11
Side Pita, 1 serving	6

▲ Power Foods	*PointsPlus®* value
Side Rice, 1 serving	9
Side Roasted Potato, 1 serving	5
Side Spanikopita, 1 serving	10

DESSERT

	PointsPlus® value
Baklava, 1	6

ORANGE JULIUS®

Power Foods	PointsPlus® value
JULIUS® FRUIT DRINKS	
Bananarilla® Julius, 1 small	10
Bananarilla® Julius, 1 medium	12
Bananarilla® Julius, 1 large	19
Blackberry Julius, 1 small	11
Blackberry Julius, 1 medium	14
Blackberry Julius, 1 large	22
Cool Cappuccino Julius, 1 small	15
Cool Cappuccino Julius, 1 medium	19
Cool Cappuccino Julius, 1 large	31
Cool Mocha Julius, 1 small	18
Cool Mocha Julius, 1 medium	22
Cool Mocha Julius, 1 large	36
Eggnog Julius, 1 small	10
Eggnog Julius, 1 medium	12
Eggnog Julius, 1 large	20
Lemon Julius, 1 small	8
Lemon Julius, 1 medium	10
Lemon Julius, 1 large	16
Mango Julius, 1 small	7
Mango Julius, 1 medium	9
Mango Julius, 1 large	14
Orange Julius, 1 small	7
Orange Julius, 1 medium	8
Orange Julius, 1 large	14
Peach Julius, 1 small	8
Peach Julius, 1 medium	10
Peach Julius, 1 large	16
Piña Colada Julius, 1 small	11
Piña Colada Julius, 1 medium	13
Piña Colada Julius, 1 large	21
Pineapple Julius, 1 small	7
Pineapple Julius, 1 medium	9
Pineapple Julius, 1 large	15
Pomegranate Julius, 1 small	7

Power Foods	PointsPlus® value
Pomegranate Julius, 1 medium	9
Pomegranate Julius, 1 large	15
Raspberry Julius, 1 small	8
Raspberry Julius, 1 medium	10
Raspberry Julius, 1 large	16
Strawberry Banana Julius, 1 small	11
Strawberry Banana Julius, 1 medium	13
Strawberry Banana Julius, 1 large	21
Strawberry Julius, 1 small	8
Strawberry Julius, 1 medium	10
Strawberry Julius, 1 large	17
Tripleberry® Julius, 1 small	11
Tripleberry® Julius, 1 medium	14
Tripleberry® Julius, 1 large	23
Tropical Julius, 1 small	11
Tropical Julius, 1 medium	13
Tropical Julius, 1 large	21
PREMIUM FRUIT SMOOTHIES	
3 Berry Blast, 1 small	7
3 Berry Blast, 1 medium	11
3 Berry Blast, 1 large	18
Banana Chill, 1 small	8
Banana Chill, 1 medium	13
Banana Chill, 1 large	17
Berry Banana Squeeze, 1 small	6
Berry Banana Squeeze, 1 medium	9
Berry Banana Squeeze, 1 large	13
Berry Lemon Lively, 1 small	7
Berry Lemon Lively, 1 medium	13
Berry Lemon Lively, 1 large	16
Blackberry Storm, 1 small	11
Blackberry Storm, 1 medium	18
Blackberry Storm, 1 large	24
Mango Passion, 1 small	5

Power Foods	PointsPlus® value
Mango Passion, 1 medium	8
Mango Passion, 1 large	11
Orange Swirl™, 1 small	10
Orange Swirl™, 1 medium	16
Orange Swirl™, 1 large	22
Peaches & Cream, 1 small	6
Peaches & Cream, 1 medium	9
Peaches & Cream, 1 large	13
Pomegranate & Berries, 1 small	6
Pomegranate & Berries, 1 medium	9
Pomegranate & Berries, 1 large	13
Raspberry Crème, 1 small	8
Raspberry Crème, 1 medium	13
Raspberry Crème, 1 large	17
Raspberry Crush, 1 small	4
Raspberry Crush, 1 medium	8
Raspberry Crush, 1 large	12
Strawberry Sensation, 1 small	7
Strawberry Sensation, 1 medium	10
Strawberry Sensation, 1 large	16
Strawberry Xtreme, 1 small	7
Strawberry Xtreme, 1 medium	9
Strawberry Xtreme, 1 large	14
Superberry, 1 small	10
Superberry, 1 medium	9
Superberry, 1 large	13
Tropi, 1 small	8
Tropi, 1 medium	14
Tropi, 1 large	19
Tropical Tango, 1 small	9
Tropical Tango, 1 medium	13
Tropical Tango, 1 large	19
Wild Blue Twist, 1 small	7
Wild Blue Twist, 1 medium	12
Wild Blue Twist, 1 large	16

Power Foods	PointsPlus® value
LIGHT PREMIUM FRUIT SMOOTHIES	
Strawberry Delight™, 1 small	3
Strawberry Delight™, 1 medium	9
Strawberry Delight™, 1 large	6
Berry Pom Twilight™, 1 small	3
Berry Pom Twilight™, 1 medium	6
Berry Pom Twilight™, 1 large	8
Pineapple Berry Daylight™, 1 small	3
Pineapple Berry Daylight™, 1 medium	6
Pineapple Berry Daylight™, 1 large	8
Tropical Sunlight™, 1 small	3
Tropical Sunlight™, 1 medium	5
Tropical Sunlight™, 1 large	7
TEA SMOOTHIES	
Blackberry White Tea, 1 small	6
Blackberry White Tea, 1 medium	9
Blackberry White Tea, 1 large	15
Peach White Tea, 1 small	8
Peach White Tea, 1 medium	10
Peach White Tea, 1 large	18
Raspberry White Tea, 1 small	7
Raspberry White Tea, 1 medium	11
Raspberry White Tea, 1 large	17
BOOSTS	
Banana, 1 serving	3
Fibre, 1 serving	0
Protein, 1 serving	1

ORANGE JULIUS®

Power Foods	PointsPlus® value
HOT DOGS	
Bacon Cheese Dog, 1	12
Cheese Dog, 1	12
Chili Cheese Dog, 1	9
Chili Melt Dog, 1	12
Classic Dog, 1	7
Pepperoni Cheese Dog, 1	12
Relish Dog, 1	11
Triple Cheese Dog, 1	14
DRINKS	
Pepsi®, 1 small	5
Pepsi®, 1 medium	6
Pepsi®, 1 large	9
Diet Pepsi, 1 small	0
Diet Pepsi, 1 medium	0
Diet Pepsi, 1 large	0
7-Up®, 1 small	5
7-Up®, 1 medium	6
7-Up®, 1 large	9
Lipton Brisk Iced Tea®, 1 small	3
Lipton Brisk Iced Tea®, 1 medium	4
Lipton Brisk Iced Tea®, 1 large	6
Minute Maid®, 1 small	6
Minute Maid®, 1 medium	7
Minute Maid®, 1 large	11
Coca, 1 small	5
Coca, 1 medium	6
Coca, 1 large	9
Diet Coca, 1 small	0
Diet Coca, 1 medium	0

Power Foods	PointsPlus® value
Diet Coca, 1 large	0
Barq's®, 1 small	5
Barq's®, 1 medium	7
Barq's®, 1 large	10
Sprite®, 1 small	5
Sprite®, 1 medium	6
Sprite®, 1 large	9
Nestea®, 1 small	3
Nestea®, 1 medium	4
Nestea®, 1 large	6
Bottled Water, 1	0

▲ Power Foods	*PointsPlus®* value
SIMPLE PIZZAS	
Cheese Hand-Tossed Crust Pizza, 1 slice	5
Cheese Multigrain Crust Pizza, 1 slice	5
Cheese Multigrain Thin Crust Pizza, 1 slice	4
Cheese Thin Crust Pizza, 1 slice	4
Garden Veggie Multigrain Crust Pizza, 1 slice	5
Ham & Pineapple Hand-Tossed Crust Pizza, 1 slice	5
Ham & Pineapple Multigrain Crust Pizza, 1 slice	5
Ham & Pineapple Multigrain Thin Crust Pizza, 1 slice	4
Ham & Pineapple Thin Crust Pizza, 1 slice	4
Pepperoni Hand-Tossed Crust Pizza, 1 slice	6
Pepperoni Multigrain Crust Pizza, 1 slice	5
Pepperoni Multigrain Thin Crust Pizza, 1 slice	4
Pepperoni Thin Crust Pizza, 1 slice	4
CARNE PIZZAS	
Bacon Cheeseburger Hand-Tossed Crust Pizza, 1 slice	7
Bacon Cheeseburger Multigrain Crust Pizza, 1 slice	6
Bacon Cheeseburger Multigrain Thin Crust Pizza, 1 slice	5
Bacon Cheeseburger Thin Crust Pizza, 1 slice	5
BBQ Steak Hand-Tossed Crust Pizza, 1 slice	6

▲ Power Foods	*PointsPlus®* value
BBQ Steak Multigrain Crust Pizza, 1 slice	6
BBQ Steak Multigrain Thin Crust Pizza, 1 slice	5
BBQ Steak Thin Crust Pizza, 1 slice	5
Beef Taco Hand-Tossed Crust Pizza, 1 slice	5
Beef Taco Multigrain Crust Pizza, 1 slice	5
Beef Taco Multigrain Thin Crust Pizza, 1 slice	4
Beef Taco Thin Crust Pizza, 1 slice	5
Chorizo Sausage & Goat Cheese Hand-Tossed Crust Pizza, 1 slice	6
Chorizo Sausage & Goat Cheese Multigrain Crust Pizza, 1 slice	5
Chorizo Sausage & Goat Cheese Multigrain Thin Crust Pizza, 1 slice	4
Chorizo Sausage & Goat Cheese Thin Crust Pizza, 1 slice	4
Deluxe Hawaiian Hand-Tossed Crust Pizza, 1 slice	6
Deluxe Hawaiian Multigrain Crust Pizza, 1 slice	6
Deluxe Hawaiian Multigrain Thin Crust Pizza, 1 slice	4
Deluxe Hawaiian Thin Crust Pizza, 1 slice	5
Genoa Classic Hand-Tossed Crust Pizza, 1 slice	6
Genoa Classic Multigrain Crust Pizza, 1 slice	6
Genoa Classic Multigrain Thin Crust Pizza, 1 slice	5
Genoa Classic Thin Crust Pizza, 1 slice	5
Italia Classic Hand-Tossed Crust Pizza, 1 slice	6
Italia Classic Multigrain Crust Pizza, 1 slice	5

PANAGO PIZZA

Carne Pizzas (cont'd)

▲ Power Foods	PointsPlus® value
Italia Classic Multigrain Thin Crust Pizza, 1 slice	5
Italia Classic Thin Crust Pizza, 1 slice	5
Meatball Hand-Tossed Crust Pizza, 1 slice	7
Meatball Multigrain Crust Pizza, 1 slice	6
Meatball Multigrain Thin Crust Pizza, 1 slice	5
Meatball Thin Crust Pizza, 1 slice	5
New York Deli Hand-Tossed Crust Pizza, 1 slice	7
New York Deli Multigrain Crust Pizza, 1 slice	7
New York Deli Multigrain Thin Crust Pizza, 1 slice	5
New York Deli Thin Crust Pizza, 1 slice	6
Panago Classic Hand-Tossed Crust Pizza, 1 slice	6
Panago Classic Multigrain Crust Pizza, 1 slice	6
Panago Classic Multigrain Thin Crust Pizza, 1 slice	5
Panago Classic Thin Crust Pizza, 1 slice	5
Pepperoni Classic Hand-Tossed Crust Pizza, 1 slice	6
Pepperoni Classic Multigrain Crust Pizza, 1 slice	5
Pepperoni Classic Multigrain Thin Crust Pizza, 1 slice	4
Pepperoni Classic Thin Crust Pizza, 1 slice	4
Philly Steak Hand-Tossed Crust Pizza, 1 slice	7
Philly Steak Multigrain Crust Pizza, 1 slice	7
Philly Steak Multigrain Thin Crust Pizza, 1 slice	6

▲ Power Foods	PointsPlus® value
Philly Steak Thin Crust Pizza, 1 slice	6
Primo Capicollo Hand-Tossed Crust Pizza, 1 slice	6
Primo Capicollo Multigrain Crust Pizza, 1 slice	6
Primo Capicollo Multigrain Thin Crust Pizza, 1 slice	5
Primo Capicollo Thin Crust Pizza, 1 slice	5
Sicilian Sausage Hand-Tossed Crust Pizza, 1 slice	6
Sicilian Sausage Multigrain Crust Pizza, 1 slice	6
Sicilian Sausage Multigrain Thin Crust Pizza, 1 slice	5
Sicilian Sausage Thin Crust Pizza, 1 slice	5
Steak Mushroom Melt Hand-Tossed Crust Pizza, 1 slice	8
Steak Mushroom Melt Multigrain Crust Pizza, 1 slice	8
Steak Mushroom Melt Multigrain Thin Crust Pizza, 1 slice	7
Steak Mushroom Melt Thin Crust Pizza, 1 slice	7
The Mediterranean Hand-Tossed Crust Pizza, 1 slice	6
The Mediterranean Multigrain Crust Pizza, 1 slice	6
The Mediterranean Multigrain Thin Crust Pizza, 1 slice	5
The Mediterranean Thin Crust Pizza, 1 slice	5
Tropical Hawaiian Hand-Tossed Crust Pizza, 1 slice	6
Tropical Hawaiian Multigrain Crust Pizza, 1 slice	6
Tropical Hawaiian Multigrain Thin Crust Pizza, 1 slice	5
Tropical Hawaiian Thin Crust Pizza, 1 slice	5

PANAGO PIZZA

▲ Power Foods	PointsPlus® value

OCEANO PIZZAS

Pesto Shrimp Hand-Tossed Crust Pizza, 1 slice	7
Pesto Shrimp Multigrain Crust Pizza, 1 slice	6
Pesto Shrimp Multigrain Thin Crust Pizza, 1 slice	6
Pesto Shrimp Thin Crust Pizza, 1 slice	6
Primo Shrimp Hand-Tossed Crust Pizza, 1 slice	5
Primo Shrimp Multigrain Crust Pizza, 1 slice	4
Primo Shrimp Multigrain Thin Crust Pizza, 1 slice	4
Primo Shrimp Thin Crust Pizza, 1 slice	4
Shrimp Club Hand-Tossed Crust Pizza, 1 slice	7
Shrimp Club Multigrain Crust Pizza, 1 slice	7
Shrimp Club Multigrain Thin Crust Pizza, 1 slice	5
Shrimp Club Thin Crust Pizza, 1 slice	5

POLLO PIZZAS

BBQ Chicken Hand-Tossed Crust Pizza, 1 slice	6
BBQ Chicken Multigrain Crust Pizza, 1 slice	6
BBQ Chicken Multigrain Thin Crust Pizza, 1 slice	5
BBQ Chicken Thin Crust Pizza, 1 slice	5
Buffalo Chicken Hand-Tossed Crust Pizza, 1 slice	5
Buffalo Chicken Multigrain Crust Pizza, 1 slice	6
Buffalo Chicken Multigrain Thin Crust Pizza, 1 slice	4

▲ Power Foods	PointsPlus® value

Buffalo Chicken Thin Crust Pizza, 1 slice	4
Chicken Club Hand-Tossed Crust Pizza, 1 slice	7
Chicken Club Multigrain Crust Pizza, 1 slice	7
Chicken Club Multigrain Thin Crust Pizza, 1 slice	6
Chicken Club Thin Crust Pizza, 1 slice	6
Chicken Taco Hand-Tossed Crust Pizza, 1 slice	6
Chicken Taco Multigrain Crust Pizza, 1 slice	5
Chicken Taco Multigrain Thin Crust Pizza, 1 slice	4
Chicken Taco Thin Crust Pizza, 1 slice	5
Chipotle Chicken Hand-Tossed Crust Pizza, 1 slice	6
Chipotle Chicken Multigrain Crust Pizza, 1 slice	6
Chipotle Chicken Multigrain Thin Crust Pizza, 1 slice	5
Chipotle Chicken Thin Crust Pizza, 1 slice	5
Primo Pollo Hand-Tossed Crust Pizza, 1 slice	6
Primo Pollo Multigrain Crust Pizza, 1 slice	6
Primo Pollo Multigrain Thin Crust Pizza, 1 slice	5
Primo Pollo Thin Crust Pizza, 1 slice	5
The Fajita Hand-Tossed Crust Pizza, 1 slice	6
The Fajita Multigrain Crust Pizza, 1 slice	5
The Fajita Multigrain Thin Crust Pizza, 1 slice	4
The Fajita Thin Crust Pizza, 1 slice	4

PANAGO PIZZA

▲ Power Foods	*PointsPlus®* value
Tropical Chicken Hand-Tossed Crust Pizza, 1 slice	6
Tropical Chicken Multigrain Crust Pizza, 1 slice	6
Tropical Chicken Multigrain Thin Crust Pizza, 1 slice	5
Tropical Chicken Thin Crust Pizza, 1 slice	5

VEGETARIANO PIZZAS

Garden Veggie Hand-Tossed Crust Pizza, 1 slice	6
Garden Veggie Multigrain Thin Crust Pizza, 1 slice	4
Garden Veggie Thin Crust Pizza, 1 slice	4
Grilled Vegetable & Goat Cheese Hand-Tossed Crust Pizza, 1 slice	5
Grilled Vegetable & Goat Cheese Multigrain Crust Pizza, 1 slice	5
Grilled Vegetable & Goat Cheese Multigrain Thin Crust Pizza, 1 slice	4
Grilled Vegetable & Goat Cheese Thin Crust Pizza, 1 slice	4
Primo Vegetarian Hand-Tossed Crust Pizza, 1 slice	6
Primo Vegetarian Multigrain Crust Pizza, 1 slice	6
Primo Vegetarian Multigrain Thin Crust Pizza, 1 slice	5
Primo Vegetarian Thin Crust Pizza, 1 slice	5
Quattro Formaggio Hand-Tossed Crust Pizza, 1 slice	5
Quattro Formaggio Multigrain Crust Pizza, 1 slice	5
Quattro Formaggio Multigrain Thin Crust Pizza, 1 slice	4
Quattro Formaggio Thin Crust Pizza, 1 slice	4

▲ Power Foods	*PointsPlus®* value
Veggie Mediterranean Hand-Tossed Crust Pizza, 1 slice	6
Veggie Mediterranean Multigrain Crust Pizza, 1 slice	5
Veggie Mediterranean Multigrain Thin Crust Pizza, 1 slice	5
Veggie Mediterranean Thin Crust Pizza, 1 slice	5
Veggie Pepperoni Hand-Tossed Crust Pizza, 1 slice	5
Veggie Pepperoni Multigrain Crust Pizza, 1 slice	5
Veggie Pepperoni Multigrain Thin Crust Pizza, 1 slice	4
Veggie Pepperoni Thin Crust Pizza, 1 slice	4

SALADS

Antipasto Salad, 1 serving	5
Caesar Salad, 1 serving	4
Chicken Caesar Salad, 1 serving	7
Chicken Garden Salad, 1 serving	7
Garden Salad, 1 serving	4
Mediterranean Salad, 1 serving	4
Shrimp Caesar Salad, 1 serving	5
Shrimp Garden Salad, 1 serving	5

WINGS

Honey Mustard Wings, 3 wings	7
Hot Buffalo Wings, 3 wings	7
Mediterranean Wings, 3 wings	7
Tikka Masala Wings, 3 wings	8

BREADSTICKS

Cinnamon Torizone Breadstick, 1	4
Rosemary Garlic Torizone Breadstick, 1	3

▲ Power Foods	*PointsPlus®* value

DIPS

Balsamic Vinaigrette Dip, 1 packet	1
Barbecue Dip, 1 packet	1
Blue Cheese Dip, 1 packet	3
Cheezy Cheedar Dip, 1 packet	4
Cheezy Formaggio Cucina Dip, 1 packet	4
Chipotle Cilantro Dip, 1 packet	5
Classic Caesar Dip, 1 packet	4
Creamy Ranch Jalapeno Cucina Dip, 1 packet	3
Frank's Original Red Hot Dip, 1 packet	0
Italian Garlic Dip, 1 packet	4
Italian Tomato Dip, 1 packet	1
Italiano Garlic Cucina Dip, 1 packet	4
Jalapeno Ranch Dip, 1 packet	4
Sweet Frost Icing Dip, 1 packet	3

SHAKERS

Chilli Shaker, 1 serving	0
Formaggio Shaker, 1 serving	1
Italiano Shaker, 1 serving	0

PIZZA DELIGHT®

	PointsPlus® value

STARTERS

BBQ Chicken Nachos, 1 serving	26
Fajita Flat'za®, 1 serving	11
Fire Bread with Spinach & Artichoke Dip, 1 serving	23
French Onion Soup, 1 serving	10
Garlic Cheese Fingers, 1 serving	9
Italiano Sausage Pinwheels, 1 serving	21
Oven-Baked Chicken Wings, 1 serving	11
Pesto Pinwheels, 1 serving	21
Southwest Flat'za®, 1 serving	13
Sun-dried Tomato & Chicken Pinwheels, 1 serving	19

FRESH SALADS

Chicken Caesar Salad, 1 serving	10
Chicken Honey Mustard Three-Leaf Salad, 1 serving	10
Chicken, Cranberry & Goat Cheese Salad, 1 serving	10
Famous Caesar Salad, 1 serving	6
Garden Salad, 1 serving	1
Grilled Chicken & Mandarin Three-leaf Salad, 1 serving	10
Hot-Top Salad®, 1 serving	13
Italian Pasta Salad, 1 serving	9
Roasted Mushroom & Grilled Chicken Salad, 1 serving	8
Tuscan® Chicken Salad, 1 serving	10

OVEN FRESH 12" SIGNATURE PIZZAS

All-Star® Meat, 1 slice	9
BBQ Chicken, 1 slice	8
Broadway® Classic, 1 slice	8
Canadian Bacon Classic Pizza, 1 slice	6
Chicken Classica, 1 slice	9
Chunky Vegetable Greek, 1 slice	6
Creamy Smoked Salmon & Shrimp, 1 slice	7
Donair Pizza, 1 slice	9
Grilled Cheese & Bacon, 1 slice	8
Hawaiian Delight, 1 slice	7
Italiano, 1 slice	6
Oven-Roasted Vegetable, 1 slice	8
Pesto & Cherry Tomato, 1 slice	6
Philly Cheese Steak Pizza, 1 slice	8
Rustic Deli, 1 slice	7
Seafood, 1 slice	7
Works, 1 slice	8

RUSTICA THIN CRUST PIZZA

Chicken Florentine Pizza, 1 slice	18
Spicy Chicken Pizza, 1 slice	17

OVEN-BAKED PASTAS

Chicken Broccoli Penne, 1 serving	18
Chicken Carbonara, 1 serving	29
Creamy Smoked Salmon & Shrimp Fettuccine, 1 serving	27

PIZZA DELIGHT®

Power Foods	PointsPlus® value
Fettuccine Alfredo with Chicken, 1 serving	16
Oven-Baked Lasagna, 1 serving	15
Parmigiana Chicken, 1 serving	24
Pasta Classica, 1 serving	19
Seafood Penne, 1 serving	18
Spaghetti Supreme, 1 serving	18
Spaghetti with Italian Meatballs, 1 serving	14
Spinach & Cheese Cannelloni, 1 serving	26

SKILLETS™ & CHICKEN

	PointsPlus® value
BBQ Chicken Skillet™, 1 serving	12
Chicken Skillet™, 1 serving	9
Oven-Roasted Ribs, 1 serving	40
Quarter Chicken Dinner, 1 serving	26
Seafood Skillet™, 1 serving	11
Super Donair Skillet™, 1 serving	25
Sweet & Sour Chicken Skillet™, 1 serving	14

DONAIRS & PANZEROTTI

	PointsPlus® value
Famous Donair, 1 serving	14
Super Donair, 1 serving	18
Classic Panzerotti, 1 serving	12
Seafood Panzerotti, 1 serving	10
Donair Panzerotti, 1 serving	17
Philly Cheese Steak Panzerotti, 1 serving	15
Italiano Sausage Panzerotti, 1 serving	16
Creamy Smoked Salmon & Shrimp Panzerotti, 1 serving	14

Power Foods	PointsPlus® value

PANINIS

	PointsPlus® value
Chicken & Green Apple Panini, 1	18
Grilled Chicken Panini, 1	15
Ham & Roasted Red Onion Panini, 1	19
Philly Cheese Steak Panini, 1	17
Sicilian Club Panini, 1	19
Tuscan Chicken Panini, 1	18
Italian Club Sandwich, 1	24
Tuscan® Chicken Sandwich, 1	12
Caesar Wrap, 1	8
Club Wrap, 1	14

KID'S MENU

	PointsPlus® value
6" Garlic Cheese Fingers, 1 serving	8
Bad Dog Pizza, 1 serving	21
Chicken Nuggets & Fries, 1 serving	13
Kitty Cat Pizza, 1 serving	10
Mac 'n Cheese, 1 serving	8
Meatball Pizza, 1 serving	13
Spaghetti & Meat Sauce, 1 serving	11

DESSERTS

	PointsPlus® value
Apple Cinnamon Sensation, 1 serving	20
Apple Skillet, 1 serving	13
Brownie Skillet Supreme, 1 serving	20
Caramel Crepe, 1 serving	15
Chocolate Crepe, 1 serving	15
Chocolate Eruption, 1 serving	23
Red Cherry Temptation, 1 serving	20

PIZZA HUT®

APPETIZERS

Breadsticks, 2 pieces	3
Breadsticks with Cheese, 2 pieces	3
Breadsticks Sauce, 1 serving	1
Bruschetta, 1 slice	5
Garlic Bread, 1 slice	4
Garlic Bread with Cheese, 1 slice	5
Pesto Chicken Spinrolls or Quesadillas, 2 pieces	8

SALADS & DRESSINGS

BLT Salad (without dressing), 1 side serving	3
Caesar Salad (with dressing), 1 side serving	9
Chicken Caesar Salad, 1 side serving	10
Garden Salad (without dressing), 1 side serving	4
Greek Salad (without dressing), 1 side serving	3
Warm Spinach Salad (with dressing), 1 entrée serving	7
Caesar Dressing, 28 g (1 oz)	3
French Dressing, 28 g (1 oz)	3
Honey Mustard Dressing, 28 g (1 oz)	1
Ranch Dressing, 28 g (1 oz)	4
Sweet Italian Dressing, 28 g (1 oz)	4

BRUSCHETTA PIZZAS

Hand Tossed, 1 slice (1/6 of 22 cm [9"] small pizza)	6
Hand Tossed, 1 slice (1/8 of 30 cm [12"] medium pizza)	5
Hand Tossed, 1 slice (1/12 of 35 cm [14"] large pizza)	5

Personal Pan Pizza®, 1 slice (1/4 of 15 cm [6"] personal pizza)	4
Personal Pan Pizza®, 1 slice (1/6 of 22 cm [9"] small pizza)	4
Personal Pan Pizza®, 1 slice (1/8 of 30 cm [12"] medium pizza)	6
Personal Pan Pizza®, 1 slice (1/12 of 35 cm [14"] large pizza)	5
Stuffed Crust, 1 slice (1/8 of 30 cm [12"] medium pizza)	8
Stuffed Crust, 1 slice (1/12 of 35 cm [14"] large pizza)	9
Thin 'N Crispy®, 1 slice (1/8 of 30 cm [12"] medium pizza)	5
Thin 'N Crispy®, 1 slice (1/12 of 35 cm [14"] large pizza)	5

CANADIAN PIZZAS

Hand Tossed, 1 slice (1/8 of 30 cm [12"] medium pizza)	7
Hand Tossed, 1 slice (1/12 of 35 cm [14"] large pizza)	7
Personal Pan Pizza®, 1 slice (1/4 of 15 cm [6"] personal pizza)	4
Personal Pan Pizza®, 1 slice (1/6 of 22 cm [9"] small pizza)	5
Personal Pan Pizza®, 1 slice (1/8 of 30 cm [12"] medium pizza)	7
Personal Pan Pizza®, 1 slice (1/12 of 35 cm [14"] large pizza)	7
Stuffed Crust Pizza, 1 slice (1/8 of 30 cm [12"] medium pizza)	11
Stuffed Crust Pizza, 1 slice (1/12 of 35 cm [14"] large pizza)	11
Thin 'N Crispy®, 1 slice (1/8 of 30 cm [12"] medium pizza)	7
Thin 'N Crispy®, 1 slice (1/12 of 35 cm [14"] large pizza)	6

▲ Power Foods	PointsPlus® value

▲ Power Foods	PointsPlus® value

CHEESE LOVER'S PLUS® PIZZAS

Hand Tossed, 1 slice
(1/8 of 30 cm [12"] medium pizza) — 7

Hand Tossed, 1 slice
(1/12 of 35 cm [14"] large pizza) — 7

Personal Pan Pizza®, 1 slice
(1/4 of 15 cm [6"] personal pizza) — 4

Personal Pan Pizza®, 1 slice
(1/6 of 22 cm [9"] small pizza) — 5

Personal Pan Pizza®, 1 slice
(1/8 of 30 cm [12"] medium pizza) — 7

Personal Pan Pizza®, 1 slice
(1/12 of 35 cm [14"] large pizza) — 7

Stuffed Crust, 1 slice
(1/8 of 30 cm [12"] medium pizza) — 10

Stuffed Crust, 1 slice
(1/12 of 35 cm [14"] large pizza) — 11

Thin 'N Crispy®, 1 slice
(1/8 of 30 cm [12"] medium pizza) — 7

Thin 'N Crispy®, 1 slice
(1/12 of 35 cm [14"] large pizza) — 7

CHEESE ONLY PIZZAS

Personal Pan Pizza®, 1 slice
(1/4 of 15 cm [6"] personal pizza) — 4

Personal Pan Pizza®, 1 slice
(1/6 of 22 cm [9"] small pizza) — 5

Personal Pan Pizza®, 1 slice
(1/8 of 30 cm [12"] medium pizza) — 7

Personal Pan Pizza®, 1 slice
(1/12 of 35 cm [14"] large pizza) — 6

Stuffed Crust Pizza, 1 slice
(1/8 of 30 cm [12"] medium pizza) — 9

Stuffed Crust Pizza, 1 slice
(1/12 of 35 cm [14"] large pizza) — 9

Thin 'N Crispy®, 1 slice
(1/8 of 30 cm [12"] medium pizza) — 6

CHICKEN CAESAR PIZZAS

Hand Tossed, 1 slice
(1/8 of 30 cm [12"] medium pizza) — 6

Hand Tossed, 1 slice
(1/12 of 35 cm [14"] large pizza) — 6

Personal Pan Pizza®, 1 slice
(1/4 of 15 cm [6"] personal pizza) — 4

Personal Pan Pizza®, 1 slice
(1/6 of 22 cm [9"] small pizza) — 5

Personal Pan Pizza®, 1 slice
(1/8 of 30 cm [12"] medium pizza) — 7

Personal Pan Pizza®, 1 slice
(1/12 of 35 cm [14"] large pizza) — 6

Stuffed Crust, 1 slice
(1/8 of 30 cm [12"] medium pizza) — 9

Stuffed Crust, 1 slice
(1/12 of 35 cm [14"] large pizza) — 10

Thin 'N Crispy®, 1 slice
(1/8 of 30 cm [12"] medium pizza) — 6

Thin 'N Crispy®, 1 slice
(1/12 of 35 cm [14"] large pizza) — 6

CHICKEN FLORENTINE PIZZAS

Hand Tossed, 1 slice
(1/8 of 30 cm [12"] medium pizza) — 6

Hand Tossed, 1 slice
(1/12 of 35 cm [14"] large pizza) — 6

Personal Pan Pizza®, 1 slice
(1/4 of 15 cm [6"] personal pizza) — 4

Personal Pan Pizza®, 1 slice
(1/6 of 22 cm [9"] small pizza) — 5

Personal Pan Pizza®, 1 slice
(1/8 of 30 cm [12"] medium pizza) — 7

Personal Pan Pizza®, 1 slice
(1/12 of 35 cm [14"] large pizza) — 6

Stuffed Crust, 1 slice
(1/8 of 30 cm [12"] medium pizza) — 9

PIZZA HUT®

▲ Power Foods	*PointsPlus®* value
Stuffed Crust, 1 slice (1/12 of 35 cm [14"] large pizza)	9
Thin 'N Crispy®, 1 slice (1/8 of 30 cm [12"] medium pizza)	6
Thin 'N Crispy®, 1 slice (1/12 of 35 cm [14"] large pizza)	6

CHICKEN LOVER'S DELUXE® PIZZAS

Hand Tossed, 1 slice (1/8 of 30 cm [12"] medium pizza)	6
Hand Tossed, 1 slice (1/12 of 35 cm [14"] large pizza)	5
Personal Pan Pizza®, 1 slice (1/4 of 15 cm [6"] personal pizza)	4
Personal Pan Pizza®, 1 slice (1/6 of 22 cm [9"] small pizza)	5
Personal Pan Pizza®, 1 slice (1/8 of 30 cm [12"] medium pizza)	6
Personal Pan Pizza®, 1 slice (1/12 of 35 cm [14"] large pizza)	6
Stuffed Crust, 1 slice (1/8 of 30 cm [12"] medium pizza)	9
Stuffed Crust, 1 slice (1/12 of 35 cm [14"] large pizza)	9
Thin 'N Crispy®, 1 slice (1/8 of 30 cm [12"] medium pizza)	6
Thin 'N Crispy®, 1 slice (1/12 of 35 cm [14"] large pizza)	6

GREEK PIZZAS

Hand Tossed, 1 slice (1/8 of 30 cm [12"] medium pizza)	6
Hand Tossed, 1 slice (1/12 of 35 cm [14"] large pizza)	5
Personal Pan Pizza®, 1 slice (1/4 of 15 cm [6"] personal pizza)	4
Personal Pan Pizza®, 1 slice (1/6 of 22 cm [9"] small pizza)	5
Personal Pan Pizza®, 1 slice (1/8 of 30 cm [12"] medium pizza)	6

▲ Power Foods	*PointsPlus®* value
Personal Pan Pizza®, 1 slice (1/12 of 35 cm [14"] large pizza)	6
Stuffed Crust, 1 slice (1/8 of 30 cm [12"] medium pizza)	9
Stuffed Crust, 1 slice (1/12 of 35 cm [14"] large pizza)	9
Thin 'N Crispy®, 1 slice (1/8 of 30 cm [12"] medium pizza)	6
Thin 'N Crispy®, 1 slice (1/12 of 35 cm [14"] large pizza)	5

GRILLED CHICKEN ITALIANO PIZZAS

Hand Tossed, 1 slice (1/8 of 30 cm [12"] medium pizza)	6
Hand Tossed, 1 slice (1/12 of 35 cm [14"] large pizza)	6
Personal Pan Pizza®, 1 slice (1/4 of 15 cm [6"] personal pizza)	4
Personal Pan Pizza®, 1 slice (1/6 of 22 cm [9"] small pizza)	5
Personal Pan Pizza®, 1 slice (1/8 of 30 cm [12"] medium pizza)	6
Personal Pan Pizza®, 1 slice (1/12 of 35 cm [14"] large pizza)	6
Stuffed Crust, 1 slice (1/8 of 30 cm [12"] medium pizza)	9
Stuffed Crust, 1 slice (1/12 of 35 cm [14"] large pizza)	9
Thin 'N Crispy®, 1 slice (1/8 of 30 cm [12"] medium pizza)	6
Thin 'N Crispy®, 1 slice (1/12 of 35 cm [14"] large pizza)	6

HAWAIIAN PIZZAS

Hand Tossed, 1 slice (1/8 of 30 cm [12"] medium pizza)	7
Personal Pan Pizza®, 1 slice (1/4 of 15 cm [6"] personal pizza)	5
Personal Pan Pizza®, 1 slice (1/6 of 22 cm [9"] small pizza)	5

▲ Power Foods	PointsPlus® value
Personal Pan Pizza®, 1 slice (1/8 of 30 cm [12"] medium pizza)	7
Personal Pan Pizza®, 1 slice (1/12 of 35 cm [14"] large pizza)	7
Stuffed Crust Pizza, 1 slice (1/8 of 30 cm [12"] medium pizza)	10
Stuffed Crust Pizza, 1 slice (1/12 of 35 cm [14"] large pizza)	10
Thin 'N Crispy®, 1 slice (1/8 of 30 cm [12"] medium pizza)	7

ITALIAN CLASSIC PIZZAS

Hand Tossed, 1 slice (1/8 of 30 cm [12"] medium pizza)	8
Hand Tossed, 1 slice (1/12 of 35 cm [14"] large pizza)	7
Personal Pan Pizza®, 1 slice (1/4 of 15 cm [6"] personal pizza)	5
Personal Pan Pizza®, 1 slice (1/6 of 22 cm [9"] small pizza)	6
Personal Pan Pizza®, 1 slice (1/8 of 30 cm [12"] medium pizza)	8
Personal Pan Pizza®, 1 slice (1/12 of 35 cm [14"] large pizza)	8
Stuffed Crust, 1 slice (1/8 of 30 cm [12"] medium pizza)	10
Stuffed Crust, 1 slice (1/12 of 35 cm [14"] large pizza)	11
Thin 'N Crispy®, 1 slice (1/8 of 30 cm [12"] medium pizza)	8
Thin 'N Crispy®, 1 slice (1/12 of 35 cm [14"] large pizza)	7

MEAT LOVER'S® PIZZAS

Hand Tossed, 1 slice (1/12 of 35 cm [14"] large pizza)	7
Personal Pan Pizza®, 1 slice (1/4 of 15 cm [6"] personal pizza)	5
Personal Pan Pizza®, 1 slice (1/6 of 22 cm [9"] small pizza)	6

▲ Power Foods	PointsPlus® value
Personal Pan Pizza®, 1 slice (1/8 of 30 cm [12"] medium pizza)	8
Personal Pan Pizza®, 1 slice (1/12 of 35 cm [14"] large pizza)	8
Stuffed Crust Pizza, 1 slice (1/8 of 30 cm [12"] medium pizza)	11
Stuffed Crust Pizza, 1 slice (1/12 of 35 cm [14"] large pizza)	11
Thin 'N Crispy®, 1 slice (1/8 of 30 cm [12"] medium pizza)	8
Thin 'N Crispy®, 1 slice (1/12 of 35 cm [14"] large pizza)	7

PEPPERONI LOVER'S® PIZZAS

Hand Tossed, 1 slice (1/8 of 30 cm [12"] medium pizza)	8
Personal Pan Pizza®, 1 slice (1/4 of 15 cm [6"] personal pizza)	5
Personal Pan Pizza®, 1 slice (1/6 of 22 cm [9"] small pizza)	6
Personal Pan Pizza®, 1 slice (1/8 of 30 cm [12"] medium pizza)	8
Personal Pan Pizza®, 1 slice (1/12 of 35 cm [14"] large pizza)	8
Stuffed Crust Pizza, 1 slice (1/8 of 30 cm [12"] medium pizza)	11
Stuffed Crust Pizza, 1 slice (1/12 of 35 cm [14"] large pizza)	12
Thin 'N Crispy®, 1 slice (1/8 of 30 cm [12"] medium pizza)	8
Thin 'N Crispy®, 1 slice (1/12 of 35 cm [14"] large pizza)	7

PEPPERONI ONLY PIZZAS

Hand Tossed, 1 slice (1/8 of 30 cm [12"] medium pizza)	7
Personal Pan Pizza®, 1 slice (1/4 of 15 cm [6"] personal pizza)	4
Personal Pan Pizza®, 1 slice (1/6 of 22 cm [9"] small pizza)	5

PIZZA HUT®

▲ Power Foods	PointsPlus® value
Personal Pan Pizza®, 1 slice (1/8 of 30 cm [12"] medium pizza)	7
Personal Pan Pizza®, 1 slice (1/12 of 35 cm [14"] large pizza)	6
Stuffed Crust Pizza, 1 slice (1/8 of 30 cm [12"] medium pizza)	9
Stuffed Crust Pizza, 1 slice (1/12 of 35 cm [14"] large pizza)	10
Thin 'N Crispy®, 1 slice (1/12 of 35 cm [14"] large pizza)	6

SUPREME LOVER'S PIZZAS

▲ Power Foods	PointsPlus® value
Personal Pan Pizza®, 1 slice (1/4 of 15 cm [6"] personal pizza)	5
Personal Pan Pizza®, 1 slice (1/6 of 22 cm [9"] small pizza)	6
Personal Pan Pizza®, 1 slice (1/8 of 30 cm [12"] medium pizza)	8
Personal Pan Pizza®, 1 slice (1/12 of 35 cm [14"] large pizza)	7
Stuffed Crust Pizza, 1 slice (1/8 of 30 cm [12"] medium pizza)	11
Stuffed Crust Pizza, 1 slice (1/12 of 35 cm [14"] large pizza)	11
Thin 'N Crispy®, 1 slice (1/8 of 30 cm [12"] medium pizza)	7

THE EDGE® PIZZAS

▲ Power Foods	PointsPlus® value
Meaty, 1 slice (1/8 of 30 cm [12"] medium pizza)	3
Meaty, 1 slice (1/12 of 35 cm [14"] large pizza)	5
The Works, 1 slice (1/8 of 30 cm [12"] medium pizza)	3
The Works, 1 slice (1/12 of 35 cm [14"] large pizza)	5
Veggie, 1 slice (1/8 of 30 cm [12"] medium pizza)	3
Veggie, 1 slice (1/12 of 35 cm [14"] large pizza)	4

TRIPLE CROWN® PIZZAS

▲ Power Foods	PointsPlus® value
Hand Tossed, 1 slice (1/8 of 30 cm [12"] medium pizza)	6
Hand Tossed, 1 slice (1/12 of 35 cm [14"] large pizza)	6
Personal Pan Pizza®, 1 slice (1/4 of 15 cm [6"] personal pizza)	4
Personal Pan Pizza®, 1 slice (1/6 of 22 cm [9"] small pizza)	5
Personal Pan Pizza®, 1 slice (1/8 of 30 cm [12"] medium pizza)	7
Personal Pan Pizza®, 1 slice (1/12 of 35 cm [14"] large pizza)	6
Stuffed Crust Pizza, 1 slice (1/8 of 30 cm [12"] medium pizza)	9
Stuffed Crust Pizza, 1 slice (1/12 of 35 cm [14"] large pizza)	10
Thin 'N Crispy®, 1 slice (1/8 of 30 cm [12"] medium pizza)	6
Thin 'N Crispy®, 1 slice (1/12 of 35 cm [14"] large pizza)	6

TUSCAN SAUSAGE PIZZAS

▲ Power Foods	PointsPlus® value
Hand Tossed, 1 slice (1/8 of 30 cm [12"] medium pizza)	7
Hand Tossed, 1 slice (1/12 of 35 cm [14"] large pizza)	6
Personal Pan Pizza®, 1 slice (1/4 of 15 cm [6"] personal pizza)	4
Personal Pan Pizza®, 1 slice (1/6 of 22 cm [9"] small pizza)	5
Personal Pan Pizza®, 1 slice (1/8 of 30 cm [12"] medium pizza)	8
Personal Pan Pizza®, 1 slice (1/12 of 35 cm [14"] large pizza)	7
Stuffed Crust, 1 slice (1/8 of 30 cm [12"] medium pizza)	10
Stuffed Crust, 1 slice (1/12 of 35 cm [14"] large pizza)	10
Thin 'N Crispy®, 1 slice (1/8 of 30 cm [12"] medium pizza)	6

▲ Power Foods	*PointsPlus®* value
Thin 'N Crispy®, 1 slice (1/12 of 35 cm [14"] large pizza)	7

VEGGIE LOVER'S PIZZAS

▲ Power Foods	*PointsPlus®* value
Hand Tossed, 1 slice (1/8 of 30 cm [12"] medium pizza)	6
Personal Pan Pizza®, 1 slice (1/4 of 15 cm [6"] personal pizza)	4
Personal Pan Pizza®, 1 slice (1/6 of 22 cm [9"] small pizza)	5
Personal Pan Pizza®, 1 slice (1/8 of 30 cm [12"] medium pizza)	6
Personal Pan Pizza®, 1 slice (1/12 of 35 cm [14"] large pizza)	6
Stuffed Crust Pizza, 1 slice (1/8 of 30 cm [12"] medium pizza)	9
Stuffed Crust Pizza, 1 slice (1/12 of 35 cm [14"] large pizza)	9
Thin 'N Crispy®, 1 slice (1/8 of 30 cm [12"] medium pizza)	6
Thin 'N Crispy®, 1 slice (1/12 of 35 cm [14"] large pizza)	5

VEGGIE MEDITERRANEAN PIZZAS

▲ Power Foods	*PointsPlus®* value
Hand Tossed, 1 slice (1/8 of 30 cm [12"] medium pizza)	6
Hand Tossed, 1 slice (1/12 of 35 cm [14"] large pizza)	5
Personal Pan Pizza®, 1 slice (1/4 of 15 cm [6"] personal pizza)	4
Personal Pan Pizza®, 1 slice (1/6 of 22 cm [9"] small pizza)	5
Personal Pan Pizza®, 1 slice (1/8 of 30 cm [12"] medium pizza)	6
Personal Pan Pizza®, 1 slice (1/12 of 35 cm [14"] large pizza)	6
Stuffed Crust, 1 slice (1/8 of 30 cm [12"] medium pizza)	8
Stuffed Crust, 1 slice (1/12 of 35 cm [14"] large pizza)	9

▲ Power Foods	*PointsPlus®* value
Thin 'N Crispy®, 1 slice (1/8 of 30 cm [12"] medium pizza)	6
Thin 'N Crispy®, 1 slice (1/12 of 35 cm [14"] large pizza)	5

VENETIAN PIZZAS

▲ Power Foods	*PointsPlus®* value
Hand Tossed, 1 slice (1/8 of 30 cm [12"] medium pizza)	7
Hand Tossed, 1 slice (1/12 of 35 cm [14"] large pizza)	7
Personal Pan Pizza®, 1 (15 cm [6"] personal pizza)	17
Personal Pan Pizza®, 1 slice (1/6 of 22 cm [9"] small pizza)	5
Personal Pan Pizza®, 1 slice (1/8 of 30 cm [12"] medium pizza)	8
Personal Pan Pizza®, 1 slice (1/12 of 35 cm [14"] large pizza)	8
Stuffed Crust, 1 slice (1/8 of 30 cm [12"] medium pizza)	10
Stuffed Crust, 1 slice (1/12 of 35 cm [14"] large pizza)	11
Thin 'N Crispy®, 1 slice (1/8 of 30 cm [12"] medium pizza)	7
Thin 'N Crispy®, 1 slice (1/12 of 35 cm [14"] large pizza)	7

DIPPING SAUCES

	PointsPlus® value
Ranch, 1 dipping cup	6
Roasted Garlic, 1 dipping cup	7
Roasted Red Pepper Dipping Sauce, 1 dipping cup	5

PZONE®

	PointsPlus® value
Canadian, 1/2 portion	19
Cheesy, 1/2 portion	21

PIZZA HUT®

PASTAS

Cheese Cavatini, 1 serving	39
Chicken Fettuccini Alfredo, 1 serving	22
Chicken Pomodoro, 1 serving	30
Fettuccini Alfredo, 1 serving	19
Spaghetti and Meat Sauce, 1 serving	18
Spaghetti and Tomato Sauce, 1 serving	12

SANDWICHES

Buffalo Chicken Sandwich, 1	21
Chicken Parmesan Sandwich, 1	26
Chicken Pesto Sandwich, 1	17
Club Sandwich, 1	14
Meatball Sandwich, 1	26

WING STREET WINGS

Bone-In Breaded, 5 wings	12
Bone-Out Breaded, 5 wings	9
Traditional, 5 wings	5

WING STREET SAUCES

Buffalo Burning Hot Wing Sauce, 1 serving	2
Buffalo Medium Wing Sauce, 1 serving	2
Buffalo Mild Wing Sauce, 1 serving	2
Honey BBQ Sauce, 1 serving	5
Spicy Asian Sauce, 1 serving	4
Spicy BBQ Sauce, 1 serving	4

WING STREET SIDE ITEMS

Taters, 1 serving	9

DESSERTS

Brownie, 1	6
Chocolate Fudge (Turtle) Cake, 1	14
Cinnaparts™, 1	6
Dessert Pizza with Apple Topping, 1	3
Dessert Pizza with Cherry Topping, 1	3
Macintosh Apple Cheesecake, 1	9

PIZZA NOVA

▲ Power Foods	*PointsPlus®* value

PIZZA

Bruschetta (herbed olive oil, diced sweet tomatoes, prepared with garlic & onion), 1 medium slice	5
Cheese, 1 medium slice	5
Hawaiian (Smoked Ham, Pineapple), 1 medium slice	5
Pepperoni, 1 medium slice	5
Pepperoni, Mushrooms, Green Peppers, 1 medium slice	5
Super Gourmet (Sun Dried Tomatoes, Grilled Chicken, Roasted Red Peppers, Feta Cheese), 1 medium slice	6
Veggie (Mushrooms, Green Peppers, Onions), 1 medium slice	5
Whole Wheat Chicken alla Bianca (Herbed Olive Oil, Grilled Chicken, Roasted Red Peppers, Parmigiano Cheese), 1 medium slice	5
Whole Wheat Thin Crust (Broccoli, Red Pepper, Artichokes), 1 medium slice	3

PEOPLE PLEASERS

Chicken Wings, 1 serving	5
Garlic Bread, 1 slice	5
Lasagna, 1 serving	15

PIZZA PIZZA

▲ Power Foods   *PointsPlus®* value   ▲ Power Foods   *PointsPlus®* value

CLASSIC PIZZAS
(SMALL PIZZA – 25 CM [10"] DIAMETER)

Bacon Double Cheeseburger Pizza, 1 slice (1/6 of pizza)	6
Big Bacon Bonanza Pizza, 1 slice (1/6 of pizza)	7
Canadian Eh! Pizza, 1 slice (1/6 of pizza)	6
Cheese Pizza, 1 slice (1/6 of pizza)	5
Classic Super Pizza, 1 slice (1/6 of pizza)	5
Garden Veggie Pizza, 1 slice (1/6 of pizza)	5
New York Pepperoni Pizza, 1 slice (1/6 of pizza)	6
Pepperoni Pizza, 1 slice (1/6 of pizza)	5
Sausage Mushroom Melt Pizza, 1 slice (1/6 of pizza)	6
Spicy BBQ Chicken Pizza, 1 slice (1/6 of pizza)	5
Sweet Heat Pizza, 1 slice (1/6 of pizza)	5
Tropical Hawaiian Pizza, 1 slice (1/6 of pizza)	7

CLASSIC PIZZAS
(MEDIUM PIZZA – 30 CM [12"] DIAMETER)

Bacon Double Cheeseburger Pizza, 1 slice (1/8 of pizza)	6
Big Bacon Bonanza Pizza, 1 slice (1/8 of pizza)	8
Canadian Eh! Pizza, 1 slice (1/8 of pizza)	6
Cheese Pizza, 1 slice (1/8 of pizza)	5
Classic Super Pizza, 1 slice (1/8 of pizza)	6
Garden Veggie Pizza, 1 slice (1/8 of pizza)	5
New York Pepperoni Pizza, 1 slice (1/8 of pizza)	6
Pepperoni Pizza, 1 slice (1/8 of pizza)	6
Sausage Mushroom Melt Pizza, 1 slice (1/8 of pizza)	6
Spicy BBQ Chicken Pizza, 1 slice (1/8 of pizza)	6
Sweet Heat Pizza, 1 slice (1/8 of pizza)	5
Tropical Hawaiian Pizza, 1 slice (1/8 of pizza)	8

CLASSIC PIZZAS
(LARGE PIZZA – 35 CM [14"] DIAMETER)

Bacon Double Cheeseburger Pizza, 1 slice (1/10 of pizza)	7
Big Bacon Bonanza Pizza, 1 slice (1/10 of pizza)	8
Canadian Eh! Pizza, 1 slice (1/10 of pizza)	7
Cheese Pizza, 1 slice (1/10 of pizza)	6
Classic Super Pizza, 1 slice (1/10 of pizza)	6
Garden Veggie Pizza, 1 slice (1/10 of pizza)	6
New York Pepperoni Pizza, 1 slice (1/10 of pizza)	7
Pepperoni Pizza, 1 slice (1/10 of pizza)	6
Sausage Mushroom Melt Pizza, 1 slice (1/10 of pizza)	7
Spicy BBQ Chicken Pizza, 1 slice (1/10 of pizza)	6
Sweet Heat Pizza, 1 slice (1/10 of pizza)	6
Tropical Hawaiian Pizza, 1 slice (1/10 of pizza)	9

CLASSIC PIZZAS
(X-LARGE PIZZA – 40 CM [16"] DIAMETER)

Bacon Double Cheeseburger Pizza, 1 slice (1/12 of pizza)	8
Big Bacon Bonanza Pizza, 1 slice (1/12 of pizza)	9

Power Foods	PointsPlus® value
Canadian Eh! Pizza, 1 slice (1/12 of pizza)	8
Cheese Pizza, 1 slice (1/12 of pizza)	6
Classic Super Pizza, 1 slice (1/12 of pizza)	7
Garden Veggie Pizza, 1 slice (1/12 of pizza)	6
New York Pepperoni Pizza, 1 slice (1/12 of pizza)	8
Pepperoni Pizza, 1 slice (1/12 of pizza)	7
Sausage Mushroom Melt Pizza, 1 slice (1/12 of pizza)	7
Spicy BBQ Chicken Pizza, 1 slice (1/12 of pizza)	7
Sweet Heat Pizza, 1 slice (1/12 of pizza)	6
Tropical Hawaiian Pizza, 1 slice (1/12 of pizza)	9

CLASSIC PIZZAS
(45 CM [18"] DIAMETER)

Bacon Double Cheeseburger Pizza, 1 walk-in slice (1/6 of pizza)	19
Big Bacon Bonanza Pizza, 1 walk-in slice (1/6 of pizza)	22
Canadian Eh! Pizza, 1 walk-in slice (1/6 of pizza)	19
Cheese Pizza, 1 walk-in slice (1/6 of pizza)	15
Classic Super Pizza, 1 walk-in slice (1/6 of pizza)	17
Garden Veggie – Classic Dough, 1 walk-in slice (1/6 of pizza)	16
Garden Veggie – Whole Wheat Multigrain Dough, 1 walk-in slice (1/6 of pizza)	15
New York Pepperoni Pizza, 1 walk-in slice (1/6 of pizza)	18
Pepperoni Pizza, 1 walk-in slice (1/6 of pizza)	16

Power Foods	PointsPlus® value
Sausage Mushroom Melt Pizza, 1 walk-in slice (1/6 of pizza)	18
Spicy BBQ Chicken Pizza, 1 walk-in slice (1/6 of pizza)	18
Sweet Heat Pizza, 1 walk-in slice (1/6 of pizza)	16
Tropical Hawaiian Pizza, 1 walk-in slice (1/6 of pizza)	22

SIGNATURE PIZZAS
(SMALL PIZZA – 25 CM [10"] DIAMETER)

Bacon Chicken Mushroom Melt Pizza, 1 slice (1/6 of pizza)	6
Chicken Bruschetta Parm, 1 slice (1/6 of pizza)	5
Grilled Veggie and Goat Cheese Pizza, 1 slice (1/6 of pizza)	5
Loaded Classic Pizza, 1 slice (1/6 of pizza)	6
Meat Supreme Pizza, 1 slice (1/6 of pizza)	7
Mediterranean Vegetarian Pizza, 1 slice (1/6 of pizza)	5
Pesto Amore Pizza, 1 slice (1/6 of pizza)	5
Pesto Con Pollo Pizza, 1 slice (1/6 of pizza)	6
Philly Cheese Steak Pizza, 1 slice (1/6 of pizza)	5
Sweet Chili Chicken Thai Pizza, 1 slice (1/6 of pizza)	5

SIGNATURE PIZZAS
(MEDIUM PIZZA – 30 CM [12"] DIAMETER)

Bacon Chicken Mushroom Melt Pizza, 1 slice (1/8 of pizza)	6
Chicken Bruschetta Parm, 1 slice (1/8 of pizza)	5
Grilled Veggie and Goat Cheese Pizza, 1 slice (1/8 of pizza)	5

PIZZA PIZZA

▲ Power Foods	PointsPlus® value
Loaded Classic Pizza, 1 slice (1/8 of pizza)	7
Meat Supreme Pizza, 1 slice (1/8 of pizza)	7
Mediterranean Vegetarian Pizza, 1 slice (1/8 of pizza)	5
Pesto Amore Pizza, 1 slice (1/8 of pizza)	4
Pesto Con Pollo Pizza, 1 slice (1/8 of pizza)	6
Philly Cheese Steak Pizza, 1 slice (1/8 of pizza)	6
Sweet Chili Chicken Thai Pizza, 1 slice (1/8 of pizza)	5

SIGNATURE PIZZAS
(LARGE PIZZA – 35 CM [14"] DIAMETER)

Power Foods	PointsPlus® value
Bacon Chicken Mushroom Melt Pizza, 1 slice (1/10 of pizza)	7
Chicken Bruschetta Parm, 1 slice (1/10 of pizza)	6
Grilled Veggie and Goat Cheese Pizza, 1 slice (1/10 of pizza)	6
Loaded Classic Pizza, 1 slice (1/10 of pizza)	8
Meat Supreme Pizza, 1 slice (1/10 of pizza)	8
Mediterranean Vegetarian Pizza, 1 slice (1/10 of pizza)	6
Pesto Amore Pizza, 1 slice (1/10 of pizza)	5
Pesto Con Pollo Pizza, 1 slice (1/10 of pizza)	7
Philly Cheese Steak Pizza, 1 slice (1/10 of pizza)	7
Shrimp Pizza, 1 slice (1/10 of pizza)	6
Sweet Chili Chicken Thai Pizza, 1 slice (1/10 of pizza)	6

SIGNATURE PIZZAS
(X-LARGE PIZZA – 40 CM [16"] DIAMETER)

▲ Power Foods	PointsPlus® value
Bacon Chicken Mushroom Melt Pizza, 1 slice (1/12 of pizza)	7
Chicken Bruschetta Parm, 1 slice (1/12 of pizza)	6
Grilled Veggie and Goat Cheese Pizza, 1 slice (1/12 of pizza)	7
Loaded Classic Pizza, 1 slice (1/12 of pizza)	8
Meat Supreme Pizza, 1 slice (1/12 of pizza)	9
Mediterranean Vegetarian Pizza, 1 slice (1/12 of pizza)	7
Pesto Amore Pizza, 1 slice (1/12 of pizza)	5
Pesto Con Pollo Pizza, 1 slice (1/12 of pizza)	8
Philly Cheese Steak Pizza, 1 slice (1/12 of pizza)	7
Sweet Chili Chicken Thai Pizza, 1 slice (1/12 of pizza)	7

SIGNATURE PIZZAS
(45 CM [18"] DIAMETER)

Power Foods	PointsPlus® value
Bacon Chicken Mushroom Melt Pizza, 1 walk-in slice (1/6 of pizza)	18
Chicken Bruschetta Parm, 1 walk-in slice (1/6 of pizza)	18
Grilled Veggie and Goat Cheese Pizza, 1 walk-in slice (1/6 of pizza)	17
Loaded Classic Pizza, 1 walk-in slice (1/6 of pizza)	19
Meat Supreme Pizza, 1 walk-in slice (1/6 of pizza)	21
Mediterranean Vegetarian Pizza, 1 walk-in slice (1/6 of pizza)	16
Pesto Amore Pizza, 1 walk-in slice (1/6 of pizza)	17
Pesto Con Pollo Pizza, 1 walk-in slice (1/6 of pizza)	20

▲ Power Foods | *PointsPlus®* value

Philly Cheese Steak Pizza,
1 walk-in slice (1/6 of pizza) — 18

Quattro Fromaggio Pizza,
1 walk-in slice (1/6 of pizza) — 16

Sweet Chili Chicken Thai Pizza,
1 walk-in slice (1/6 of pizza) — 17

SQUARE PIZZAS

Cheese Pizza,
1 slice (1/6 of pizza) — 12

Classic Super Pizza,
1 slice (1/6 of pizza) — 12

Garden Veggie Pizza,
1 slice (1/6 of pizza) — 12

**Mediterranean Vegetarian
Pizza,** 1 slice (1/6 of pizza) — 13

Pepperoni Pizza, 1 slice
(1/6 of pizza) — 12

Tropical Hawaiian Pizza,
1 slice (1/6 of pizza) — 17

CRUST ONLY
(LARGE PIZZA – 35 CM [14"] DIAMETER)

Gluten Free Crust – Crust Only,
1 slice (1/10 of pizza) — 2

**Whole Wheat Multigrain
Crust Only,** 1 slice (1/10 of pizza) — 4

PANZEROTTI

Cheese Panzerotti, 1 serving — 20

Cheese and Pepperoni Panzerotti,
1 serving — 25

CHICKEN ITEMS

Boneless Chicken Bites, 1 serving — 5

Chicken Strips, 1 serving — 8

Classic Wings, 1 serving — 10

Crispy Breaded Wings, 1 serving — 20

▲ Power Foods | *PointsPlus®* value

STUFFED SANDWICH

Bacon Cheeseburger, 1 — 9

Basic Cheese and Sauce, 1 — 8

Classic Super, 1 — 9

Garden Veggie, 1 — 8

Mediterranean Vegetarian, 1 — 8

Pepperoni, 1 — 9

Tropical Hawaiian, 1 — 16

COOL & FRESH SALADS
(WITHOUT DRESSING)

Caesar Salad, 1 small salad — 1

Caesar Salad, 1 large salad — 3

▲ **Garden Salad,** 1 small salad — 1

▲ **Garden Salad,** 1 large salad — 1

Mediterranean Greek Salad,
1 small salad — 2

Mediterranean Greek Salad,
1 large salad — 5

SALAD DRESSING

Renee's Asian Sesame Vinaigrette,
1 packet — 4

Renee's Balsamic Vinaigrette,
1 packet — 3

**Renee's Buttermilk Ranch Salad
Dressing,** 1 packet — 5

Renee's Caesar Salad Dressing,
1 packet — 8

Renee's Greek Feta, 1 packet — 7

**Renee's Light Caesar Salad
Dressing,** 1 packet — 4

**Renee's Ravin Raspberry
Vinaigrette,** 1 packet — 2

**Renee's Spring Herb Italian
Salad Dressing,** 1 packet — 2

PIZZA PIZZA

PointsPlus® value

PointsPlus® value

SIDES

Garlic Bread / Toast, 2 pieces	7
Garlic Stick, 2 sticks	10
Onion Rings, 1 serving	7
Regular Fries, 1 serving	8
Jumbo Fries, 1 serving	24

DESSERTS

Apple Pie / Turnover, 1 serving	6
Cinnamon Poppers, 2 buns	5
Two-Bite Brownies, 1 serving	2

SAUCES & DIPS

Blue Cheese, 1 serving	8
Bruschetta, 1 serving	2
Classic Tomato, 1 serving	1
Creamy Garlic, 1 serving	10
Homestyle Pizzaletto, 1 serving	1
Honey Garlic, 1 serving	3
Honey Mustard, 1 serving	7
Hot Wing Sauce, 1 serving	2
Italian Marinara, 1 serving	1
Jalapeno Cheddar, 1 serving	6
Mild Wing Sauce, 1 serving	2
Peppercorn Ranch, 1 serving	9
Pesto Sauce, 1 serving	5
Plum Sauce, 1 serving	3
Poutine Sauce, 1 serving	0
Seafood Sauce, 1 serving	2
Smokey BBQ, 1 serving	3
Sweet Chili Thai, 1 serving	3

▲ Power Foods | *PointsPlus*® value

APPETIZERS

Chicken Wings, 4 wings	5
Fried Cheese Sticks, 4 sticks	10
Mini Spring Rolls – Vegetable, 4 rolls	4
Small Caesar Salad (without dressing), 1 serving	3

SOUPS

Chicken and Noodle Soup (with soda crackers), 1 serving	4
Chicken and Rice Soup (with soda crackers), 1 serving	4
Chicken Cream Soup (with soda crackers), 1 serving	3
Vegetable Soup (with soda crackers), 1 serving	2

ROASTED CHICKEN

Roasted Chicken – Leg, 1 serving	8
Roasted Chicken – Double Leg, 1 serving	17
Roasted Chicken – Breast, 1 serving	9

RIBS

St-Hubert Ribs, 1 serving	20
St-Hubert Ribs with Quarter Chicken Breast, 1 serving	29
St-Hubert Ribs with Quarter Chicken Leg, 1 serving	28

FROM OUR GRILL

Fajitas on the griddle (moderate portion), 1 serving	30
Top Sirloin Steak, 200 g (7 oz)	21

▲ Power Foods | *PointsPlus*® value

SANDWICHES

Chicken Fillets, 2 fillets	3
Chicken Fillet Wrap, 1	13
Club Burger, 1	12
Club Sandwich (dark meat, whole wheat bread), 1 sandwich	15
Hot Chicken Sandwich (dark meat, whole wheat bread), 1/2 sandwich	5

GARDEN FRESH

Bangkok Salad with Breaded Chicken Fillets (without dressing), 1 moderate serving	8
Bangkok Salad with Satay Chicken Fillets (without dressing), 1 moderate serving	8
Caesar Salad with Chicken and Mandarins (without dressing), 1 moderate serving	11
Californian Salad (without dressing), 1 serving	9
Mexican Salad (without dressing), 1 serving	11
St-Hubert Classic Salad: Roasted chicken breast on Caesar salad (without dressing), 1 serving	9

ST-HUBERT

Garden Fresh (cont'd)

▲ Power Foods	PointsPlus® value
St-Hubert Classic Salad: roasted chicken breast on fresh lettuce (without dressing), 1 serving	9
Warm Spinach Salad with Chicken (with dressing), 1 moderate serving	13

DRESSINGS

Balsamic Dressing, 30 ml (approx 2 Tbsp)	3
Caesar Dressing, 55 ml (approx 3 Tbsp)	10
Californian Dressing, 30 ml (approx 2 Tbsp)	4
Mexican Dressing, 30 ml (approx 2 Tbsp)	3

COLESLAW

Creamy St-Hubert Coleslaw, 1 serving	5
Traditional St-Hubert Coleslaw, 1 serving	3

SIDE ORDERS

Caesar Salad (without dressing), 1 serving	1
▲ **Garden Salad (without dressing)**, 1 serving	0
Julienne Vegetables, 1 serving	3
Mashed Potatoes, 1 serving	2
Oven Baked Potato (without toppings), 1	7
Fries, 1 serving	8
Sweet Potato Fries, 1 serving	8
Pilaf Rice, 1 serving	4
Hamburger Bun, 1	2

SAUCES

BBQ Sauce, 100 ml	2
Fruity Sauce, 1 packet	1

▲ Power Foods	PointsPlus® value
Guacamole, 40 ml	2
Honey Garlic Sauce, 40 ml	2
Mustard Sauce, 1 packet	1
Pepper Sauce, 40 ml	1
Salsa Sauce, 15 ml (1 Tbsp)	0
Sour Cream (14% M.F.), 30 ml (2 Tbsp)	1
Spicy BBQ Sauce, 1 packet	1
St-Hubert Wing Sauce, 40 ml	2
Sweet and Sour Sauce, 1 packet	1

DESSERTS

Apple Temptation, 1 serving	14
Chocolate and Raspberry Muffin, 1	6
Chocomousse, 1 serving	13
Chômeur Pudding, 1 regular portion (2 pieces with "sucre à la crème" and a scoop of ice cream)	24
Fruit Salad with Wafer Cigar, 1 serving	4
Hot Date Swoon, 1 regular portion (2 squares with garnish)	25
Millefeuille, 1 millefeuille with chocolate sauce	16
Mini Desserts in Verrine, 3 verrines	8
Super Sundae with Wafer Cigar, 1 scoop with "sucre à la crème" sauce	10
Sweet Desire (sugar pie), 1 slice of pie with "sucre à la crème" sauce	14
The 7th Heaven, 1 serving	19
The Chocolate Mountain, 1 square with a scoop of ice cream and chocolate sauce	24
The New Yorker (cheesecake) (with sides), 1 serving	12
Volcano Cake, 1 volcano with chocolate sauce	19
Yogurt with Fruits, 1 regular portion	4

Power Foods	PointsPlus® value

6" SUBS WITH 6 GRAMS OF FAT OR LESS

Black Forest Ham, 1	7
Oven Roasted Chicken, 1	8
Roast Beef, 1	7
Subway Club, 1	7
Sweet Onion Chicken Teriyaki, 1	9
Turkey Breast, 1	7
Turkey Breast & Black Forest Ham, 1	7
Veggie Delite, 1	6

6" SUBS

Chicken & Bacon Ranch, 1	13
Chicken Pizziola, 1	11
Cold Cut Combo, 1	13
Italian BMT, 1	12
Meatball Marinara, 1	15
Pizza Sub, 1	12
Spicy Italian, 1	14
Steak & Cheese, 1	10
Subway Melt, 1	9
Tuna, 1	14

MINI SUBS

Black Forest Ham, 1	5
Roast Beef, 1	5
Tuna (includes cheese), 1	9
Turkey Breast, 1	5

BREADS

9-Grain Wheat Bread, 1 (15 cm [6"])	5
Hearty Italian Bread, 1 (15 cm [6"])	6
Honey Oat, 1 (15 cm [6"])	6
Italian (White) Bread, 1 (15 cm [6"])	5
Italian Herbs & Cheese, 1 (15 cm [6"])	6
Monterey Cheddar, 1 (15 cm [6"])	6
Parmesan Oregano Bread, 1 (15 cm [6"])	6
Roasted Garlic, 1 (15 cm [6"])	6
Flatbread, 1 (15 cm [6"])	6
▲ Light Wheat English Muffin, 1 (15 cm [6"])	3

CHEESES

Cheddar Cheese Product, Processed, 1 serving	1
Feta, 1 serving	1
Monterey Cheddar, Shredded, 1 serving	2
Monterey Jack, 1 serving	1
Mozzarella, Shredded, 1 serving	1
Natural Cheddar, 1 serving	1
Swiss, 1 serving	1

SANDWICH CONDIMENTS

Chipotle Southwest Sauce, 1 serving	2
Honey Mustard Sauce, Fat Free, 1 serving	1
House Sandwich Sauce, 1 serving	3
Mustard, yellow or deli brown, 10 ml (2 tsp)	0
Light Mayonnaise-Type Dressing, 15 ml (1 Tbsp)	2
Mayonnaise, 15 ml (1 Tbsp)	3
Ranch Dressing, 1 serving	1
Sweet Onion Sauce, Fat Free, 1 serving	1

SUBWAY®

▲ Power Foods   *PointsPlus®* value

SALADS

Black Forest Ham, 1	3
Oven Roasted Chicken Breast, 1	3
Roast Beef, 1	3
Subway Club, 1	3
Sweet Onion Chicken Teriyaki, 1	5
Turkey Breast, 1	2
Turkey Breast & Black Forest Ham, 1	3
Veggie Delite, 1	1

SALAD DRESSING

Fat Free Italian, 1 serving	1
Ranch, 1 serving	8

BREAKFAST SANDWICHES

Bacon & Cheese English Muffin Sandwich (with egg white), 1	5
Cheese English Muffin Sandwich (with egg white), 1	4
Ham & Cheese English Muffin Sandwich (with egg white), 1	4
Mega English Muffin Sandwich (with egg white), 1	8
Sausage & Cheese English Muffin Sandwich (with egg white), 1	7

▲ Power Foods | *PointsPlus®* value

STARTERS

Caesar Salad (with dressing), 1 serving	12
Chalet Chicken Soup, 1 bowl	4
Chalet Chicken Wings, 8 wings	15
Cheese Perogies, 7 pieces	11
Chicken Spring Rolls, 4 pieces	11
Crispy Dry Ribs, 1 serving	24
Garlic Cheese Loaf, 1 serving	24
Garlic Loaf (no cheese), 1 serving	18
Greek Salad (without dressing), 1 serving	2
Hearty Chicken Minestrone Soup, 1 bowl	4

ROTISSERIE CHICKEN

Chicken Pot Pie, 1 serving	18
Classic Double Leg (with skin), 1 serving	16
Classic Half Chicken (with skin), 1 serving	16
Classic Quarter Chicken Breast (skinless), 1 serving	4
Classic Quarter Chicken Breast (with skin), 1 serving	7
Classic Quarter Chicken Leg (skinless), 1 serving	6
Classic Quarter Chicken Leg (with skin), 1 serving	8
Health Check™ Classic Quarter Chicken (with white meat, Chalet dipping sauce, fresh vegetables or garden salad with no dressing; no oil), 1 serving	8

▲ Power Foods | *PointsPlus®* value

FROM THE GRILL

1/3 Rack BBQ Ribs, 1 serving	11
Half Rack BBQ Ribs, 1 serving	17
Full Rack BBQ Ribs, 1 serving	34

ENTRÉE SALADS & STIR FRIES

Bacon Ranch Salad, 1	14
Chalet Chopped Salad, 1	12
Chicken Stir Fry (with rice), 1	20
Chicken Stir Fry (without rice), 1	12
Crispy Tortilla Strips, 1 serving	4
Fresh Vegetable Stir Fry (without rice), 1	9
Grilled Chicken Caesar Salad, 1	18
Spinach Chicken Salad (with fat-free dressing and no tortillas), 1	4

WRAPS, SANDWICHES & BURGERS
(EXCLUDING SIDE SERVINGS)

Chargrilled Bacon Cheese Burger (with bun only), 1	24
Chargrilled Bacon Cheeseburger (without bun and garnishes), 1	18
Chargrilled Hamburger (with bun only), 1	19

SWISS CHALET

▲ Power Foods	*PointsPlus®* value
Chargrilled Hamburger (without bun and garnishes), 1	13
Chargrilled Veggie Burger (with bun only), 1	11
Chargrilled Veggie Burger (without bun and garnishes), 1	6
Chicken Caesar Wrap, 1	23
Chicken on a Kaiser (dark meat), 1	13
Chicken on a Kaiser (white meat without sauce), 1	11
Chipotle Chicken Sandwich, 1	13
Classic Hot Chicken Sandwich (dark meat), 1	11
Classic Hot Chicken Sandwich (white meat), 1	9
Rotisserie Chicken Club Wrap, 1	22
Rotisserie Chicken Quesadilla (without salsa and sour cream), 1	16

SIDE SERVINGS

	PointsPlus® value
Butter, 1 serving	2
Creamy Coleslaw, 1 serving	5
Fresh Vegetable Medley, 1 serving	0
Fresh, Hand-Cut Fries (cooked in trans-fat free oil), 1 serving	14
Freshly Sauteed Mushrooms, 1 serving	6
Garlic Breadsticks, 1 serving	4
Gravy, 1 serving	1
Mashed Potatoes, 1 serving	4
Multigrain Roll, 1	3

▲ Power Foods	*PointsPlus®* value
Oven-Baked Potato, 1	5
Ramekin of Creamy Coleslaw, 1 serving	2
Real Sour Cream & Chives, 1 serving	2
Seasoned Rice, 1 serving	6
Side Caesar Salad (with dressing), 1 serving	6
Side Garden Salad (without dressing), 1 serving	0
Side Greek Salad (without dressing), 1 serving	1
Sweet Kernel Corn, 1 serving	4
White Roll, 1	3

SALAD DRESSINGS & DIPS

	PointsPlus® value
Balsamic Vinaigrette, 1 serving	2
Blue Cheese Dip, 1 serving	2
Caesar Dressing, 1 serving	2
Cajun Sauce Dip, 1 serving	3
Chalet Dipping Sauce, 1 serving	1
Chalet Dressing, 1 serving	2
Fat-Free Raspberry Vinaigrette, 1 serving	0
Greek Dressing, 1 serving	2
Lemon Garlic Dressing, 1 serving	1
Light Italian Dressing, 1 serving	0
Light Mayonnaise, 1 serving	1
Plum Sauce, 1 serving	1
Ranch Dressing, 1 serving	2
Sweet Chili Sauce, 1 serving	3

▲ Power Foods

PointsPlus®
value

KIDS' MEALS (EXCLUDING SIDE SERVINGS)

Cheesy Pizza, 1 serving	10
Chicken Strips, 3 strips	8
Chicken Thigh & Drumstick (with skin), 1 serving	8
Mini Burgers, 1 serving	10
Mini Chicken Sandwiches, 1 serving	8

DESSERTS

Baked Apple Crumble, 1 serving	13
Caramel Pecan Cheesecake, 1 serving	18
Chocolate Lava Cake, 1 serving	12
Classic Apple Pie, 1 serving	12
Classic Fudge Cake, 1 serving	20
Coconut Cream Pie, 1 serving	15
Cranberry Raspberry Frozen Yogurt, 1 serving	3
Ice Cream – Chocolate, 1 serving	3
Ice Cream – Vanilla, 1 serving	3
Lemon Meringue Pie, 1 serving	11
Old Fashioned Carrot Cake, 1 serving	17
Pecan Pie, 1 serving	16
Sauce – Butterscotch, 1 serving	3
Sauce – Chocolate, 1 serving	2
Sauce – Strawberry, 1 serving	1

TACO BELL®

FRESCO STYLE BURRITOS

1/2 Lb. Beef & Bean Burrito Fresco, 1	9
7 Layer Burrito Fresco, 1	8
Burrito Supreme® Fresco, 1	8
Chicken Burrito Supreme® Fresco, 1	8
Fajita Stuft Burrito-Chicken Fresco, 1	11
Fajita Stuft Burrito-Steak Fresco, 1	11
Spicy Chicken Burrito Fresco, 1	7
Steak Burrito Supreme® Fresco, 1	7

FRESCO STYLE CRUNCHWRAPS

Crunchwrap Supreme® Fresco, 1	10
Spicy Chicken Crunchwrap Supreme™ Fresco, 1	10

FRESCO STYLE GORDITAS

Beef Gordita Supreme Fresco, 1	6
Chicken Gordita Supreme Fresco, 1	6
Steak Gordita Supreme Fresco, 1	6

FRESCO STYLE TACOS

Beef Hard Taco Fresco, 1	4
Beef Soft Taco Fresco, 1	4
Chicken Soft Taco Fresco, 1	4
Double Decker Taco Fresco, 1	7
Steak Soft Taco Fresco, 1	3

BIG BELL VALUE MENU™

1/2 Lb. Beef & Bean Burrito, 1	10
1/2 Lb. Beef & Potato Burrito, 1	13
Cheesy Fiesta Potatoes, 1 serving	9
DOUBLE DECKER® Taco, 1	8
Spicy Chicken Burrito, 1	9

BURRITOS

Burrito Supreme®, 1	10
Fajita Grilled Stuft Burrito – Chicken, 1	12
Fajita Grilled Stuft Burrito – Steak, 1	12

GORDITAS

Beef Gordita Supreme, 1	8
Cheesy Gordita Crunch, 1	13
Chicken Gordita Supreme, 1	8
Steak Gordita Supreme, 1	8

TACOS

Beef Hard Taco, 1	4
Beef Soft Taco, 1	4
Beef Soft Taco Supreme®, 1	6
Beef Taco Supreme®, 1	6
Steak Soft Taco, 1	7

SPECIALTIES

Fiesta Taco Salad®, 1	22
Fiesta Taco Salad™ (without shell), 1	12
MexiMelt®, 1	6
Spicy Chicken Crunchwrap Supreme™, 1	12

SIDES

Cheese Fries, 1 serving	12
Chili Cheese Fries, 1 serving	13
Fries, 1 serving	10
Fries Supreme, 1 serving	15

▲ Power Foods *PointsPlus®* value

FAMOUS TERIYAKI
(COOKED WITH WATER & NO SAUCE ADDED)

Beef Teriyaki, 1 serving	14
Beef & Shrimp Teriyaki, 1 serving	15
Chicken Teriyaki, 1 serving	13
Chicken & Beef Teriyaki, 1 serving	15
Chicken & Shrimp Teriyaki, 1 serving	14
Shrimp Teriyaki, 1 serving	13
Tofu Teriyaki, 1 serving	17
Vegetable Teriyaki, 1 serving	10

PAN-ASIAN UDON NOODLES
(COOKED WITH WATER & NO SAUCE ADDED)

Beef Pan Asian, 1 serving	10
Beef & Shrimp Pan Asian, 1 serving	10
Chicken Pan Asian, 1 serving	9
Chicken & Beef Pan Asian, 1 serving	11
Chicken & Shrimp Pan Asian, 1 serving	9
Shrimp Pan Asian, 1 serving	8
Tofu Pan Asian, 1 serving	12
Vegetable Pan Asian, 1 serving	6

YAKISOBA NOODLES
(COOKED WITH WATER & NO SAUCE ADDED)

Beef & Shrimp Yakisoba, 1 serving	13
Beef Yakisoba, 1 serving	12
Chicken Yakisoba, 1 serving	11
Chicken & Beef Yakisoba, 1 serving	13
Chicken & Shrimp Yakisoba, 1 serving	12
Shrimp Yakisoba, 1 serving	11
Tofu Yakisoba, 1 serving	15
Vegetable Yakisoba, 1 serving	8

▲ Power Foods *PointsPlus®* value

SPICY UDON NOODLE SOUP BOWL

Beef, 1 serving	8
Chicken, 1 serving	8
Gyoza, 1 serving	10
Shrimp, 1 serving	7
Tofu, 1 serving	9
Vegetable, 1 serving	6

YAKISOBA NOODLE SOUP BOWL

Beef, 1 serving	11
Chicken, 1 serving	10
Gyoza, 1 serving	12
Shrimp, 1 serving	10
Tofu, 1 serving	12
Vegetable, 1 serving	9

GYOZA

Gyoza, 2 pieces	3
Gyoza, 6 pieces	8

TERIYAKI EXPERIENCE®

▲ Power Foods   *PointsPlus®* value

WRAPS

Chicken, 1 serving	14
Beef, 1 serving	16
Shrimp, 1 serving	14
Tofu, 1 serving	18

SUSHI

California Roll with Roasted Sesame Seeds, 8 pieces	18
California Roll with Tobiko, 8 pieces	11
Smoked Salmon Nigiri, 8 pieces	15
Tuna Nigiri, 8 pieces	13
Vegetable and Avocado, 8 pieces	18

INDIVIDUAL ITEMS

Brown Rice, 1 serving	8
White Rice, 1 serving	9
Udon Noodles, 1 serving	4
Yakisoba Noodles, 1 serving	7
Chicken, 1 serving	3
Beef, 1 serving	4
Shrimp, 1 serving	2
Tofu, 1 serving	6
Pan-Asian Vegetable Mix, 1 serving	1
Teriykai & Yakisoba Vegetable Mix, 1 serving	1

SAUCES

Asian Cooking Sauce, 1 serving	2
Hot & Spicy Sauce, 1 serving	6
Pan-Asian Sauce, 1 serving	2
Pineapple Sauce, 1 serving	2
Sweet Chili Sauce, 1 serving	3
Teriyaki Sauce, 1 serving	2
Teriyaki Sauce – 50% Less Sodium, 1 serving	3

THE GREAT CANADIAN BAGEL™

▲ Power Foods   *PointsPlus®* value

BAGELS

Apple Cinnamon, 1	9
Blueberry – Whole Berries, 1	8
Blueberry – Flakes, 1	10
Flax and Honey, 1	7
Honey Raisin Multigrain, 1	8
Muesli, 1	8
Multigrain, 1	7

SODIUM REDUCED BAGELS

Asiago, 1	9
Cheddar Bacon, 1	11
Cheddar Herb, 1	7
Cheddar Jalapeno, 1	8
Cheddar Onion, 1	11
Cheddar Salsa, 1	11
Cheddar Swiss, 1	7
Chocolate Chip, 1	7
Cinnamon Raisin, 1	7
Everything, 1	8
French Toast, 1	8
Maple, 1	8
Plain, 1	7
Poppy, 1	8
Pumpernickel, 1	7
Sesame, 1	8
Sour Dough, 1	7
Tomazzo, 1	9
Tomazzo (hot), 1	9
Whole Wheat, 1	7

CREAM CHEESE SPREAD

Lactantia Cream Cheese Spread*, 56 g (2 oz)	5
Lactantia Cream Cheese Spread (Lite)*, 56 g (2 oz)	4

*Ingredients used for flavoured cream cheese vary; average *PointsPlus* value used.

▲ Power Foods   *PointsPlus®* value

MUFFINS – FRUIT SENSATIONS

Banana, 1	11
Blueberry, 1	10
Carrot, 1	10
Cranberry Lemon, 1	9
Fruit Extreme, 1	8
Lemon Swirl with Poppy Seeds, 1	10
Orange Almond, 1	10
Peach Raspberry Swirl, 1	9
Pumpkin, 1	10
Raspberry Yogurt, 1	10
Strawberries and Cream, 1	10
Summer Berry, 1	10

MUFFINS – SLIM SENSATIONS

Blueberry, 1	8
Carrot Pineapple, 1	9
Cranberry Orange, 1	8
Double Chocolate, 1	9
Low Fat Cranberry Orange, 1	8
Sunny Bran and Raisin, 1	8

THE GREAT CANADIAN BAGEL™

▲ Power Foods   *PointsPlus*®
value

MUFFINS – SWEET SENSATIONS

Banana Chocolate Chunk, 1	11
Caramel Coffeecake Swirl, 1	10
Chunks O'Chocolate, 1	11
Cinnamon Raisin Swirl, 1	11
Coconut Cream, 1	10
Double Chocolate, 1	10
Maple Walnut, 1	11
Pralines and Cream, 1	11

MUFFINS – WHOLESOME GRAIN SENSATIONS

Cornmeal, 1	11
Dark Bran, 1	9
Golden Bran & Raisin, 1	9
Morning Glory, 1	11
Oatmeal and Baked Apple, 1	10
Oatmeal Date Delight, 1	10

THE OLD SPAGHETTI FACTORY

THE OLD SPAGHETTI FACTORY

Entrées (cont'd)

▲ Power Foods	*PointsPlus*® value
Red Thai Linguine with Chicken, 1 serving	18
Red Thai Linguine with Prawns, 1 serving	17
Seafood Fettuccine Alfredo, 1 serving	24
Seafood Linguine Marinara, 1 serving	18
Spicy Chorizo Penne al Fresca, 1 serving	17
Spicy Meat Sauce Spaghetti, 1 serving	17
Tomato Spaghetti, 1 serving	11
Tortellini Pomodoro, 1 serving	23
Veal a la Parmigiana, 1 serving	18
Vegetarian Lasagna, 1 serving	20

CHILDREN'S MEALS

Chicken & Fries, 1 serving	18
Lasagna, 1 serving	18
Spaghetti Meat, 1 serving	9
Spaghetti Meatballs, 1 serving	15
Spaghetti Mushroom, 1 serving	7
Spaghetti Spicy, 1 serving	9
Spaghetti Tomato, 1 serving	7
Tort Meat Sauce, 1 serving	11

THE PITA PIT

▲ Power Foods	PointsPlus® value
SALADS	
Caesar, 1 small serving	1
Caesar, 1 large serving	2
Garden, 1 small serving	3
Garden, 1 large serving	5
Greek, 1 small serving	2
Greek, 1 large serving	4

SALAD DRESSING	
French, 15 ml (1 Tbsp)	2
French, 30 ml (2 Tbsp)	4
Italian, 15 ml (1 Tbsp)	1
Italian, 30 ml (2 Tbsp)	2
Light Caesar, 15 ml (1 Tbsp)	1
Light Caesar, 30 ml (2 Tbsp)	2
Light Italian, 15 ml (1 Tbsp)	0
Light Italian, 30 ml (2 Tbsp)	1
Light Ranch, 15 ml (1 Tbsp)	1
Light Ranch, 30 ml (2 Tbsp)	2
Special Greek, 15 ml (1 Tbsp)	3
Special Greek, 30 ml (2 Tbsp)	5
Thousand Islands, 15 ml (1 Tbsp)	2
Thousand Islands, 30 ml (2 Tbsp)	3

PITAS	
Pita Bread–White, 1 (22 cm [9"]) Pita	5
Pita Bread–Whole Wheat, 1 (22 cm [9"]) Pita	5

MEAT TOPPINGS	
B.L.T., 1 serving	7
BBQ Rib, 1 serving	7
▲ **Chicken Breast,** 1 serving	3

▲ Power Foods	PointsPlus® value
Chicken Caesar, 1 serving	5
Chicken Crave, 1 serving	5
Chicken Souvlaki, 1 serving	2
Club, 1 serving	4
Dagwood, 1 serving	3
Gyros, 1 serving	9
▲ **Ham,** 1 serving	3
Philly Steak, 1 serving	4
Roast Beef, 1 serving	2
Southwestern Chicken, 1 serving	4
Southwestern Steak, 1 serving	6
Spicy Buffalo Chicken, 1 serving	5
▲ **Tuna,** 1 serving	2
▲ **Turkey Breast,** 1 serving	2

VEGGIE TOPPINGS	
▲ **Alfalfa Sprouts,** 8 g (approx 1/4 oz)	0
Babaganoush, 60 ml (1/4 cup)	2
Black Olives, 15 g (1/2 oz)	1
▲ **Cucumbers,** 42 g (approx 1 1/2 oz)	0
▲ **Falafel,** 94 g (3 1/3 oz)	7
▲ **Garden mix,** 1 serving	1
Green Olives, 15 g (1/2 oz)	0
▲ **Green Peppers,** 18 g (approx 2/3 oz)	0
▲ **Hot Peppers,** 20 g (3/4 oz)	0
▲ **Jalapeños,** 20 g (3/4 oz)	0
▲ **Lettuce – Iceberg,** 30 g (approx 1 oz)	0
▲ **Lettuce – Romaine,** 30 g (approx 1 oz)	0
▲ **Mushrooms,** 15 g (1/2 oz)	0
▲ **Onions,** 20 g (approx 2/3 oz)	0
▲ **Pickles,** 40 g (approx 1 1/2 oz)	0
▲ **Pineapple,** 30 g (approx 1 oz)	0
▲ **Spinach,** 30 g (approx 1 oz)	0
▲ **Tomatoes,** 45 g (approx 1 1/2 oz)	0

THE PITA PIT

EXTRAS

Bacon, 1 serving	3
Cheddar, 28 g (1 oz)	3
Feta, 28 g (1 oz)	2
Hummus, 60 ml (1/4 cup)	4
Parmesan, 1 serving	1
Swiss, 28 g (1 oz)	3

BREAKFAST PITAS

Awakin' With Bacon, 1	7
Ham 'N' Eggs, 1	6
Meat The Day, 1	12
Morning Glory, 1	4
Sausage Sunrise, 1	8

SAUCES & CONDIMENTS

Ancho Chipotle, 15 ml (1 Tbsp)	1
Babaganoush, 60 ml (1/4 cup)	2
BBQ Sauce, 15 ml (1 Tbsp)	1
Honey Mustard, 15 ml (1 Tbsp)	0
Horseradish Dijon, 15 ml (1 Tbsp)	2
Hot Sauce, 5 ml (1 tsp)	0
Light Caesar, 15 ml (1 Tbsp)	1
Light Mayonnaise, 15 ml (1 Tbsp)	1
Light Ranch, 15 ml (1 Tbsp)	1
Mustard, 7 ml (1 1/2 tsp)	0
Special Sauce, 15 ml (1 Tbsp)	3
Teriyaki, 15 ml (1 Tbsp)	1
Tzatziki, 30 ml (2 Tbsp)	1

SMOOTHIES

5 Berry Immuniforce, 1 serving (480 ml)	8
Banana Pineapple 'n' Fibre, 1 serving (480 ml)	9
Mango Probiotic, 1 serving (480 ml)	8
Pomberry Antioxia, 1 serving (480 ml)	8
Strawberry/Kiwi Omega 3, 1 serving (480 ml)	8

TIM HORTON'S®

CAKE DONUTS

Chocolate Glazed, 1	7
Old Fashion Glazed, 1	9
Old Fashion Plain, 1	7
Sour Cream Plain, 1	7

FILLED DONUTS

Blueberry, 1	6
Boston Cream, 1	7
Canadian Maple, 1	7
Strawberry, 1	6
Strawberry Vanilla, 1	8

YEAST DONUTS

Apple Fritter, 1	8
Blueberry Fritter, 1	9
Chocolate Dip, 1	6
Dutchie, 1	7
Honey Dip, 1	6
Maple Dip, 1	6

OTHER DONUTS

Honey Cruller, 1	9
Walnut Crunch, 1	10

CAKE TIMBITS

Chocolate Glazed, 1	2
Old Fashion Plain, 1	2
Sour Cream Glazed, 1	3

FILLED TIMBITS

Blueberry, 1	2
Lemon, 1	2
Raspberry, 1	2

Strawberry, 1	2
Apple Fritter, 1	1
Dutchie, 1	2

YEAST TIMBITS

Honey Dip, 1	2

MUFFINS

Banana Nut, 1	10
Blueberry, 1	9
Chocolate Chip, 1	11
Cranberry Blueberry Bran, 1	9
Fruit Explosion, 1	9
Low Fat Double Berry, 1	7
Raisin Bran, 1	11
Strawberry Sensation, 1	9
Triple Chocolate, 1	12
Whole Grain Blueberry, 1	10
Whole Grain Carrot Orange, 1	10
Whole Grain Raspberry, 1	11

COOKIES

Caramel Chocolate Pecan, 1	6
Chocolate Chunk, 1	6
Oatmeal Raisin Spice, 1	6
Peanut Butter, 1	7
Trail Mix Cookie with Fruit and Nuts, 1	6
Triple Chocolate, 1	7
White Chocolate Macadamia Nut, 1	7

SPECIALTY BAKED GOODS

Cheese Croissant, 1	9
Cherry Cheese Danish, 1	9
Chocolate Danish, 1	13
Cinnamon Roll – Frosted, 1	13

TIM HORTON'S®

▲ Power Foods	PointsPlus® value
Cinnamon Roll – Glazed, 1	12
Maple Pecan Danish, 1	11
Plain Croissant, 1	7
Plain Tea Biscuit, 1	6
Raisin Tea Biscuit, 1	8

BAGELS

12 Grain, 1	8
Blueberry, 1	7
Cheddar Cheese, 1	6
Everything Cinnamon, 1	7
Onion, 1	7
Plain, 1	7
Raisin, 1	7
Sesame Seed, 1	7
Wheat 'N Honey, 1	8

CREAM CHEESE

Herb and Garlic, 43 g (1 1/2 oz)	4
Light Plain, 43 g (1 1/2 oz)	3
Light Strawberry, 43 g (1 1/2 oz)	3
Plain, 43 g (1 1/2 oz)	4

SOUPS & CHILI

Beef Barley with Portobello Mushroom, 1 serving	3
Chicken Noodle, 1 serving	3
Chicken Vegetable & Rice, 1 serving	3
Cream of Broccoli, 1 serving	4
Creamy Field Mushroom, 1 serving	4
Hearty Potato Bacon, 1 serving	6
Hearty Vegetable, 1 serving	2
Minestrone, 1 serving	3
Turkey and Wild Rice, 1 serving	3
Chili, 1 serving	9

▲ Power Foods	PointsPlus® value

'TIM'S OWN®' SANDWICHES

BLT Sandwich, 1	11
Chicken Caesar Sandwich, 1	10
Chicken Salad Sandwich, 1	9
Egg Salad Sandwich, 1	9
Ham & Swiss Sandwich, 1	10
Toasted Chicken Club Sandwich, 1	9
Turkey Bacon Club Sandwich, 1	9
Turkey Caesar Sandwich, 1	9

TIM HORTON'S CHICKEN WRAP SNACKERS

BBQ Chicken, 1	5
Chicken Ranch, 1	5

BREAKFAST SANDWICHES

Bacon, Egg, Cheese, 1	11
Breakfast Sausage & Biscuit, 1	11
Egg, Cheese, 1	10
English Muffin, Egg, Bacon, Cheese, 1	9
English Muffin, Egg, Cheese, 1	8
English Muffin, Egg, Sausage, Cheese, 1	12
Sausage, Egg, Cheese, 1	14

BREAKFAST WRAPS

Sausage, Egg, Cheese, 1	11
Bacon, Egg, Cheese, 1	8
Egg and Cheese, 1	7

BREAKFAST OTHER

Bagel BELT, 1	12
Hashbrown, 1	3
Oatmeal – Maple, 1 serving	6
Oatmeal – Mixed Berries, 1 serving	6

TIM HORTON'S®

▲ Power Foods | *PointsPlus®* value

REAL FRUIT SMOOTHIES

Mixed Berry (No Yogurt),
300 ml (10 fl oz) — 4

Mixed Berry with Yogurt,
300 ml (10 fl oz) — 4

Strawberry Banana (No Yogurt),
300 ml (10 fl oz) — 4

Strawberry Banana with Yogurt,
300 ml (10 fl oz) — 4

YOGURT & BERRIES

Creamy Vanilla with Berries,
1 serving — 4

Strawberry with Berries, 1 serving — 4

BEVERAGES

Coffee (1 cream, 1 sugar),
300 ml (10 fl oz) — 2

Steeped Tea (1 milk, 1 sugar),
300 ml (10 fl oz) — 1

Hot Chocolate, 300 ml (10 fl oz) — 6

French Vanilla Cappuccino,
300 ml (10 fl oz) — 7

Iced Cappuccino, 300 ml (10 fl oz) — 7

Iced Cappuccino (Milk), 300 ml
(10 fl oz) — 4

Iced Coffee (Cream), 300 ml
(10 fl oz) — 3

Iced Coffee (Milk), 300 ml (10 fl oz) — 2

Café Mocha, 300 ml (10 fl oz) — 5

Flavour Shot, 1 shot — 0

TOPPER'S PIZZA™

SALAD (WITHOUT DRESSING)

Caesar Salad, 1 serving	3
Greek Salad, 1 serving	2
Spinach Salad, 1 serving	4
▲ **Add Chicken to Salads,** 45 g (1 1/2 oz)	1

SALAD DRESSINGS

Caesar Dressing, 1 serving	4
Greek Dressing, 1 serving	5
Spinach Salad Dressing, 1 serving	6

▲ Power Foods   *PointsPlus®* value

PIZZA

Canadiana, 1/8 of a medium, 30 cm [12"] pizza	6
Chicken Parmesan, 1/8 of a medium, 30 cm [12"] pizza	5
Deluxe, 1/8 of a medium, 30 cm [12"] pizza	6
Greek, 1/8 of a medium, 30 cm [12"] pizza	6
Hawaiian, 1/8 of a medium, 30 cm [12"] pizza	6
Mexican, 1/8 of a medium, 30 cm [12"] pizza	6
Pepperoni, 1/8 of a medium, 30 cm [12"] pizza	4
Plain Cheese, 1/8 of a medium, 30 cm [12"] pizza	5
Turkey Pepperoni Sensation – Multi Grain, 1/8 of a medium, 30 cm [12"] pizza	4
Turkey Pepperoni Sensation – Reg, 1/8 of a medium, 30 cm [12"] pizza	4
Veggie, 1/8 of a medium, 30 cm [12"] pizza	6

WENDY'S®

GARDEN SENSATIONS SALADS

Apple Pecan Chicken Salad, 1/2 serving	5
Apple Pecan Chicken Salad, 1 serving	9
Baja Salad, 1/2 serving	8
Baja Salad, 1 serving	15
BLT Cobb Salad, 1/2 serving	6
BLT Cobb Salad, 1 serving	12
Spicy Chicken Caesar Salad, 1/2 serving	6
Spicy Chicken Caesar Salad, 1 serving	11

SALAD DRESSINGS & TOPPINGS

Avocado Ranch Dressing, 1 serving	3
Creamy Red Jalapeño Dressing, 1 serving	3
Fat Free Italian Vinaigrette, 1 serving	1
Lemon Garlic Caesar Dressing, 1 serving	3
Light Classic Ranch, 1 serving	1
Pomegranate Vinaigrette Dressing, 1 serving	2
Gourmet Croutons, 1 serving	2
Roasted Pecans, 1 serving	3
Seasoned Tortilla Strips, 1 serving	2

SANDWICHES

Bacon Deluxe Double, 1	24
Bacon Deluxe/Big Bacon Classic®, 1	18
Baconator®, Single, 1	17
Baconator, Double, 1	26
Double Stack, 1	10
Double with Everything and Cheese, 1	21
Homestyle Chicken Breast Sandwich, 1	12
Jr. Bacon Cheeseburger, 1	9
Jr. Cheeseburger Deluxe, 1	8
Jr. Hamburger Deluxe, 1	7
Single with Everything and Cheese, 1	15
Spicy Chicken Breast Sandwich, 1	12
Triple with Everything and Cheese, 1	28
Ultimate Chicken Grill Sandwich, 1	9
BLT Fresh Wrap, 1	9
Pico Grilled Chicken Fresh Wrap, 1	7
Spicy Chicken BLT Fresh Wrap, 1	10
Hamburger, Kids' Meal, 1	6
Cheeseburger, Kids' Meal, 1	7

SANDWICH BREADS

Sandwich Bun, 1	3
Premium Bun, 1	5
Tortilla, 1	3

SANDWICH MEATS

Jr. Hamburger Patty, 1	3
1/4 lb. Hamburger Patty, 1	6
Ultimate Chicken Grill Breast, 1	3
Spicy Chicken Breast, 1	6
Homestyle Chicken Breast, 1	6

SANDWICH TOPPINGS

Applewood Smoked Bacon, 1 strip	1
Cheddar Pepper Jack Cheese Blend, Shredded, 1 serving	2
Dill Pickles, 4 pieces	0
Honey Mustard Sauce, 1 serving	1
Iceburg Lettuce Leaf, 1 serving	0
Ketchup, 1 serving	0

WENDY'S®

Sandwich Toppings (cont'd)
▲ Power Foods

	PointsPlus® value
Mayonnaise, Lite, 1 serving	1
Mustard, 1 serving	0
▲ **Onion,** 4 rings	0
▲ **Pico de Gallo,** 1 serving	0
Processed Cheese Slice, 1 serving	1
Ranch Sauce, 1 serving	1
▲ **Tomato,** 1 slice	0

CRISPY CHICKEN NUGGETS, CRISPY ALL-WHITE MEAT CHICKEN

Homestyle Chicken Strips, 1 serving	10
Kids' Meal Nuggets, 4 pieces	5
Nuggets, 5 pieces	6
Nuggets, 10 pieces	11

DIPPING SAUCES

Heartland Ranch Sauce, 1 serving	3
Barbecue Sauce, 1 serving	1
Sweet & Sour Sauce, 1 serving	1
Honey Mustard Sauce, 1 serving	4
Wild Buffalo Ranch Sauce, 1 serving	4

BAKED POTATOES

Bacon & Cheese Sauce Baked Potato, 1	11
Broccoli & Cheese Sauce Baked Potato, 1	8
▲ **Plain Baked Potato,** 1	7
Sour Cream & Chives Baked Potato, 1	9

CHILI

Small Chili, 1	5
Large Chili, 1	4

▲ Power Foods | PointsPlus® value

FRIES

Kids' Fries, 1	6
Small Fries, 1	9
Medium Fries, 1	11

OTHER SIDES & CONDIMENTS

Becel® Margarine, 1 serving	2
Caesar Side Salad, 1 serving	2
Cheddar Cheese, shredded, 1 serving	2
Garden Side Salad, 1 serving	1
Hot Chili Seasoning, 1 serving	0
Saltine Crackers, 1 serving	1
Strawberry Yogurt, 1 serving	4

FROSTY™ TREATS

Chocolate Frosty, Junior, 1	4
Chocolate Frosty, Small, 1	8
Chocolate Fudge Frosty Shake, Small, 1	11
Chocolate Fudge Frosty Shake, Large, 1	15
Coffee Toffee Twisted Frosty, Chocolate, 1	15
Coffee Toffee Twisted Frosty, Vanilla, 1	15
Frosty™-cino, Small, 1	10
Frosty™-cino, Large, 1	14
M&M's® Twisted Frosty, Chocolate, 1	15
M&M's Twisted Frosty, Vanilla, 1	15
Oreo® Twisted Frosty, Chocolate, 1	12
Oreo Twisted Frosty, Vanilla, 1	12
Strawberry Frosty Shake, Small, 1	11
Strawberry Frosty Shake, Large, 1	14
Vanilla Bean Frosty Shake, Small, 1	10

▲ Power Foods	PointsPlus® value
Vanilla Bean Frosty Shake, Large, 1	14
Vanilla Frosty, Junior, 1	4
Vanilla Frosty, Small, 1	8
Vanilla Frosty Float with Barq's Root Beer, 1	11
Vanilla Frosty Float with Coca-Cola, 1	11
Vanilla Frosty Float with Fresca, 1	7
Vanilla Frosty Float with Fruitopia Strawberry Passion Awareness, 1	11

BEVERAGES

1% M.F. Partly Skimmed Chocolate Milk, 1	3
2% M.F. Partly Skimmed Milk, 1	3
Barq's® Root Beer, Small Cup, 1	5
Coca-Cola Classic®, Small Cup, 1	5
Coffee, Regular Cup, 1	0
Dasani® Bottled Water, 1	1
Diet Coke®, Small Cup, 1	0
Fresca®, Small Cup, 1	0
Hot Specialty Teas, Regular Cup, Orange Pekoe, Orange Pekoe Decaf, Chai, Green Tea, Earl Grey, Peppermint, 1	0
Minute Maid® Orange Juice, 1	4
Minute Maid Apple Juice, 1	4
Nestea® Sweetened Lemon Iced Tea, Small Cup, 1	4
Sprite®, Small Cup, 1	4

WILD WING®

▲ Power Foods	*PointsPlus*® value
FROZEN YOGURT	
Low Fat Vanilla Frozen Yogurt, 160 ml (2/3 cup)	3
Low Fat Chocolate Frozen Yogurt, 160 ml (2/3 cup)	3
No Fat Vanilla Frozen Yogurt, 160 ml (2/3 cup)	3
No Fat Tart Frozen Yogurt, 160 ml (2/3 cup)	3
No Sugar Added Vanilla Frozen Yogurt, 160 ml (2/3 cup)	3
Non Dairy Sorbet, 160 ml (2/3 cup)	4

NOTE: *PointsPlus* values will vary depending on serving size and addition of fruit and toppings.